HOW TO MAKE A MONSTER

CASANOVA NOBODY FRANKENSTEIN
GLENN PEARCE

FANTAGRAPHICS BOOKS   SEATTLE, WASHINGTON

Fantagraphics Books Inc.
7563 Lake City Way NE
Seattle, WA 98115
www.fantagraphics.com
@fantagraphics

Editor: Gary Groth
Designer: Justin Allan-Spencer
Production: Christina Hwang
Promotion: Jacq Cohen
VP / Associate Publisher: Eric Reynolds
President / Publisher: Gary Groth

ISBN: 978-1-68396-571-8
Library of Congress Control Number: 2021951171
First Fantagraphics Books edition: June 2022
Printed in China

HOW TO MAKE A MONSTER.

BY CASANOVA NOBODY FRANKENSTEIN.

TRANSCRIBED FROM THE VOID BY GLENN PEARCE.

SPECIAL THANK YOU TO GREGOR FERGIE, MATTHEW MAKMAN, AUSTIN ENGLISH AND GARY GROTH.

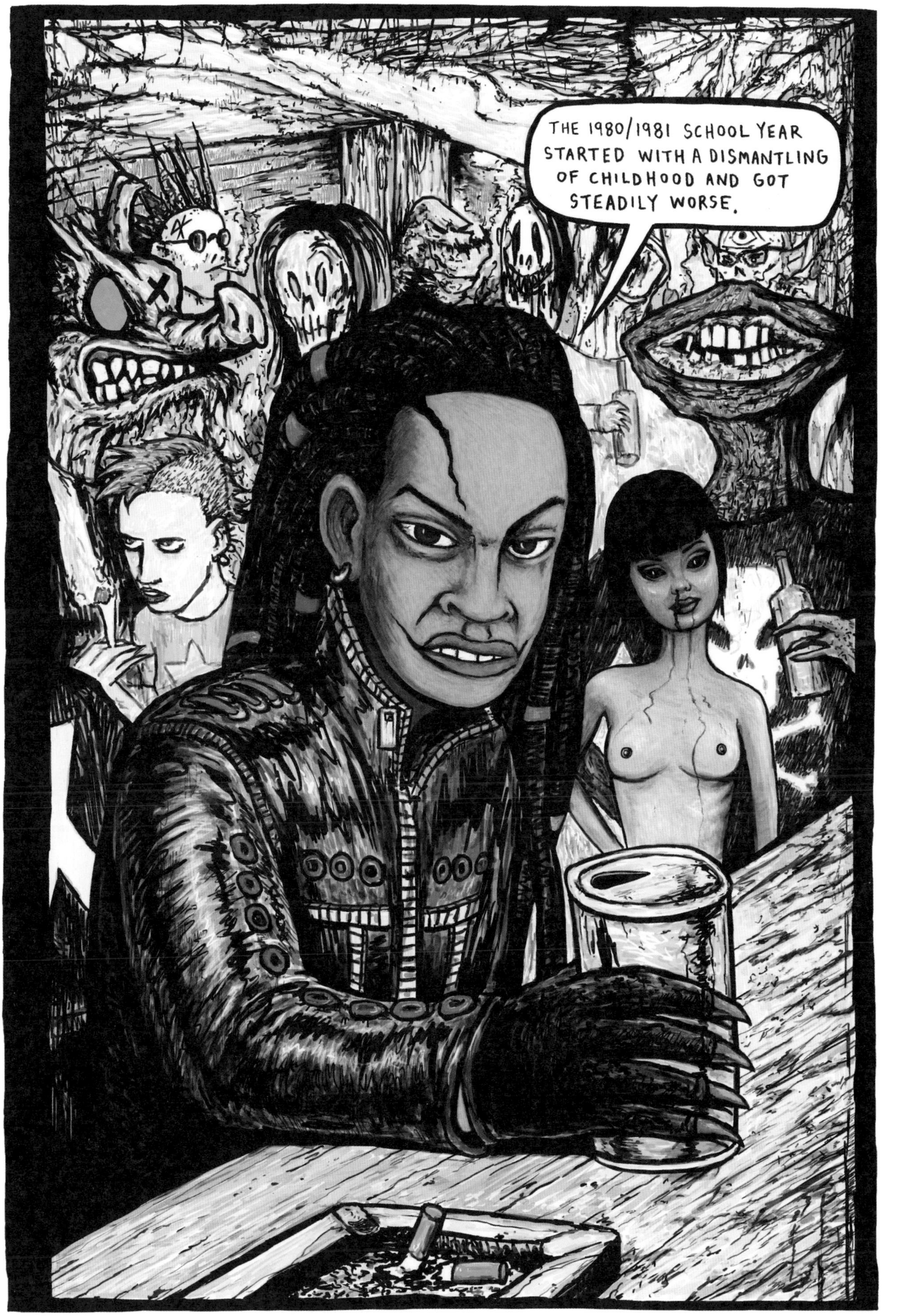
THE 1980/1981 SCHOOL YEAR STARTED WITH A DISMANTLING OF CHILDHOOD AND GOT STEADILY WORSE.

THE POWER OF NEGATIVE THINKING

I'D MANAGED TO MAKE IT THROUGH THE 13 YEARS OF MY LIFE UNTIL THAT POINT, FEELING AS THOUGH I WERE PRETTY NORMAL.

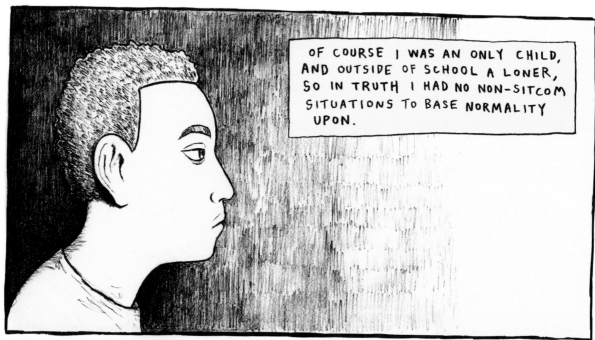

OF COURSE I WAS AN ONLY CHILD, AND OUTSIDE OF SCHOOL A LONER, SO IN TRUTH I HAD NO NON-SITCOM SITUATIONS TO BASE NORMALITY UPON.

BUT CONSIDERING THAT I WASN'T AN ANIMAL TORTURER, OR THE POSSESSOR OF MULTIPLE SYBIL-LIKE PERSONALITIES, I FIGURED IT WAS A SAFE BET THAT I WAS FAR FROM "WEIRD".

BUT SOMETHING HAD CHANGED OVER THE SUMMER.

SOMETHING OUTSIDE OF ME WAS SLINKING INTO MY LIFE LIKE A MALIGNANT TUMOR ON THE CEILING OF OUR CLASSROOM, WHOSE TENDRILS SNAKED DOWN INTO THE SKULLS OF THE BOYS AROUND ME.

THE NUTS HAD FALLEN. NOT FROM THE TREES TO THE GROUND BUT FROM THE TAINTS TO THE SACS. ALL AROUND ME BOYS WERE SUCCUMBING TO THE CHEMICALS OF PUBERTY, IN A HORRIBLE WAY. IT WAS LIKE WATCHING A ROOM FULL OF WEREWOLVES IN MID-TRANSFORMATION.

BOYS THAT WERE REASONABLE KIDS JUST A FEW MONTHS EARLIER WERE NOW STALKING JACKALS PLAYING ALPHA. I WATCHED IN AMAZEMENT AS THEY FELL INTO A PATTERN OF LEADER AND PACK.

I COULDN'T FIGURE OUT THEIR THINKING AS THOSE THEY PUT ON THE TOP STRUCK ME AS LACKING IN BASIC HUMANITY.

THESE WERE MY FIRST LESSONS IN "ADULT" SOCIALIZATION.

THE SOCIOPATHS ROSE TO THE TOP. THEIR LACK OF SHAME AND EMPATHY WAS A BEACON OF CONFIDENCE TO THE BETAS, WHO IN TURN ATTEMPTED THEIR OWN MANUFACTURED VERSIONS OF PERSONALITY DISORDERS.

WE ATTENTED IMMANUEL LUTHERAN SCHOOL, A THREE STORY SCAB-COLORED BRICK PRISON IN A MEXICAN NEIGHBORHOOD ON THE SOUTHEAST SIDE. THE RECESS/EXERCISE YARD WAS A VACANT PARKING LOT. EVERYTHING WAS GREY AND OVERCAST. COMPARE THIS TO THE SUNNY SUMMERTIME LAWNS AND OPEN SPACES OF THE SUBURBS AND YOU CAN ALMOST FEEL THE MIND FLEXING ITS SCHIZOPHRENIC DUALITY MUSCLES.

I WAS IN THE EIGHTH GRADE.

OUR CLASSROOM WAS ON THE NORTH SIDE OF THE TOP FLOOR.

ID SPENT THE PREVIOUS SCHOOL YEAR IN THAT ROOM AS A 7TH GRADER.

SEVERAL ELEMENTS COMBINED IN 1980/81 TO MOLD THE EIGHTH GRADE INTO THE PERFECT SHIT-STORM OF ARTISTIC-ANGST.

FIRSTLY, BEING AN OVER-PROTECTED LONER, I'D MISSED THE OPPORTUNITY TO INGRATIATE MYSELF INTO THE CONFIDENCE OF THE ALPHAS. BECAUSE I DIDN'T HANG OUT WITH MY CLASSMATES, OR CALL THEM ON THE PHONE I'D MISSED OUT ON THE SOCIO-SEXUAL ALCHEMY THAT SEEMED TO CHANGE ALL THE OTHERS INTO LEAD.

SECOND WAS MY INABILITY TO PLAY ANY SORT OF SPORT. SPORTS, IT TURNED OUT, WAS THE RELIGION OF THE IDIOCRACY.

FOR SOME REASON AT IMMANUEL LUTHERAN SCHOOL, GYM WAS REQUIRED OF STUDENTS AND GYM CONSISTED OF A SERIES OF ORGANIZED SPORTS.

PERHAPS MY INABILITY TO FIND A PLACE AT THE TOP OR THE MIDDLE OF THE HIERARCHY COULD BE BLAMED ON MY MOSTLY FRIENDLESS LIFE.

I HAD NO IDEA HOW TO INTERACT PROPERLY WITHIN A GROUP. AT LEAST NOT A GROUP OUTSIDE OF AN IDEALIZED COMIC BOOK REALITY.

IT SEEMED THAT AS I SPENT THE SUMMER IN THE MOSTLY WHITE SUBURB OF HOMEWOOD, ILLINOIS; RIDING BIKES CLIMBING TREES, AND LOOKING AT GREEN THINGS AND WATCHING CARTOONS ON CHANNEL 32, MY BLACK CLASSMATES WERE BACK IN THE CITY, DECIDING THAT THEY WANTED TO HIT THINGS WITH THEIR FISTS AND PUT THEIRS DICKS INTO VAGINAS.

I WAS THE SON OF A MAN THAT DIDN'T LIKE SPORTS. A COP THAT LIKED BOOZE AND WAR MOVIES AND COMIC BOOKS, BUT NOT SPORTS.

THIS MENT I KNEW NOTHING ABOUT SPORTS.

KIDS DON'T LEARN ABOUT GROUP ACTIVITIES IN A VACUUM.

YET KIDS ARE EXPECTED BY THEIR TEACHERS, TO COME PRE-PROGRAMMED WITH THE KNOWLEDGE OF THE RULES TO ALL SPORTS.

ESPECIALLY A BLACK KID.

BASKETBALL WAS A RELIGION, AS WAS FOOTBALL. AIR JORDANS WERE A SACRAMENT. BLESS ME DITKA FOR I KNOW NOT WHAT THE FUCK YOU DID.

SO MY AFTERNOONS WERE SPENT TRYING TO PIECE TOGETHER THE RULES OF SOFTBALL WHILE I WAS BEING FORCED TO PLAY IT, WHICH WAS LIKE TRYING TO LEARN DOG TRAINING WHILE BEING ATTACKED BY A WOLF. I'D TRIED TO LEARN THE ONLY WAY I'D KNOWN AT THE TIME, BY READING ABOUT THESE SPORTS IN THE ENCYCLOPEDIA SET BY MY BEDSIDE.

THAT HAD BEEN AN UTTER FAILURE BECAUSE THE RULES OF THE GAMES AS DESCRIBED IN THE WORLD BOOK ENCYCLOPEDIA OF 1977 WERE A DAMNABLE SOUP OF SPORTS JARGON AND PRECONCEPTION. I PRIDED MYSELF ON BEING REASONABLY INTELLIGENT BACK THEN, BUT EVEN SO I FELT FROM TRYING TO READ UP ON THESE GAMES THAT I'D ALMOST HAVE TO LOOK UP EVERY OTHER WORD IN THE DESCRIPTION, JUST TO GET TO THE POINT OF BEING HORRIBLY CONFUSED.

THAT WAS MY THIRD STRIKE (TO KEEP WITH THE ANOLOGY); IT HELPED ME NOT A BIT THAT MY HAND WAS ALWAYS UP TO ANSWER QUESTIONS IN CLASS. I HADN'T BEEN INFORMED YET THAT ALONG WITH COMIC BOOKS AND DRAWING, PARTICIPATING IN CLASS WAS NOW SOMETHING DONE ONLY BY "FAGGOTS".

DO YOU KNOW WHAT "BLACK PRIDE" WAS BACK THEN? NEITHER DID THEY, NOT REALLY.

IF YOU BROKE DOWN THE 70'S PRIDE MOVEMENT YOU HAD TO FIRST DEFINE "BLACKNESS", WHICH WAS SOMETHING IMPOSSIBLE TO DO, SO THEY DID THE NEXT BEST THING, THEY MADE BLACKNESS THE ANTITHESIS OF WHITENESS.

UNFORTUNATELY "WHITENESS" BECAME COMMUNICATING EFFECTIVELY (TALKING WHITE), DOING WELL IN SCHOOL (ACTING WHITE), AND ENJOYING ANYTHING OUT-SIDE OF THE PREDETERMINED ART OF INTERESTS OF A STREET HUSTLER (TRYING TO BE WHITE).

HVSTLA

BAT BAT BAT BAT

IT WASN'T LIKE I NEEDED THIS OUTSIDE PRESSURE. I'M PRETTY SURE I WAS CRACKING UP EVEN BACK THEN. FOR EXAMPLE, I WAS DEEPLY RELIGIOUS BUT MY BRAIN WOULDN'T STOP FUCKING WITH ME.

. I HEARD IN ONE OF THE MYRIAD DEVIL MOVIES OF THE 70'S THAT SAYING THE LORD'S PRAYER BACKWARDS WAS ONE OF THE MOST HORRIBLE AND SATANIC THINGS A PERSON COULD DO, SO OF COURSE AS I LAY IN BED AFTER SAYING MY PRAYERS, "AMEN... EVER... AND... FOREVER... GLORY... THE... AND... POWER..." WOULD FORCE ITSELF INTO MY SCREAMING, HORRIFIED MIND, AND I WOULD BEG GOD TO FORGIVE ME.

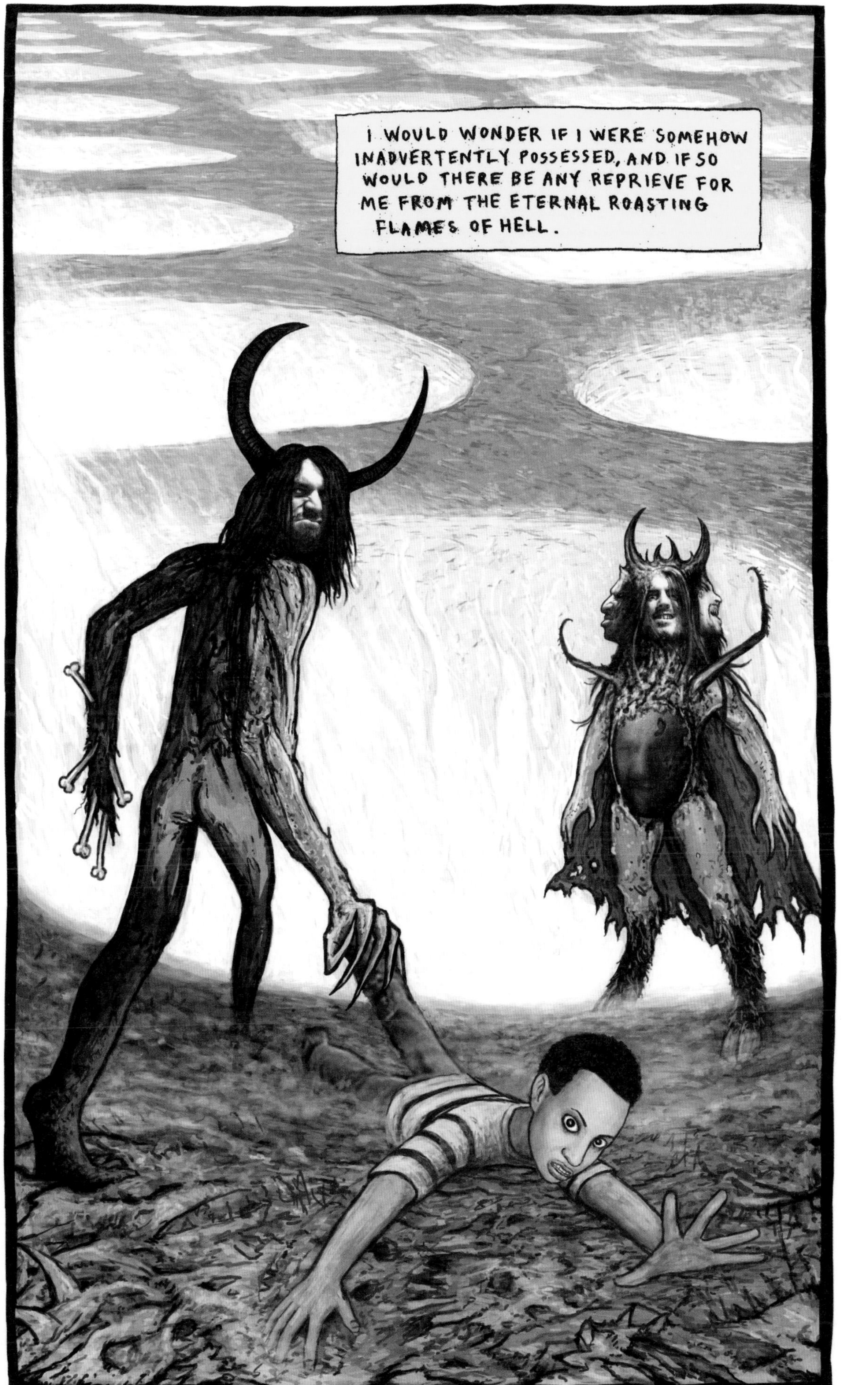
I WOULD WONDER IF I WERE SOMEHOW INADVERTENTLY POSSESSED, AND IF SO WOULD THERE BE ANY REPRIEVE FOR ME FROM THE ETERNAL ROASTING FLAMES OF HELL.

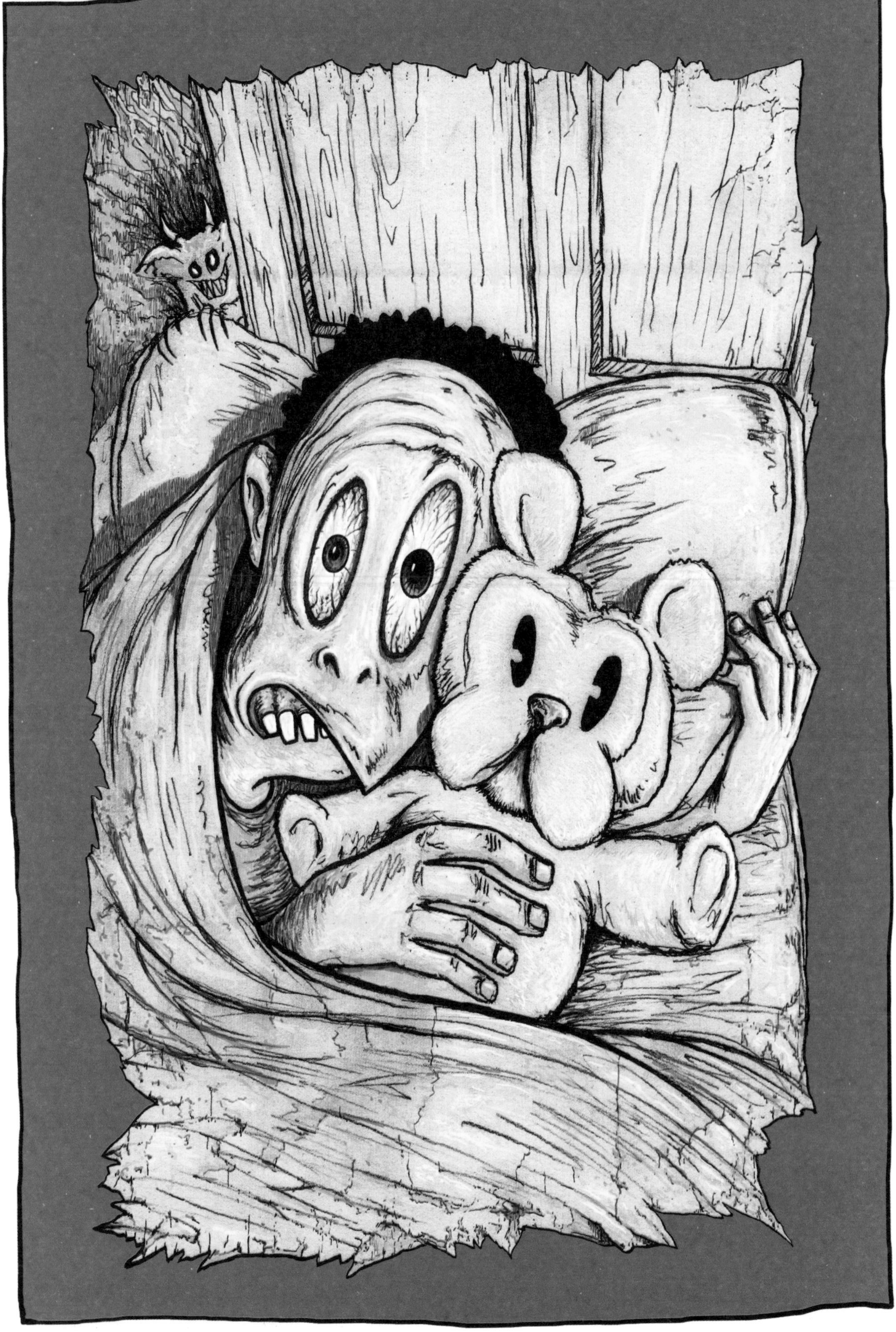

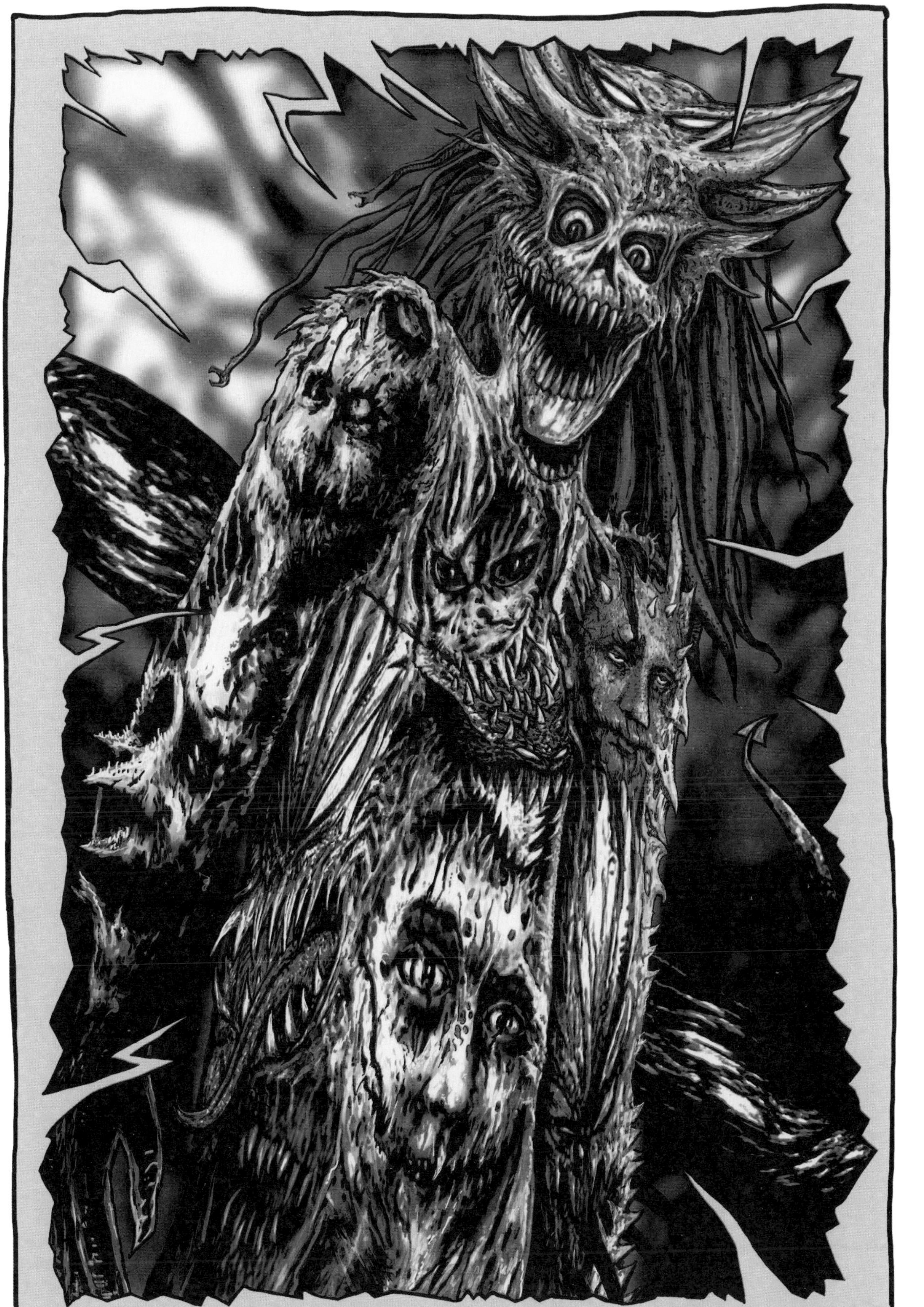

I SPENT THE AUTUMN DAYS OUT IN THE EMPTY PARKING LOT WITH THE OTHERS WHO WERE EAGERLY SWINGING THE BAT OR WAITING TO CATCH A POP-FLY.

THEY JOKED AND TALKED AS THEY WAITED FOR THEIR TURN TO BAT, WHILE I STOOD UNDER THE RAISED PORCH OF A HOUSE THAT SAT NEXT TO IMMANUEL LUTHERAN CHURCH, WHICH WAS NEXT TO IMMANUEL LUTHERAN SCHOOL. THE PORCH WAS SUPPORTED BY 4x4'S. I WOULD HIDE UNDER THERE, BEHIND THE OTHERS, TRYING TO WILL IT ALL TO BE OVER WITH.

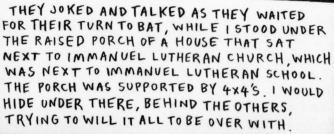

IF WE HAD BEEN WHITE STUDENTS OR BLACK STUDENTS IN THE 60'S WE'D HAVE PRODUCED A LARGE CROP OF ENGINEERS OR MATHEMATICIANS, BUT BEING AS WE WERE RIDING THE FIRST WAVE OF SOCIALLY-MANDATED NIGNORANCE, THAT WAS NEVER GOING TO HAPPEN. INSTEAD THOSE SADISTIC SAVANTS USED THEIR RAIN MAN-LIKE GEOMETRY SKILLS TO FIRE POP-UP FOULS THAT WOULD ARC DIRECTLY TOWARDS MY DAYDREAMING HEAD AND SHOULDERS.

AS BAD AS IT WAS THAT FALL SEMESTER I WASN'T YET A LOSER. I STILL HAD MY CONFIDENCE IN MY ABILITY TO DEFEND MYSELF. THAT WAS YET TO BE RIPPED AWAY FROM ME LIKE A MANIAC CANNIBAL RUNNING OFF WITH A DOWNS SYNDROME WOMAN'S NEWBORN INFANT.

OUR SMALL CLASS WAS RULED BY A GANG OF FOUR. FOUR FRIENDS WHO WERE PRACTICING THEIR LOWEST-COMMON-DENOMINATOR ACTS AS THOUGH THEY WERE TRYING TO ISOLATE A FORMULA FOR CONCENTRATED NIGGARDRY.

ROBERT GRAHAM: TALL THIN AND DARK, I THOUGHT FOR THE LONGEST TIME THAT ROBERT WAS THE ALPHA.

ON THE SURFACE HE HAD ALL OF THE VISUAL CUES. HE WAS ATHLETIC, FLASHY AND GIRLS LIKED HIM. HE WORE BUTTON-DOWN SATIN SHIRTS, BAGGY PANTS AND SKINNY-TIES. HE WORE DESIGNER GLASSES AND POINTY SHOES. HE PUT TENNIS BALLS IN HIS ARM-PITS SO THAT HIS ARM-VEINS WOULD SWELL UP. HE ALWAYS HAD A NASTY MOCK-ING LAUGH FOR THOSE OF US ON THE OUTSIDE.

QUINTON DAVIS: ROBERTS BEST FRIEND. QUINTON WAS A PERFECT EXAMPLE OF COOL BY ASSOCIATION. HE WAS GOOFY AND SOMEWHAT INSECURE AND HE MAY HAVE MANAGED AN INDE-PENDENT PERSONALITY IF HE HADN'T BEEN SO EAGER TO PLEASE THE CROWD. I ONCE, IN THE SEVENTH GRADE, MISSED MY PLAYFUL PUNCH (WHICH WAS AIMED AT HIS SHOULDER) AND ACCIDENTALLY KNOCKED A BLOW-POP HALFWAY DOWN HIS THROAT. IT WAS TERRIFYING TO WATCH HIM HAUL IT OUT.

EDSEL PARKS: (SOMEONE ACTUALLY NAMED THEIR CHILD EDSEL PARKS) HE WAS THE TALLEST AND BIGGEST KID IN CLASS. EASILY AS BIG AS ANY OF THE TEACHERS. HE LOOKED LIKE A BLACK VERSION OF ADAM BALDWIN FROM THE MOVIE MY BODYGUARD, WHICH WAS A DAMMED SHAME BECAUSE IT SOMEWHAT RUINED THAT MOVIE FOR ME, LATER WHEN I SO IDENTIFIED WITH THE BULLYING-VICTIM IN THE FILM.

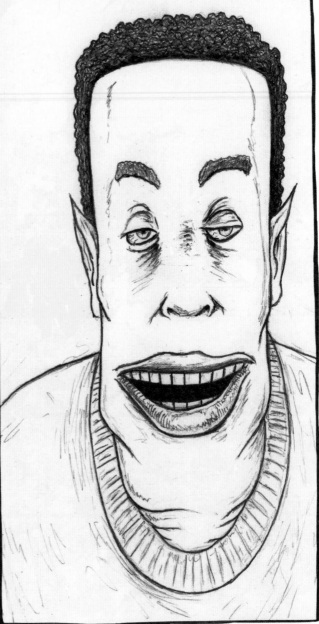

FAGGOT!
EDSEL WAS THE QUINTESSENTIAL BIG DUMB KID. HE WAS A GOOD ATHLETE, A GOOD FOLLOWER AND TERRIFYING.
HA HA HA HA HA HA HA HA HA HA HA HA HA HA HA HA HA HA HA HA

KYLE SCROGGINS: KYLE WAS ACTUALLY IN THE 7TH GRADE BUT HE WAS STILL A FULL MEMBER OF THE GANG OF FOUR. THIS FACT ALONE SHOULD GIVE YOU SOME INSIGHT TO THE PERSONALITY OF KYLE.

IT TOOK ME YEARS TO FIGURE OUT THAT HE WAS PROBABLY THE DRIVING FORCE BEHIND MY ALL-OUT REJECTION. KYLE LIVED ABOUT THREE BLOCKS AWAY FROM ME IN A MODEST RANCH HOUSE WITH HIS SINGLE MOTHER. I USED TO WONDER IF HE WAS SUCH A PRICK BECAUSE HE HAD NO FATHER TO KEEP HIM IN LINE. I HAD NO IDEA WHERE HIS FATHER WAS.

I IMAGINED HE WAS IN PRISON, OR MAYBE HE LEFT BECAUSE HE HATED HIS SON.

THINGS CAME TO AN UGLY HEAD IN THE EARLY WINTER OF 1980. KYLE HAD BEEN TAUNTING ME, MOCKING ME AND BEING A LITTLE PRICK. I DID'T KNOW WHY. I'D VISITED HIS HOUSE ONCE BACK IN THE EARLY FALL, AND THOUGHT WE WERE ON SPEAKING TERMS. BUT WE WEREN'T. NOT AT ALL. I WAS TOO NAIVE TO SEE WHAT WAS GOING ON. HE WAS TRYING TO GOAD ME INTO A FIGHT.

NOTE TO ED: DRAWING OF SCROGGINS BY C.N.F. ALSO MONSTER ISLAND MOTHER FUCKERS.

THERE WERE TWO BUS ROUTES I COULD HAVE TAKEN HOME EACH DAY FROM SCHOOL. BECAUSE KYLE LIVED SO CLOSE TO ME THERE WAS NO ESCAPING HIM IF HE WANTED TO ANNOY ME ON MY WAY HOME. NOT REALLY, BUT I TRIED ANYWAY.

IT WAS A FRUSTRATING GAME OF GHETTO CHESS. THE MORE POPULAR BUS WE COULD CATCH IN FRONT OF THE CANDY STORE, WHICH WAS A BLOCK AWAY FROM THE SCHOOL. THE STUDENTS WOULD LOAD UP ON LIK-EM-AID, OR FUNYUNS, OR BAGS OF JAY'S (THE CHICAGO BRAND) POTATO CHIPS, INTO WHICH THE CHUBBY MEXICAN SHOPKEEPER WOULD PUMP SQUIRTS OF BRIGHT RED HOT-SAUCE FROM A GALLON JUG. IF I DECIDED TO GO THIS ROUTE THEN I HAD TWO ADVANTAGES:

FIRSTLY, I HAD AN OPPORTUNITY TO TRY AND FIGURE OUT THE EXOTIC COMIC BOOK "NOVELLAS", WITH THE LURID PAINTED COVERS AND SPANISH WORDS.

CAN CAIN LA REVISTA DE LAS BURBUJAS

SWAP PANOCHA Len inherited his papa's peppers swappers

la POLIZIOTTA

JOE CRACK

YO VAMPIRO

El ENCAPUCHADO

El ENCAPUCHADO LUCHA CONTRA EL LOCO

EL ZORRO

Bri ES

SECONDLY, TAKING THIS ROUTE MADE ME SEEM BRAVER, BECAUSE I WOULD HAVE TO SIT THROUGH THE INSULTS AND TEASING AS THE FACT THAT WE TRAVELED DOWN 87TH STREET.

THE ALTERNATE ROUTE HAD ITS OWN POSITIVES AND NEGATIVES.

ON THE NEGATIVE SIDE, I HAD TO WALK THREE BLOCKS FURTHER TO GET TO A STOP WHERE I COULD NOT BE SEEN FROM THE SCHOOL.

THREE COLD BLOCKS IN THE WINTERS.

THREE QUIET LONG BLOCKS TO THINK THOUGHTS LIKE, "DID I LEAVE AT THE RIGHT TIME SO THAT KYLE CAN'T FOLLOW ME?"

"CAN I TIME IT RIGHT SO THAT I WON'T TRANSFER TO THE SAME JEFFREY BUS THAT HE IS ON, OR SHOULD I SKIP THE FINAL TRANSFER AND WALK THE LAST FOUR BLOCKS AND HAVE TO GO UNDER THE VIADUCT?"

"HOW FIRED UP TO FUCK WITH ME WILL HE BE SINCE I TOOK THE PUSSY ROUTE TODAY, INSTEAD OF MY MEDICINE?"

WERE THEY GOING TO MAKE FUN OF ME ON THE OTHER BUS? SHOULD I TURN BACK AND TAKE THE OTHER ROUTE? WOULD THEY STILL BE AT THE STOP, OR WOULD THEY HAVE LEFT ALREADY?"

LEAVING SCHOOL EVERY DAY WAS LIKE ENGINEERING A PRISON BREAK.

OPEN

THE POSITIVES OF THE QUIET (EXCEPT FOR MY HEAD) ROUTE WERE THAT I WAS BEING LEFT ALONE WHILE I WAS ON THE BUS TRAVELLING DOWN 93 RD ST. THIS SECTION OF THE CITY WAS AS STRANGELY QUIET AS A POST-APOCALYPTIC WASTELAND OF OLD GREY 1930'S STYLE DEPARTMENT-STORES AND THE ANCIENT YMCA.

ALSO THERE WAS AN OLD-FASHIONED NEWSSTAND ON THE WAY.

DEPARTMENT STORE

DEPARTMENT STORE

BEING 13, MY TASTES WERE VARIED.

MOSTLY I READ MONSTER MAGAZINES OR HUMOR MAGAZINES LIKED CRACKED, MAD, OR MY SUBVERSIVE FAVORITE: CRAZY.

LAUGHS AND GORE ASIDE, BEING 13 ALSO MEANT THAT I WAS MAYBE NOT READY FOR ACTUAL SEX, BUT DEFINITELY READY TO GET MY HANDS ON A HUSTLER MAGAZINE.

SO AT THE AGE OF THIRTEEN I PRESENTED MYSELF TO THE OLD JEWISH GUY IN THE KIOSK AND VERY CASUALLY HANDED HIM A COPY OF FANGORIA, A CRAZY MAGAZINE AND POINTED TO THE RACK IN THE DIM RECESSES OF HIS CAVE SAYING.

GIMMIE ONE OF THOSE HUSTLERS TOO.

HE LOOKED AT ME FOR A SECOND, ALL 115 lbs. OF ME WITH MY BOOK-BAG, BABY-FACE AND BAGGY ARMY FIELD-JACKET AND HE SAID.

HOW OLD ARE YOU?

STANDING UP TO MY FULL FIVE-FEET-FOUR, I INTONED A NONCHALANT.

EIGHTEEN!

IT WAS GOOD ENOUGH FOR HIM.

HE GOT HIS MONEY AND I GOT MY BOOKS. I GUESS HE FIGURED THAT MY BLACK PARENTS WOULDN'T BE PARTICULARLY UPSET BY MY CHOICE OF READING MATTER. I TOOK MY MAGAZINES AND (SWALLOWING MY HEART) MADE MY WAY TO THE BUS STOP.

THE BUS TOOK ME FROM SOUTH CHICAGO STREET TO JEFFERY BLVD, WHERE I HAD TO DECIDE TO EITHER TRANSFER OR WALK THE FINAL FOUR BLOCKS, WHICH MENT WALKING UNDER THE DREADED VIADUCT.

IF I WAITED ON THE STREET TO TRANSFER I RAN THE RISK OF GETTING ON THE SAME BUS THAT KYLE WAS ON. I ALSO HAD A DECENT CHANCE OF HAVING GANG BANGERS SHAKE ME DOWN AND RIFLE THROUGH MY POCKETS.

IF I DECIDED TO WALK UNDER THE VIADUCT I FELT LIKE ANY HORRIBLE THING WAS POSSIBLE.

THE VIADUCT RAN THE LENGTH OF THE SOUTH 9400 BLOCK, UNDER A TRAIN-YARD. IT WAS A NOISY, DAMP, POORLY-LIT TRACK. THERE WERE TWO NARROW LANES OF TRAFFIC RUNNING IN EITHER DIRECTION ON BRICK PAVED STREETS. PADESTRIANS HAD WALKWAYS ALONG THE SIDE.

IT WAS FRIGHTENING TO A KID. OR AT LEAST TO ME AS MY MIND CONJURED PEDOPHILE RAPISTS, RATS, GANGSTERS, JOHN WAYNE GACY, OR PERHAPS, WORSE OF ALL, KYLE.

THIS WAS MY DAILY CHOICE. I USUALLY JUST HALVED IT OUT SO THAT THREE DAYS I'D GO HOME ALONE AND TWO DAYS I'D RIDE WITH THE FOUR HORSEMEN AND THEIR DISEASED MINIONS.

IT WAS ABOUT A WEEK AFTER THE FIRST SNOWFALL THAT THINGS WENT PAST THE POINT OF NO-RETURN. AS I'VE SAID, I WASN'T COMPLETELY ASS-OUT BECAUSE I STILL KNEW I HAD THE OPTION OF FIGHTING.

YET SOMEHOW I'D AVOIDED IT UNTIL THAT POINT.

I'D HAD A FEW FIGHTS AS A KID AND HANDLED MYSELF PRETTY WELL, BUT I HADN'T BEEN PHYSICALLY PROVOKED AS OF YET BY THE GANG OF FOUR. YES, THEY'D SPITBALL ME, OR THWUNK MY EARS, BUT NO PUNCHES HAD COME MY WAY. IN MY MIND A PERSON HAD TO BE SWUNG ON FIRST FOR IT TO BE "SELF-DEFENSE". THIS PARTICULAR DAY I'D DECIDED TO TAKE THE BUS WITH THE CROWD.

THERE WAS THE USUAL LAUGHING AND CUTTING-UP AS WE ALL TRIED TO BE AS LOUD AND BLACK AS WE COULD BE.

A FEW OF US STOOD ON THE CORNER OF 87TH AND JEFFREY, AND WAITED FOR THE BUS. THE BENCH WAS COLD AND DIRTY SO WE STOOD. THE OTHERS WERE TALKING AS I LOOKED AROUND ME AT THE FILTHY REMNANT SNOW, THE OVERCAST GREY SKIES AND DIRTY STREET.

LIVING IN THAT PART OF THE CITY SEEMED TO BE LIKE LIVING INSIDE ONE OF A SMOKER'S CANCEROUS LUNGS.

THE BUS CAME SLOSHING UP AND STOPPED FOR US IN THE SHALLOW POOL OF CHURNING SEWAGE-COLORED SALTWATER. WE STEPPED ABOARD, FLASHED OUR TRANSFERS (THE DRIVER HAVING PUT THE BUS IN MOTION) AND LURCHED OUR WAY BACK.

THE BUS ROCKED LIKE A SHIP ON ROUGH SEAS AND WE HAD TO GRAB FROM RAIL TO RAIL, LIKE ORANGUTANS ON A JUNGLE-JIM AS WE FOUND OUR SEATS.

THE BASIC RULE WAS THAT BAD (COOL) PEOPLE SAT IN THE BACK OF THE BUS IF THERE WAS ROOM. I SAT IN THE MIDDLE AS KYLE AND TWO OTHERS HEADED FOR THE BACK.

JUST SITTING BY MYSELF MADE ME AN OUTCAST.

WHO DID I THINK I WAS? DID I THINK I WAS BETTER THAN THEM OR SOMETHING?

"I ALREADY TALKED "WHITE" AND HAD MY HAND UP IN CLASS ALL THE TIME, LIKE A PUNK. MAYBE THAT'S WHY KYLE HATED ME. OUR TWO OTHER CLASS-MATES GOT OFF THE BUS AT THEIR STOPS BEFORE WE HIT 93RD STREET.

KYLE CAME FROM HIS SEAT IN THE BACK AND SAT ACROSS FROM ME.

HE STARED AT ME. TAUNTING, MOCKING. WHAT DID HE WANT? IT WAS OBVIOUS. HE WAS BEGGING FOR A FIGHT, AS HE SAT THERE SMILING EVILLY. I COULD HAVE GOTTEN OFF ON 96TH OR 97TH. KYLE'S STOP WAS 96TH.

I PULLED THE CORD FOR THE 96TH STREET STOP, LOOKED AT KYLE AND SAID (AS STEADILY AS POSSIBLE).

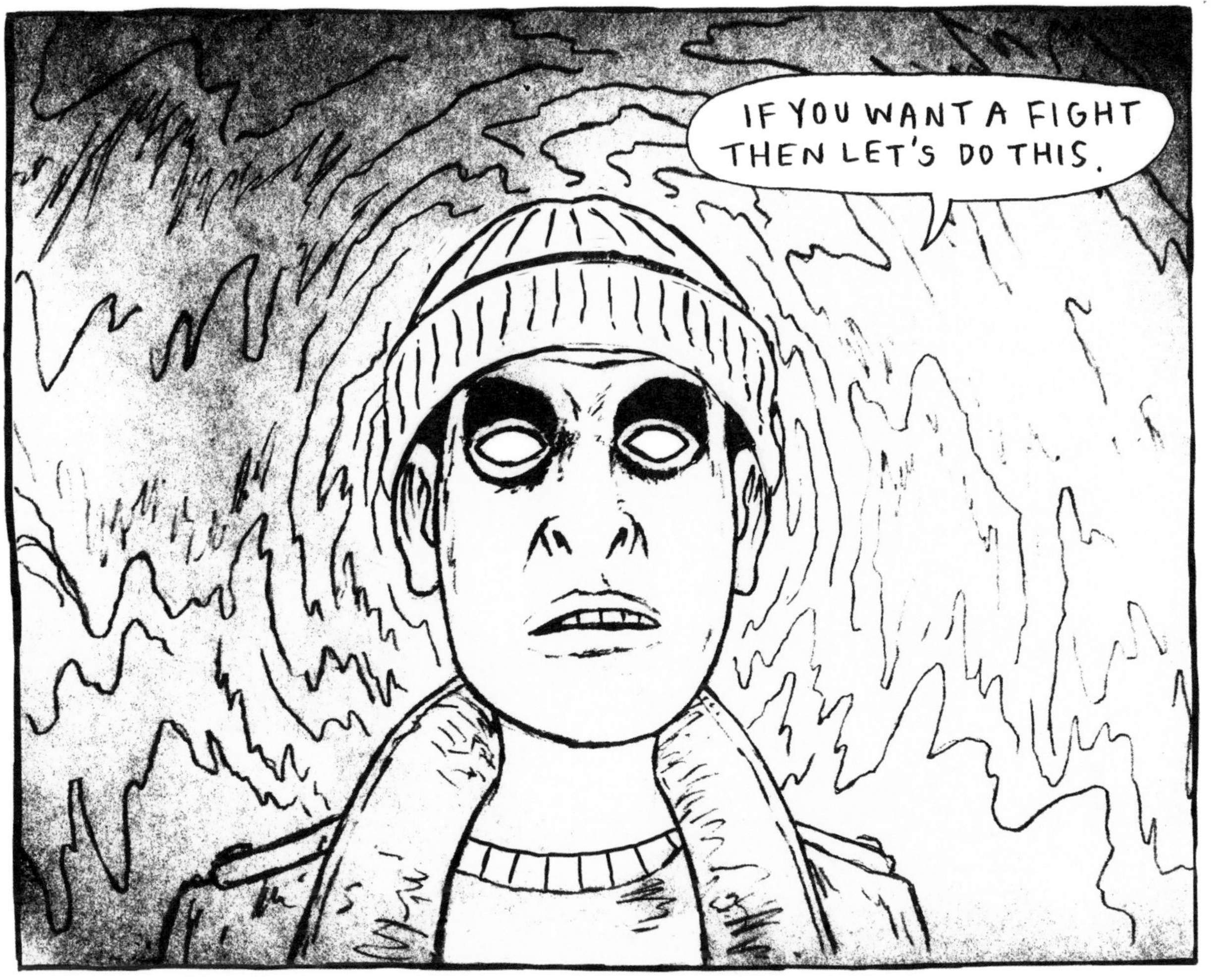
IF YOU WANT A FIGHT THEN LET'S DO THIS.

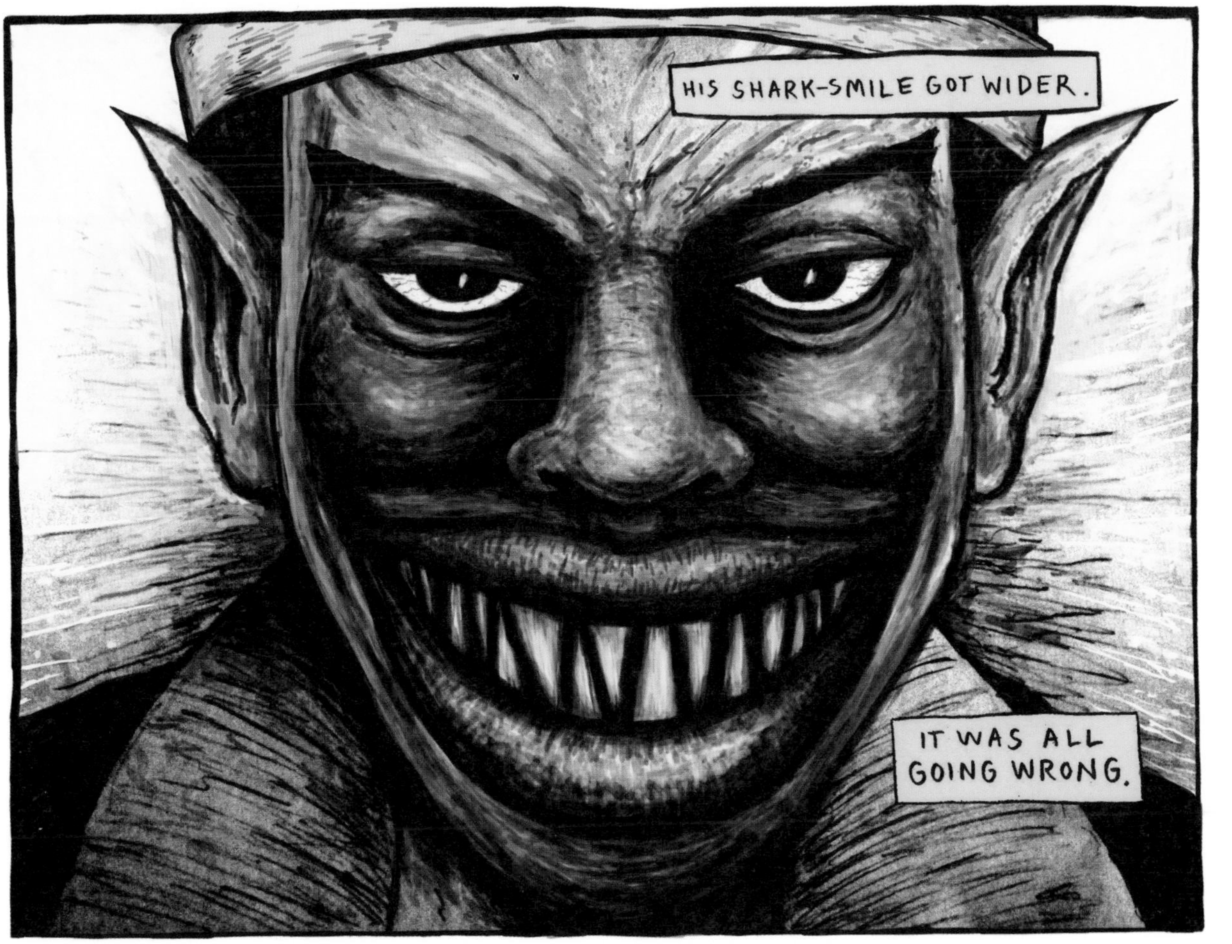
HIS SHARK-SMILE GOT WIDER.
IT WAS ALL GOING WRONG.

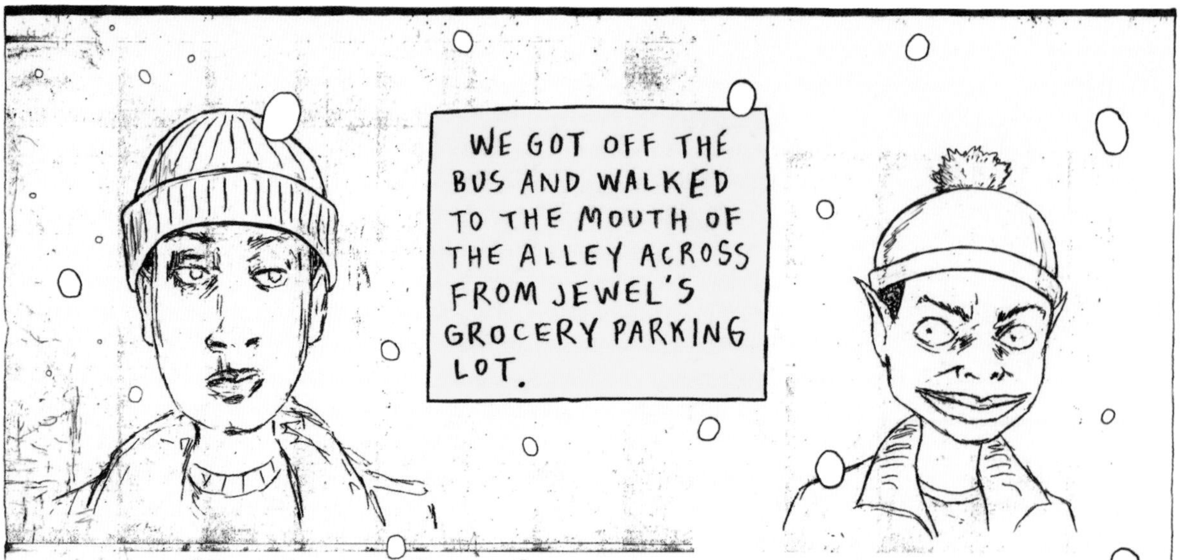
WE GOT OFF THE BUS AND WALKED TO THE MOUTH OF THE ALLEY ACROSS FROM JEWEL'S GROCERY PARKING LOT.

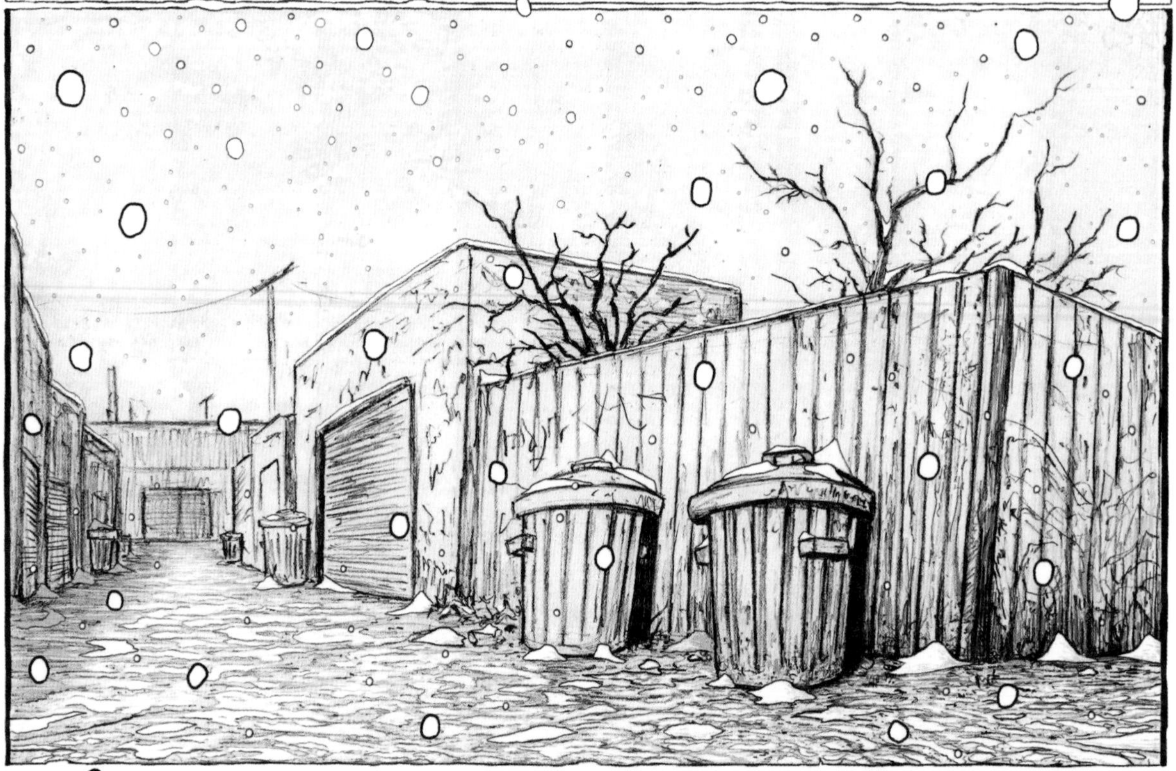

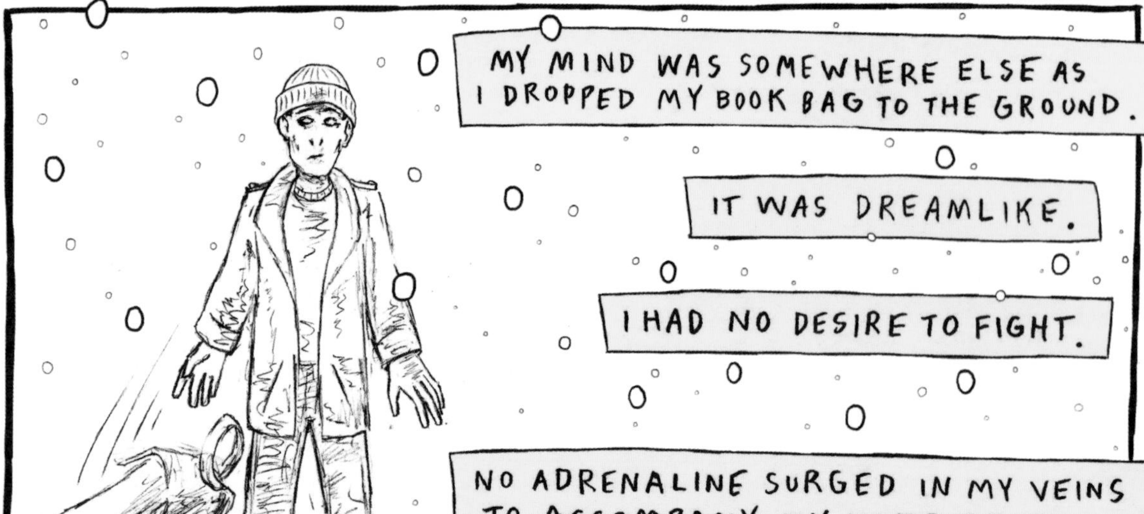
MY MIND WAS SOMEWHERE ELSE AS I DROPPED MY BOOK BAG TO THE GROUND.
IT WAS DREAMLIKE.
I HAD NO DESIRE TO FIGHT.
NO ADRENALINE SURGED IN MY VEINS TO ACCOMPANY MY NUMB FEAR.

IT WAS LIKE I WAS PILOTING MY BODY BY REMOTE.

I GUESS I COULDN'T BELIEVE THAT IT WAS ACTUALLY REAL SINCE IT WAS ALL SO ILLOGICAL.

MY BODY FELT HEAVY AND UNRESPONSIVE.

I HALF-HEARTELY SWUNG.

TAP

IT WENT WIDE AND GRAZED KYLE'S SHOULDER.

I GUESS HE WASN'T FEELING THE SURREAL WORLD AROUND US BECAUSE HE LANDED A SOLID RIGHT TO MY MOUTH.

I'D NEVER BEEN HIT IN THE FACE BEFORE.

I HAD HOWEVER FALLEN ON THE STAIRS AT HOME BEFORE AND SMASHED MY LIPS AGAINST MY TEETH.

THIS WAS JUST LIKE THAT.

IT WAS SHOCKING.

IT THREW ME OFF AS MY MIND TRIED TO MAKE SENSE OF IT.

AS MY MIND WANDERED, MY AUTOPILOT PUNCHES SEEMED TO KEEP MISSING, OR IF THEY LANDED THEY LACKED POWER.

IT WAS LIKE MY BRAIN AND HEART HAD ALREADY GIVEN UP.

MY MIND WAS FOCUSING ON MY SURROUNDINGS AS THOUGH THIS FIGHT WASN'T HAPPENING.

THE HARD GROUND, THE GALVANIZED TRASH-CANS BY THE BACKYARD FENCES ALONG THE ALLEY, THE WEATHERED PAINT-PEELING GARAGES, THE RAT-ABATEMENT PROGRAM POSTERS THAT THE CITY HAD STAPLED TO THE TELEPHONE POLES, THE SKELETAL FINGERED BLACK TREES.

EVERYTHING EXCEPT THE BATTLE AT HAND.

MAYBE IT WAS THE LOOK ON KYLE'S FACE.

LIKE I WAS NOTHING.

HIS FACE WAS EASY AND EMOTIONLESS, EXCEPT FOR A PERMANENT NONCHALANT HALF-SMILE, LIKE THIS WAS NO BIG DEAL FOR HIM.

I COULD TASTE BLOOD IN MY MOUTH AND FEEL THE TATTERED SHARDS OF MY LIPS, WHICH HIS FIST HAD SPLIT OPEN.

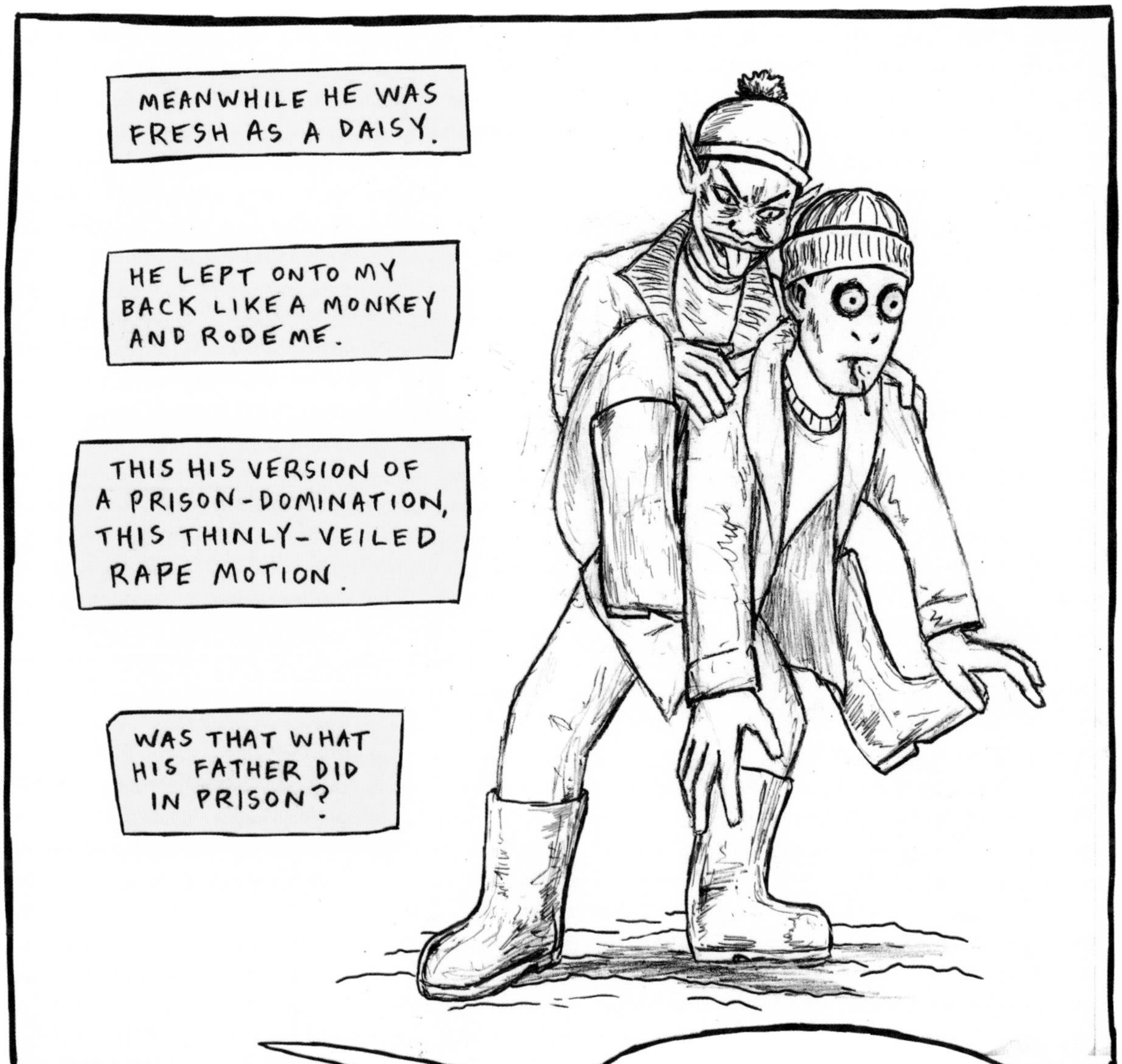
MEANWHILE HE WAS FRESH AS A DAISY.
HE LEPT ONTO MY BACK LIKE A MONKEY AND RODE ME.
THIS HIS VERSION OF A PRISON-DOMINATION, THIS THINLY-VEILED RAPE MOTION.
WAS THAT WHAT HIS FATHER DID IN PRISON?

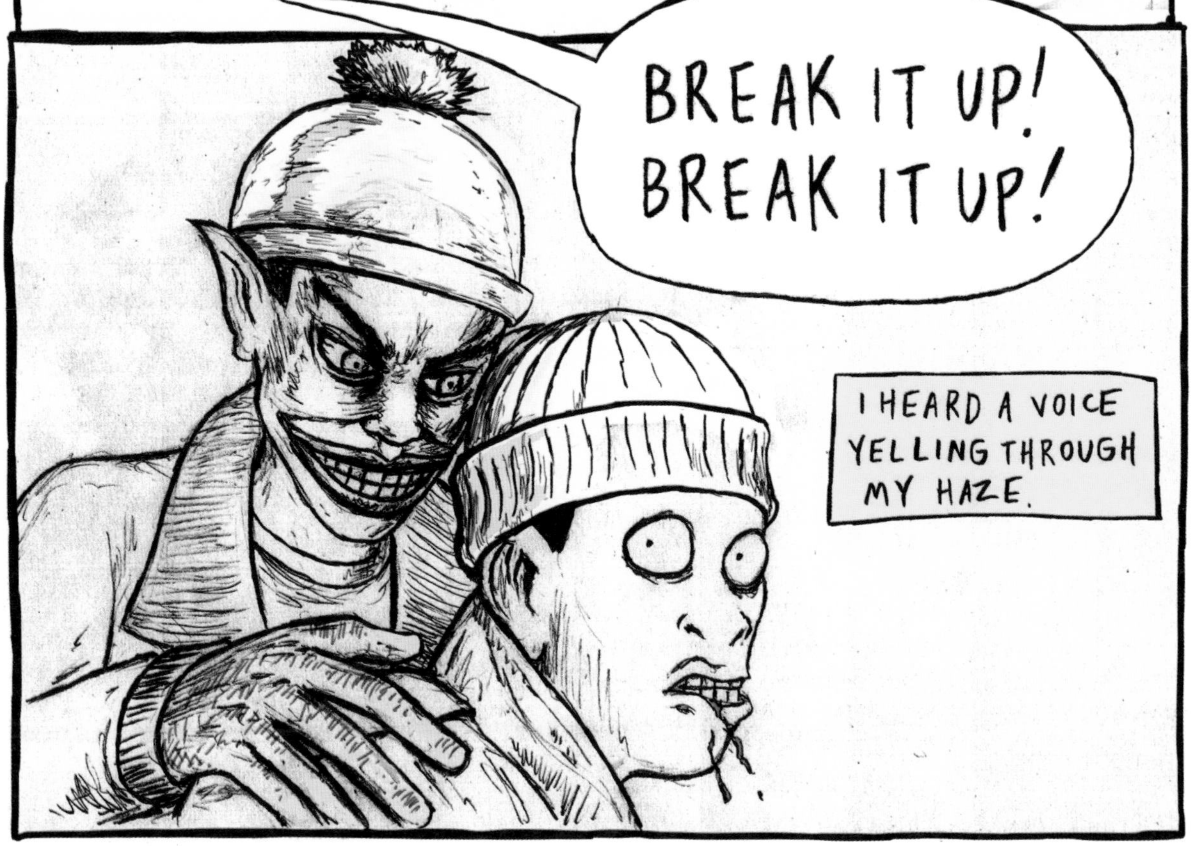
BREAK IT UP! BREAK IT UP!
I HEARD A VOICE YELLING THROUGH MY HAZE.

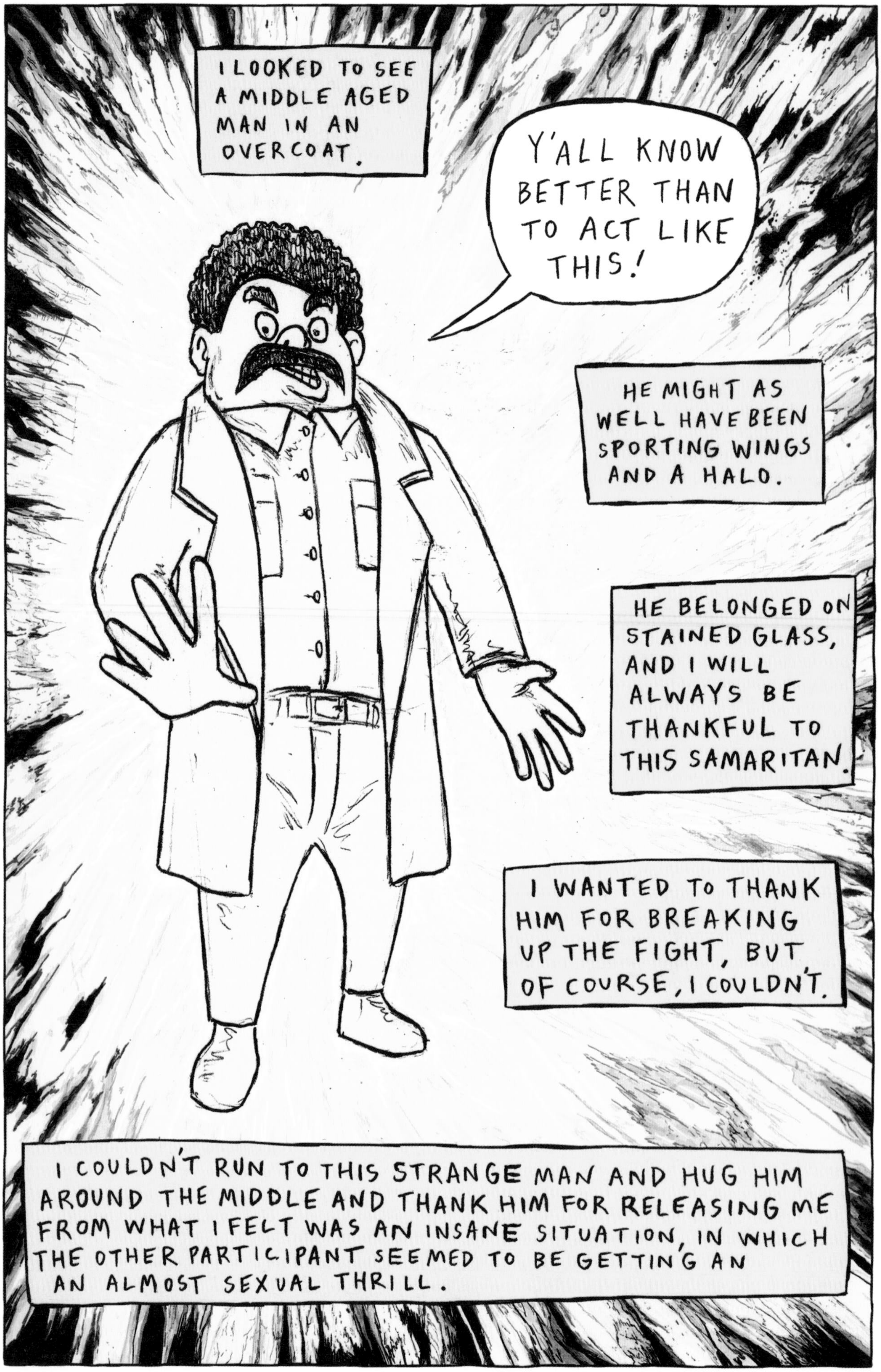
I LOOKED TO SEE A MIDDLE AGED MAN IN AN OVERCOAT.
Y'ALL KNOW BETTER THAN TO ACT LIKE THIS!
HE MIGHT AS WELL HAVE BEEN SPORTING WINGS AND A HALO.
HE BELONGED ON STAINED GLASS, AND I WILL ALWAYS BE THANKFUL TO THIS SAMARITAN.
I WANTED TO THANK HIM FOR BREAKING UP THE FIGHT, BUT OF COURSE, I COULDN'T.
I COULDN'T RUN TO THIS STRANGE MAN AND HUG HIM AROUND THE MIDDLE AND THANK HIM FOR RELEASING ME FROM WHAT I FELT WAS AN INSANE SITUATION, IN WHICH THE OTHER PARTICIPANT SEEMED TO BE GETTING AN AN ALMOST SEXUAL THRILL.

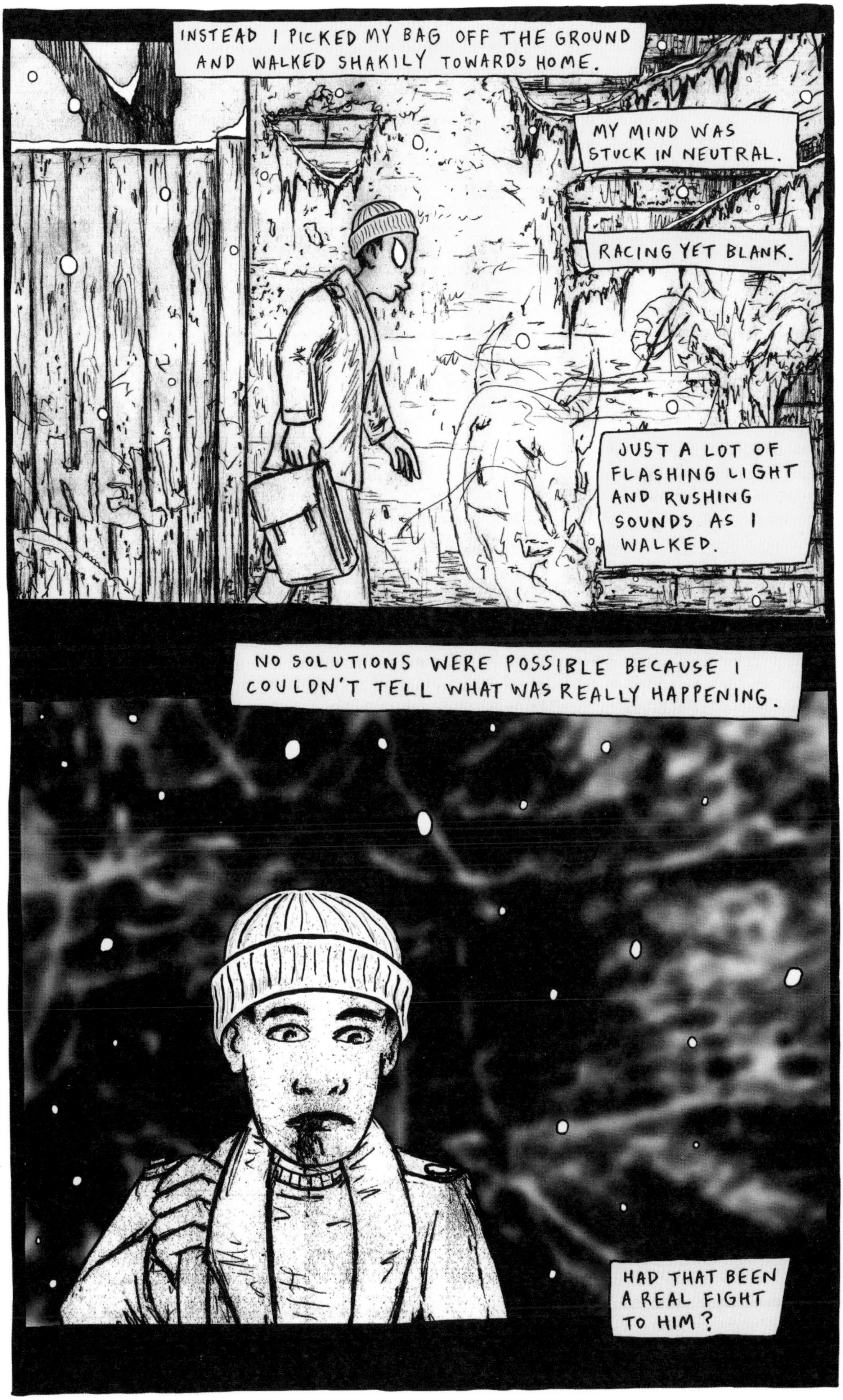
INSTEAD I PICKED MY BAG OFF THE GROUND AND WALKED SHAKILY TOWARDS HOME.
MY MIND WAS STUCK IN NEUTRAL.
RACING YET BLANK.
JUST A LOT OF FLASHING LIGHT AND RUSHING SOUNDS AS I WALKED.
NO SOLUTIONS WERE POSSIBLE BECAUSE I COULDN'T TELL WHAT WAS REALLY HAPPENING.
HAD THAT BEEN A REAL FIGHT TO HIM?

HE WAS LAUGHING THE WHOLE TIME AND I'D TURNED IN SUCH A WEAK PERFORMANCE THAT I WOULDN'T HAVE FOOLED THE MOST GULLIBLE PRO-WRESTLING AUDIENCE.

I'D ONLY MADE IT ABOUT HALF A BLOCK WHEN I WAS FLANKED BY TWO OLDER TEEN BOYS. ROUGH-LOOKING ASHY BLACK MOTHERFUCKERS IN DARK CLOTHES.

WHY YOU FIGHTIN' WITH OUR LITTLE COUSIN?

THE ONE ON THE RIGHT ASKED ME.

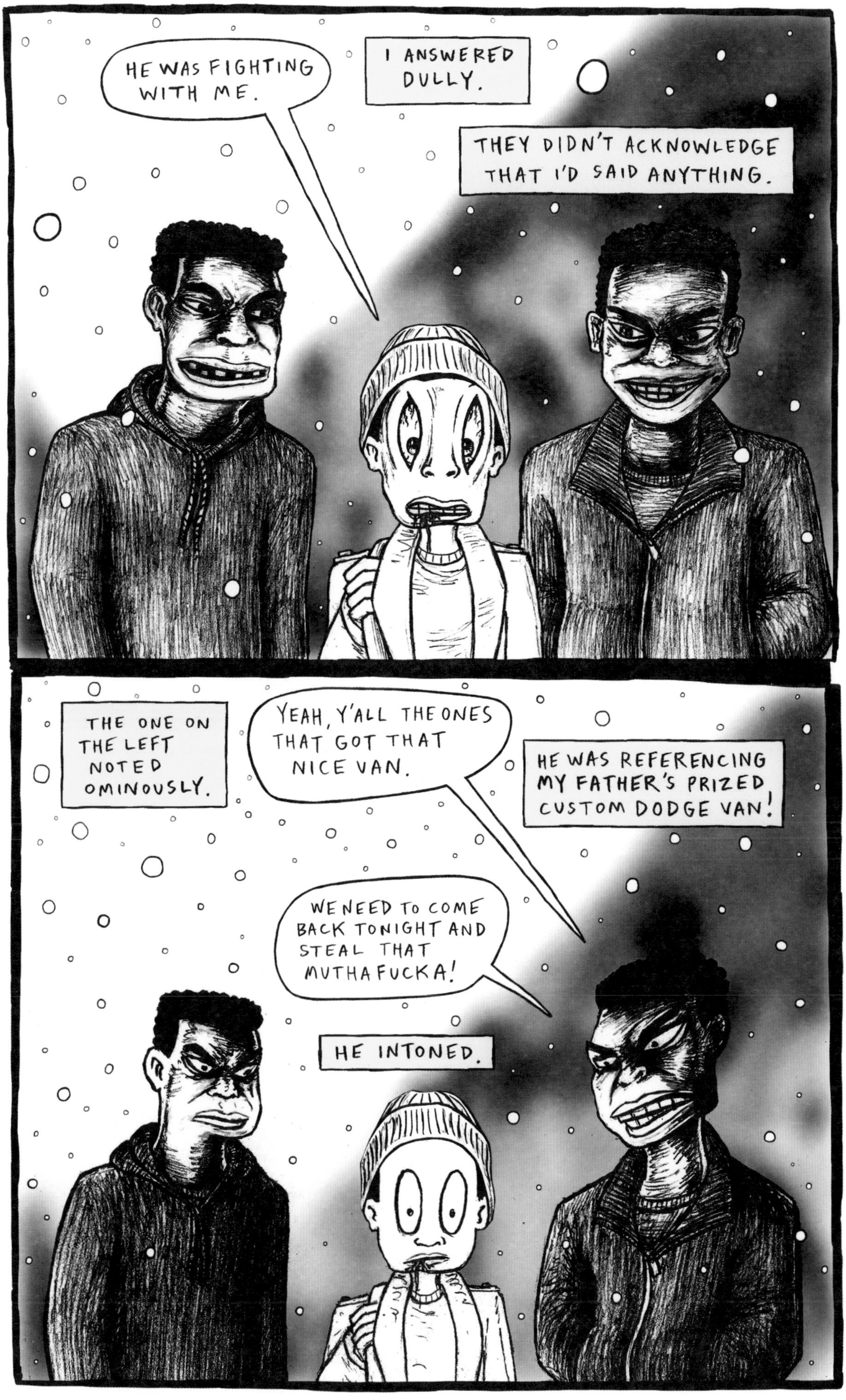
HE WAS FIGHTING WITH ME.
I ANSWERED DULLY.
THEY DIDN'T ACKNOWLEDGE THAT I'D SAID ANYTHING.
THE ONE ON THE LEFT NOTED OMINOUSLY.
YEAH, Y'ALL THE ONES THAT GOT THAT NICE VAN.
HE WAS REFERENCING MY FATHER'S PRIZED CUSTOM DODGE VAN!
WE NEED TO COME BACK TONIGHT AND STEAL THAT MUTHAFUCKA!
HE INTONED.

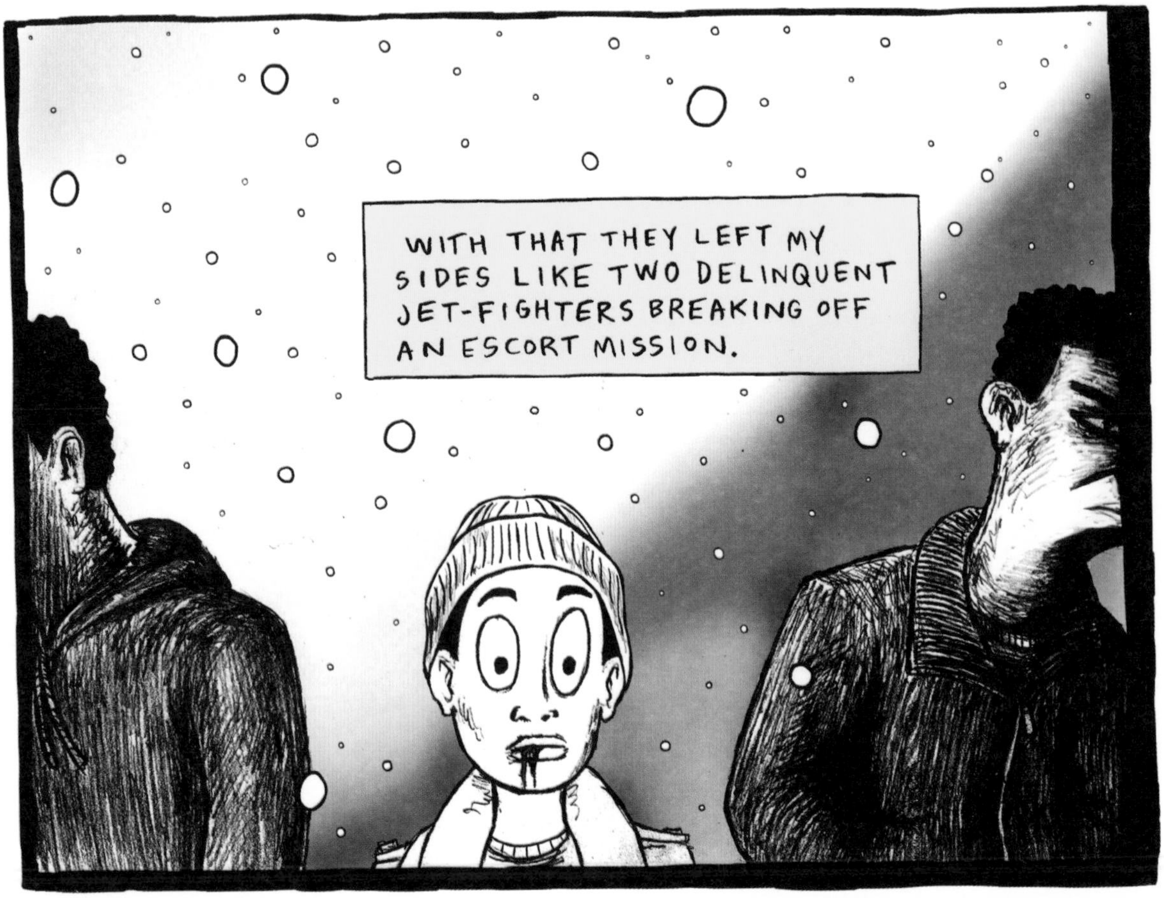
WITH THAT THEY LEFT MY SIDES LIKE TWO DELINQUENT JET-FIGHTERS BREAKING OFF AN ESCORT MISSION.

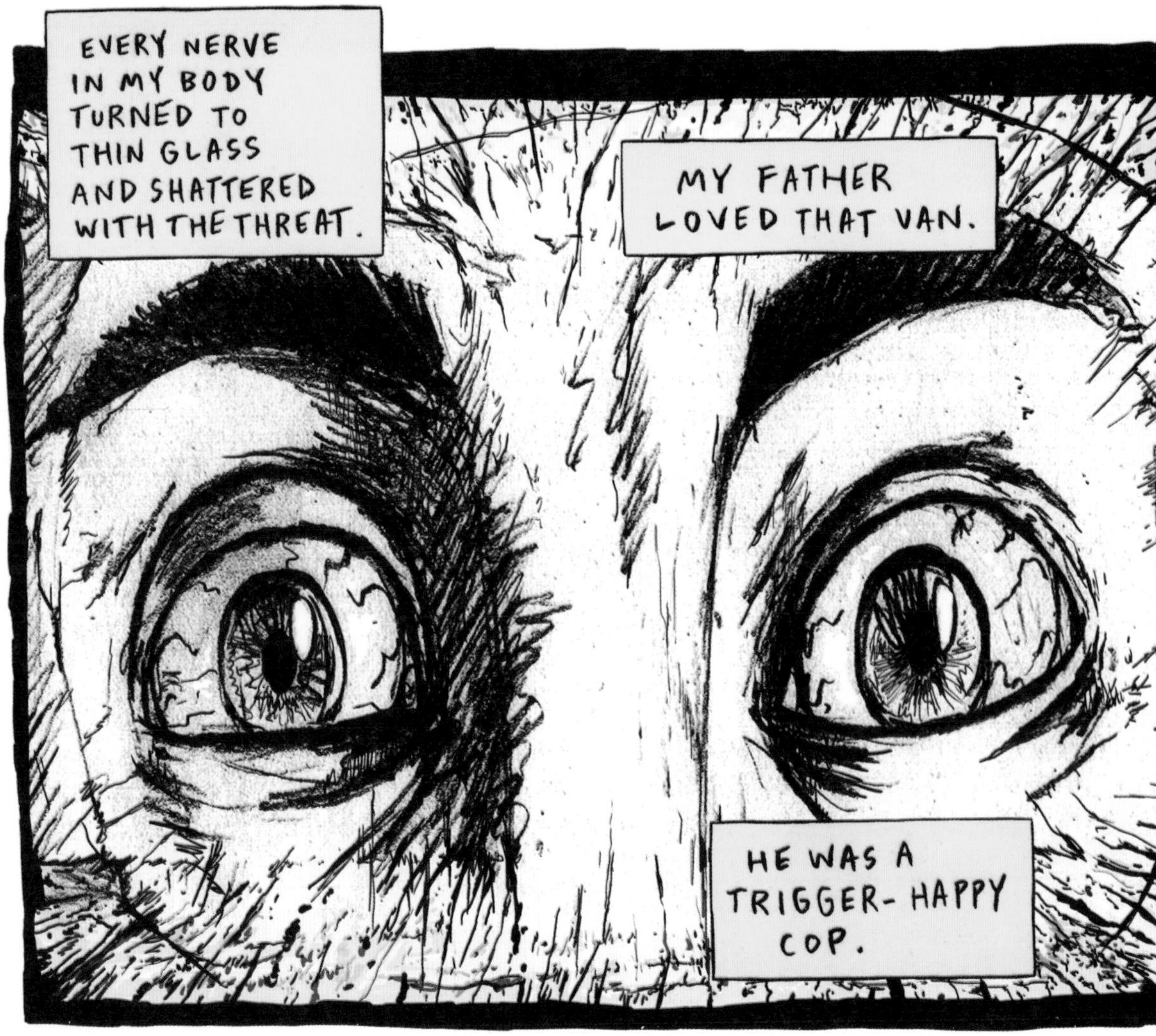
EVERY NERVE IN MY BODY TURNED TO THIN GLASS AND SHATTERED WITH THE THREAT.
MY FATHER LOVED THAT VAN.
HE WAS A TRIGGER-HAPPY COP.

ON A MORNING A FEW YEARS PRIOR HE'D BEEN AWAKENED BY THE SOUND OF A CAR ALARM GOING OFF ON THE STREET OUTSIDE OUR HOUSE.

MY COUSIN TOOTSIE LIVED TWO DOORS DOWN FROM US.

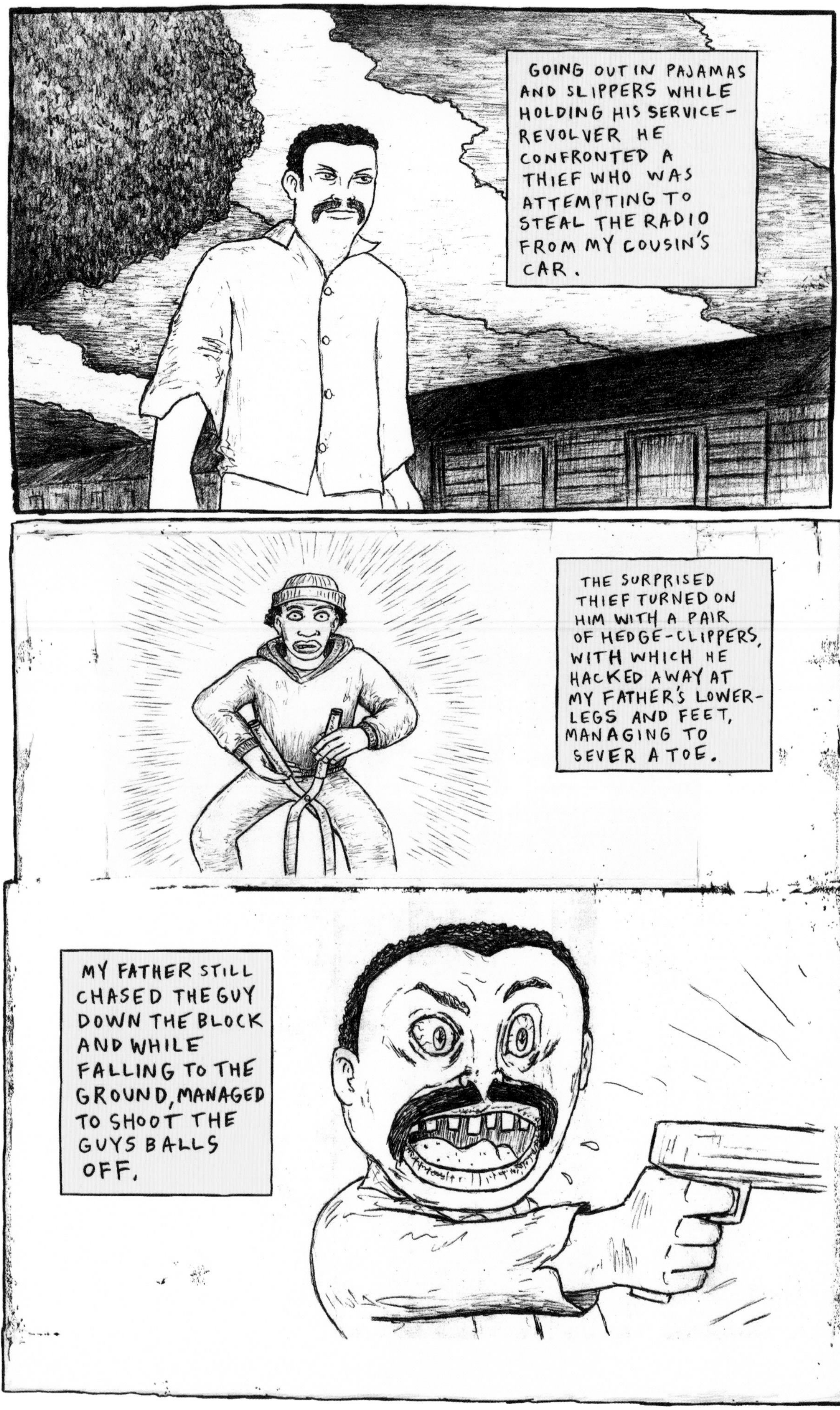
GOING OUT IN PAJAMAS AND SLIPPERS WHILE HOLDING HIS SERVICE-REVOLVER HE CONFRONTED A THIEF WHO WAS ATTEMPTING TO STEAL THE RADIO FROM MY COUSIN'S CAR.
THE SURPRISED THIEF TURNED ON HIM WITH A PAIR OF HEDGE-CLIPPERS, WITH WHICH HE HACKED AWAY AT MY FATHER'S LOWER-LEGS AND FEET, MANAGING TO SEVER A TOE.
MY FATHER STILL CHASED THE GUY DOWN THE BLOCK AND WHILE FALLING TO THE GROUND, MANAGED TO SHOOT THE GUYS BALLS OFF.

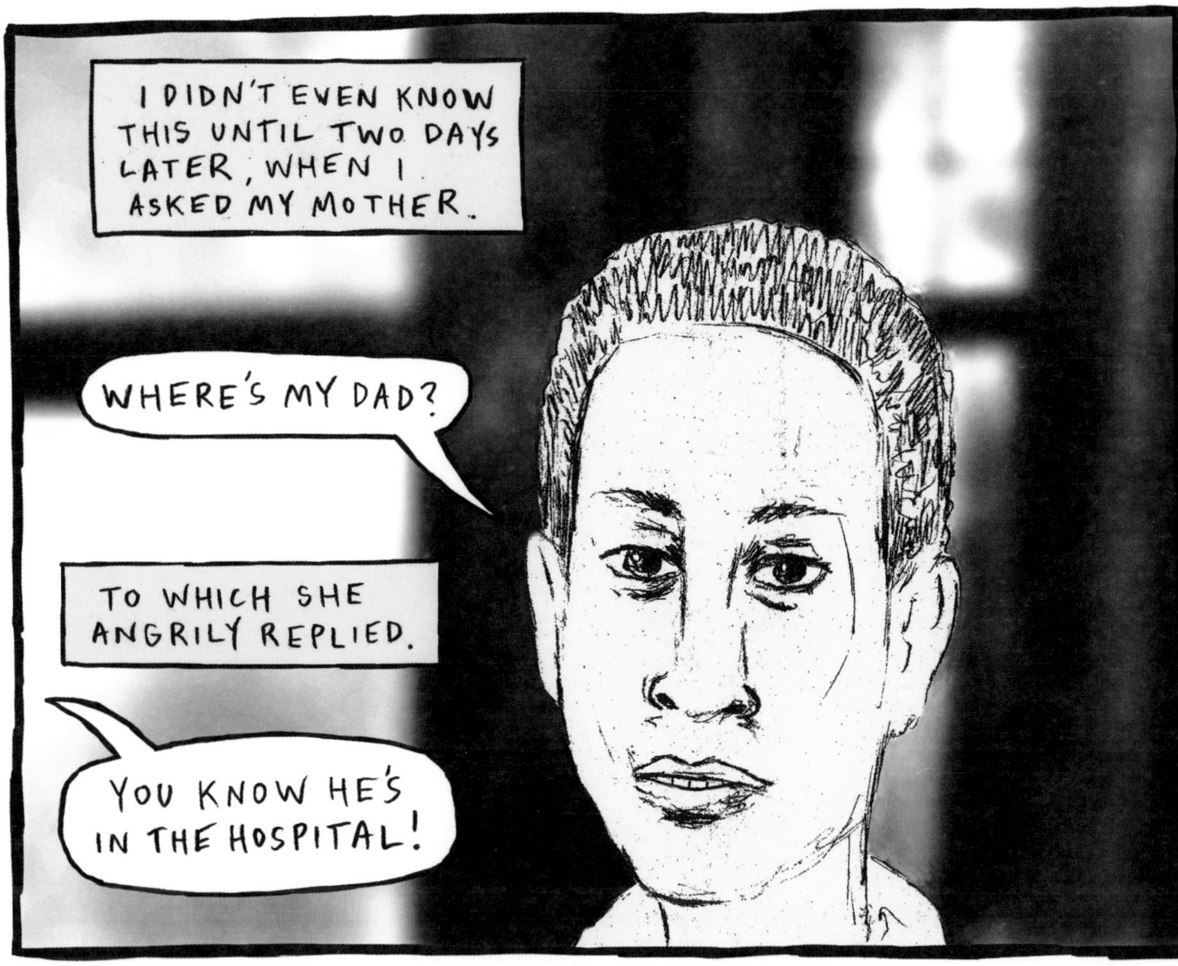
I DIDN'T EVEN KNOW THIS UNTIL TWO DAYS LATER, WHEN I ASKED MY MOTHER.
WHERE'S MY DAD?
TO WHICH SHE ANGRILY REPLIED.
YOU KNOW HE'S IN THE HOSPITAL!

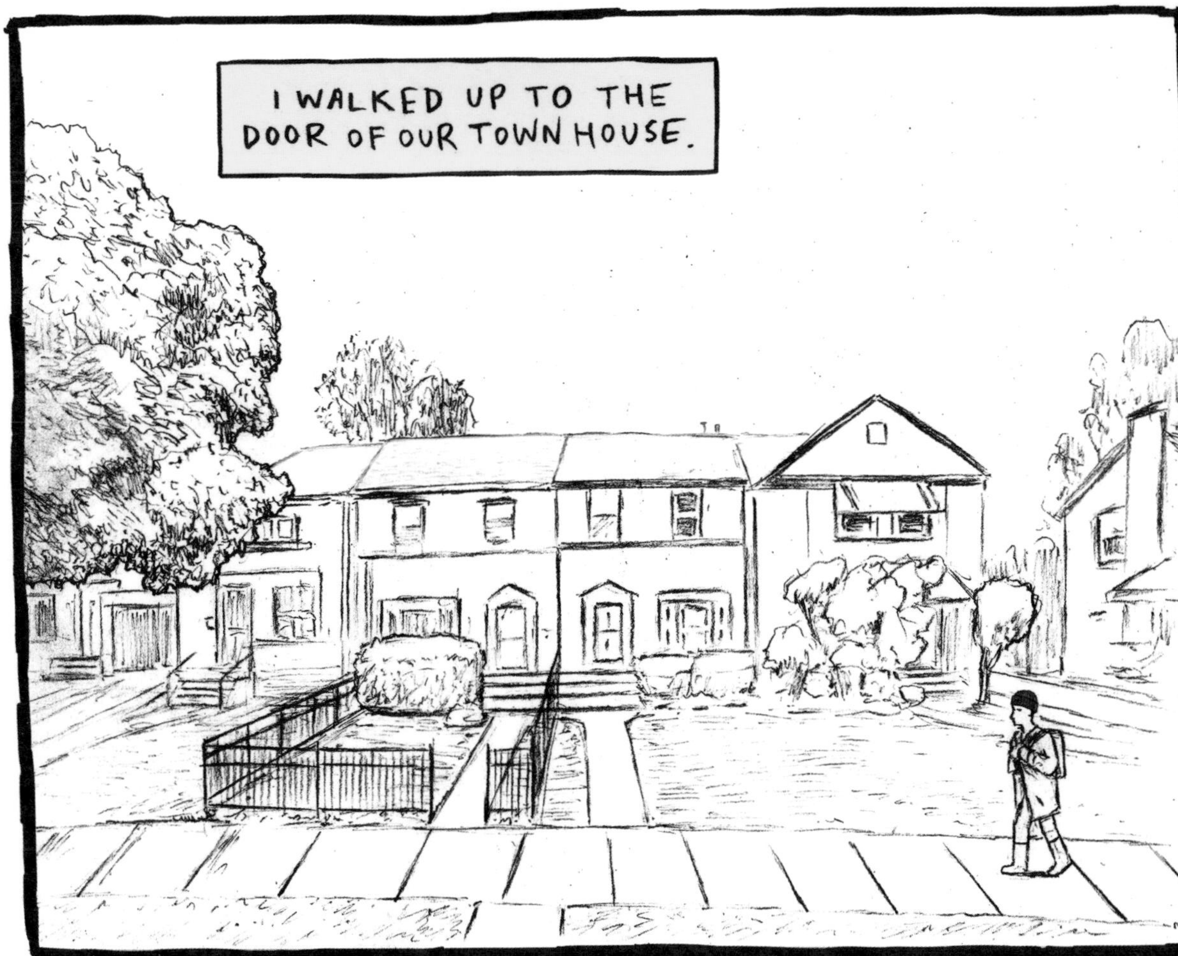
I WALKED UP TO THE DOOR OF OUR TOWN HOUSE.

THINKING THAT MY ACTIONS IN CHOOSING TO FIGHT COULD POSSIBLY GET MY FATHER KILLED.

OR SOMEONE ELSE KILLED.

OR AT THE VERY LEAST GET HIS BELOVED EXTENDED-REAR CUSTOMIZED DODGE VAN STOLEN OR DAMAGED.

I UNLOCKED THE DOOR AND KEYED IN THE ALARM PAD CODE.

IF ANYONE TRIED TO STEAL HIS VAN HE WOULD FIND OUT THAT IT WAS MY FAULT AND PUT ME IN THE HOSPITAL.

BUT IF I WARNED HIM HE'D BEAT THE SHIT OUT OF ME FOR GETTING THE SITUATION STARTED.

I WENT UPSTAIRS TO MY ROOM AND FELL ONTO MY BED.

BECAUSE I WAS NO LONGER SUPPORTING MY VERTICAL POSITION I WAS ABLE TO FALL APART.

I BEGAN TO SHAKE.

MY BODY FELT COLD AND SICK.

HOT TEARS RAN FROM MY EYES AND SOAKED INTO THE PILLOW.

I RAN THE FIGHT THROUGH MY MIND IN A LOOP.

I LOST.

I LOST TO A KID WHO WAS SMALLER THAN ME.

BUT I STOOD UP FOR MYSELF!

...BUT I HAD LOST THE FIGHT.

I WASN'T A FIGHTER.

I HAD NO HEART FOR IT, NOT EVEN AS I WAS DOING IT.

AN ANALYTICAL MIND IS THE ENEMY OF THE WARRIOR.

I'D BEEN BUSY EXAMINING MOTIVES AND SURROUNDINGS AND CONSEQUENCES WHEREAS A TRUE FIGHTER WOULD HAVE JUST TRIPPED KYLE AND STOMPED HIS HEAD INTO THE SIDEWALK.

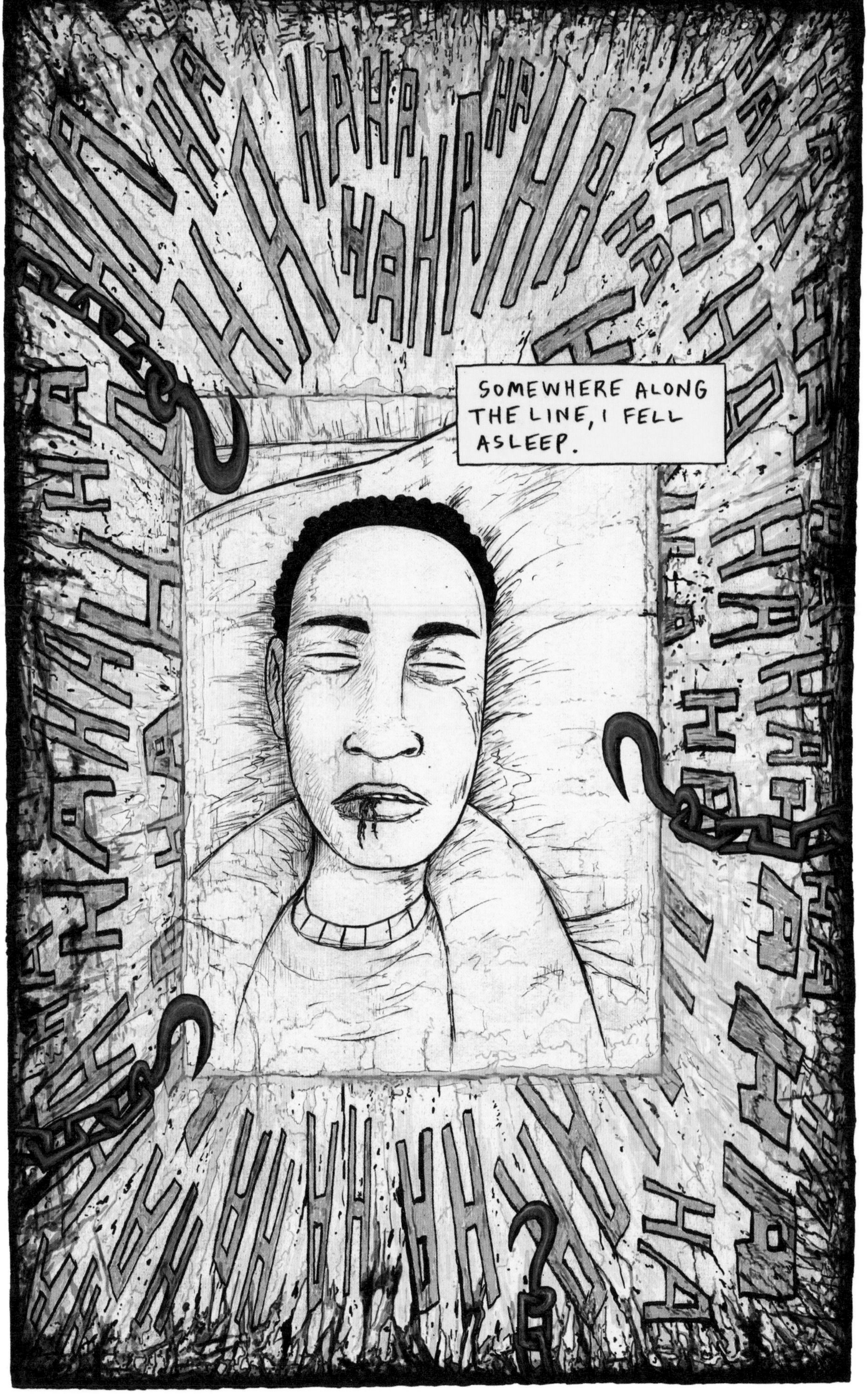
SOMEWHERE ALONG THE LINE, I FELL ASLEEP.

MY MOTHER WAS THE FIRST OF MY PARENTS TO GET HOME FROM WORK.

SHE WORKED DOWNTOWN FOR CHUBB AND SONS INSURANCE COMPANY.

SHE RATTLED AROUND FOR A WHILE, DOWN ON THE FIRST FLOOR, BEFORE COMING UPSTAIRS.

MY PARENTS' BEDROOM WAS NEXT TO MINE.

I HEARD HER MAKE AN INQUISITIVE SOUND THAT I TOOK TO BE A QUESTION.

I DIDN'T REALLY HEAR HER.

I WAS SLOW TO ANSWER.

I NEEDED HER TO COME TO ME AND GIVE ME COMFORT.

INSTEAD SHE OPENED MY DOOR AND ASKED.

DON'T YOU HEAR ME TALKING TO YOU?

I'M NOT FEELING GOOD.

I REPLIED THROUGH MUCOUS HEAVY NASAL-PASSAGES.

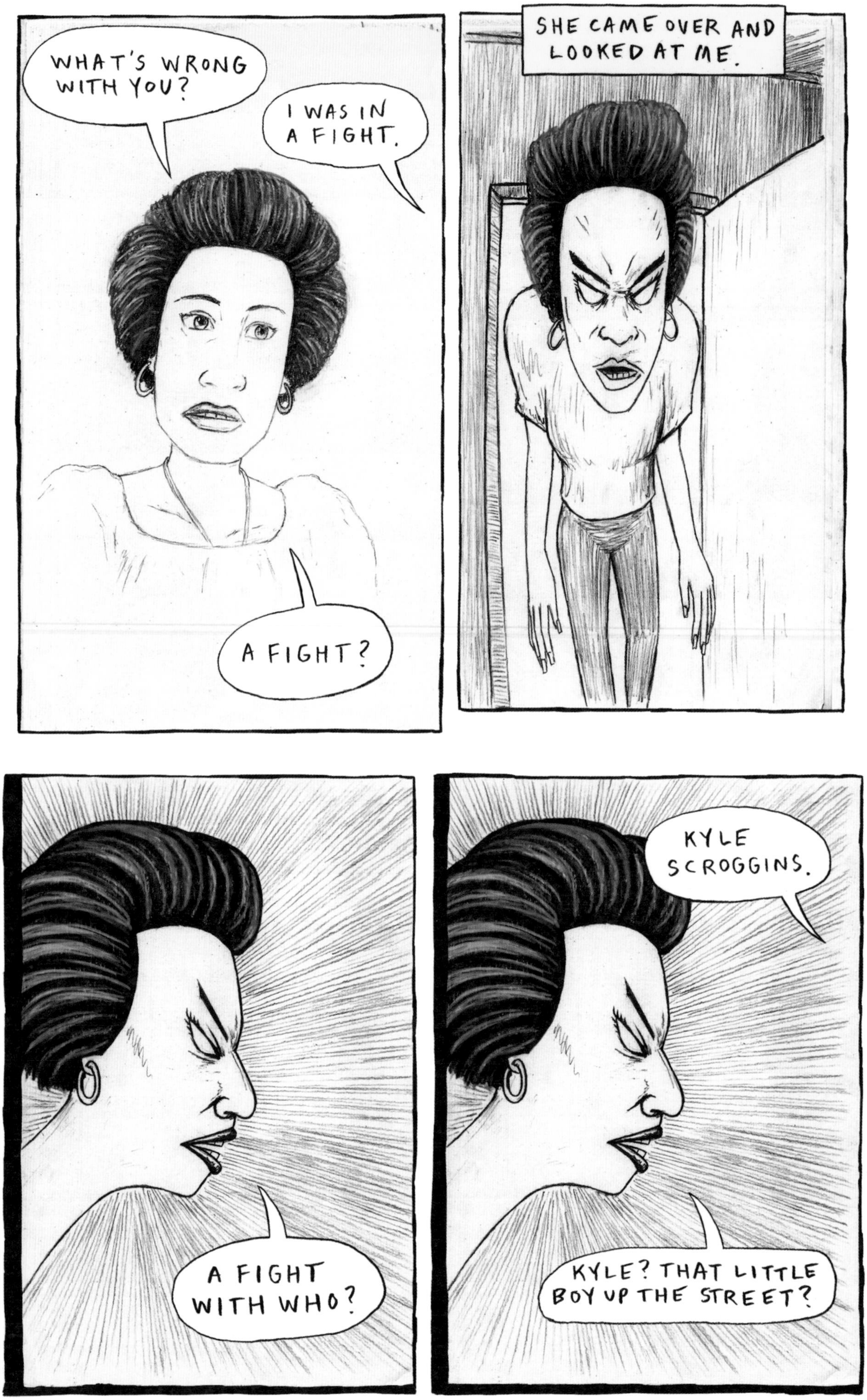
WHAT'S WRONG WITH YOU?
I WAS IN A FIGHT.
A FIGHT?
SHE CAME OVER AND LOOKED AT ME.
A FIGHT WITH WHO?
KYLE SCROGGINS.
KYLE? THAT LITTLE BOY UP THE STREET?

YES...

DID YOU WIN?

WHAT WAS SHE ASKING ME?

I'D BEEN IN A FIGHT.

MY MOUTH WAS BLOODY.

I WAS CRYING AND FEELING LIKE SHIT.

I DON'T KNOW.

I SAID.

...YOU DON'T KNOW? WHAT DO YOU MEAN YOU DON'T KNOW? BOY DON'T YOU COME UP IN THIS HOUSE IF YOU LOSE A FIGHT TO SOMEONE SMALLER THAN YOU.

I WAS FLOORED. I NEVER EXPECTED THIS RESPONSE.

THIS WAS NOTHING LIKE THE MOTHERS ON TV. NOT EVEN FLORIDA EVANS.

THIS WAS TERRIBLE.

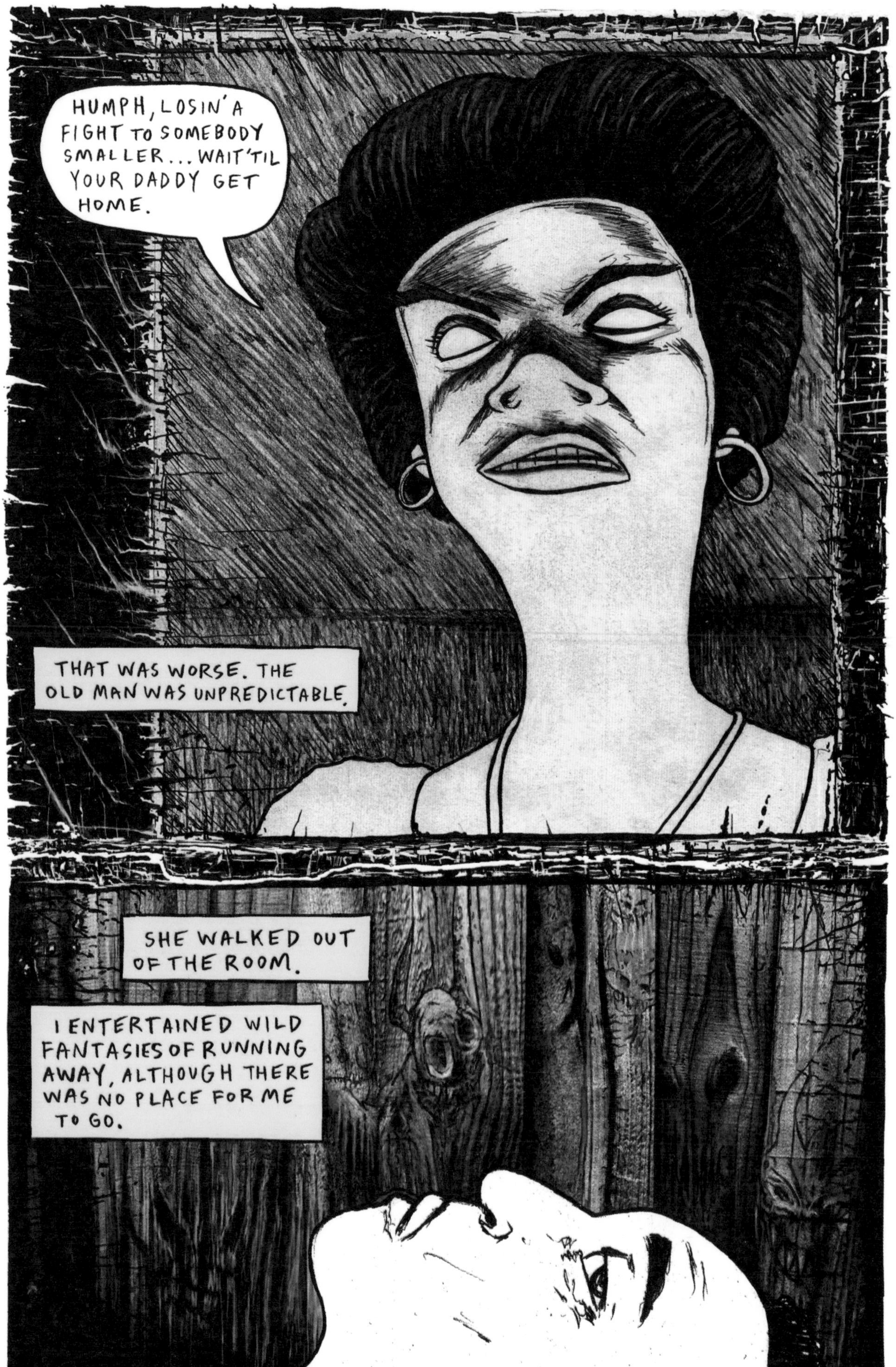
HUMPH, LOSIN' A FIGHT TO SOMEBODY SMALLER... WAIT 'TIL YOUR DADDY GET HOME.
THAT WAS WORSE. THE OLD MAN WAS UNPREDICTABLE.
SHE WALKED OUT OF THE ROOM.
I ENTERTAINED WILD FANTASIES OF RUNNING AWAY, ALTHOUGH THERE WAS NO PLACE FOR ME TO GO.

I'D RAN AWAY THE YEAR BEFORE, WHEN I GOT WHIPPED FOR SOME IMAGINED WRONG.

I GOT ON MY BICYCLE AND LEAVING THE GARAGE DOOR WIDE OPEN IN A NO-RETURNS, SYMBOLIC KIND OF "FUCK YOU" WAY, I MADE MY WAY TO THE EXPRESSWAY, WHERE I HEADED TOWARDS MY GRANDMOTHER'S HOUSE IN HOMEWOOD.

ACTUALLY MY GRANDMOTHER LIVED THERE WITH MY GREAT-GRANDPARENTS, PLUS AN ANCIENT GREAT-AUNT AND GREAT-UNCLE.

I'D GOTTEN MAYBE 20 MINUTES AWAY WHEN MY GRANDMOTHER'S CAR STOPPED AND PICKED ME UP.

I STAYED IN HOMEWOOD FOR A FEW DAYS BUT DECIDED THAT I DIDN'T WANT TO GO THROUGH THE SHAKEUP OF ACTUALLY GOING TO LIVE THERE PERMANENTLY.

THE SUMMERS THERE WERE NICE, BUT A PERMANENT SETTLEMENT AMONGST THOSE RACIST LITTLE KIDS AND THEIR PARENTS WAS AN OVERWHELMING PROSPECT.

IF I'D ONLY KNOWN HOW THINGS WOULD WORK OUT AT IMMANUEL LUTHERAN...

MY FATHER USUALLY STOPPED OFF FOR A COUPLE OF DRINKS BEFORE COMING HOME. I WAS NEVER SURE WHAT HE'D HAD TO DRINK AND THEREFORE NEVER WAS ABLE TO FORECAST WHAT HIS MOOD WOULD BE.

I HEARD HIM AS HE CAME IN.

HIS KEY TURNING THE LOCK WAS ALWAYS OVERLY-NOISY.

IT SOUNDED LIKE LARGE ROCKS FALLING DOWN A CLIFF-FACE.

MY ROOM WAS DARK.

I HADN'T TURNED THE LIGHT ON WHEN I CAME IN AND THE SUN HAD LONG SINCE GONE DOWN.

I DIDN'T KNOW IF THE ROOM WOULD BE MORE OR LESS DEPRESSING WITH THE LIGHT ON.

I COULD HEAR MY MOTHER'S VOICE DOWNSTAIRS, BUT I COULDN'T MAKE OUT WHAT WAS BEING SAID.

MY FATHER DIDN'T COME IMMEDIATELY IN.

HE ALWAYS HUNG UP HIS UNIFORM BEFORE HE DID ANYTHING.

HE WAS A REAL ANAL-RETENTIVE, A COP THROUGH AND THROUGH.

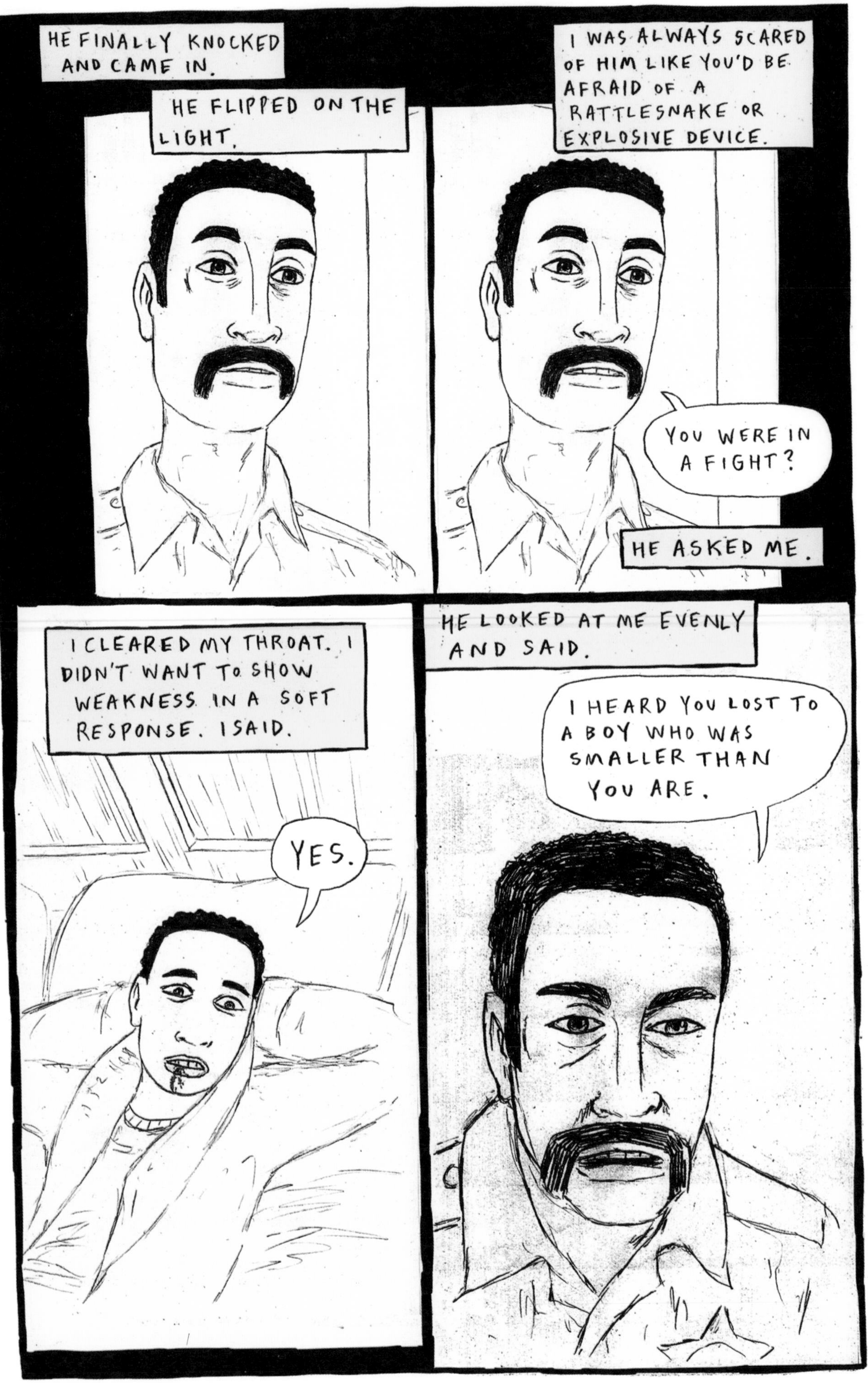
HE FINALLY KNOCKED AND CAME IN.
HE FLIPPED ON THE LIGHT.
I WAS ALWAYS SCARED OF HIM LIKE YOU'D BE AFRAID OF A RATTLESNAKE OR EXPLOSIVE DEVICE.
YOU WERE IN A FIGHT?
HE ASKED ME.
I CLEARED MY THROAT. I DIDN'T WANT TO SHOW WEAKNESS IN A SOFT RESPONSE. I SAID.
YES.
HE LOOKED AT ME EVENLY AND SAID.
I HEARD YOU LOST TO A BOY WHO WAS SMALLER THAN YOU ARE.

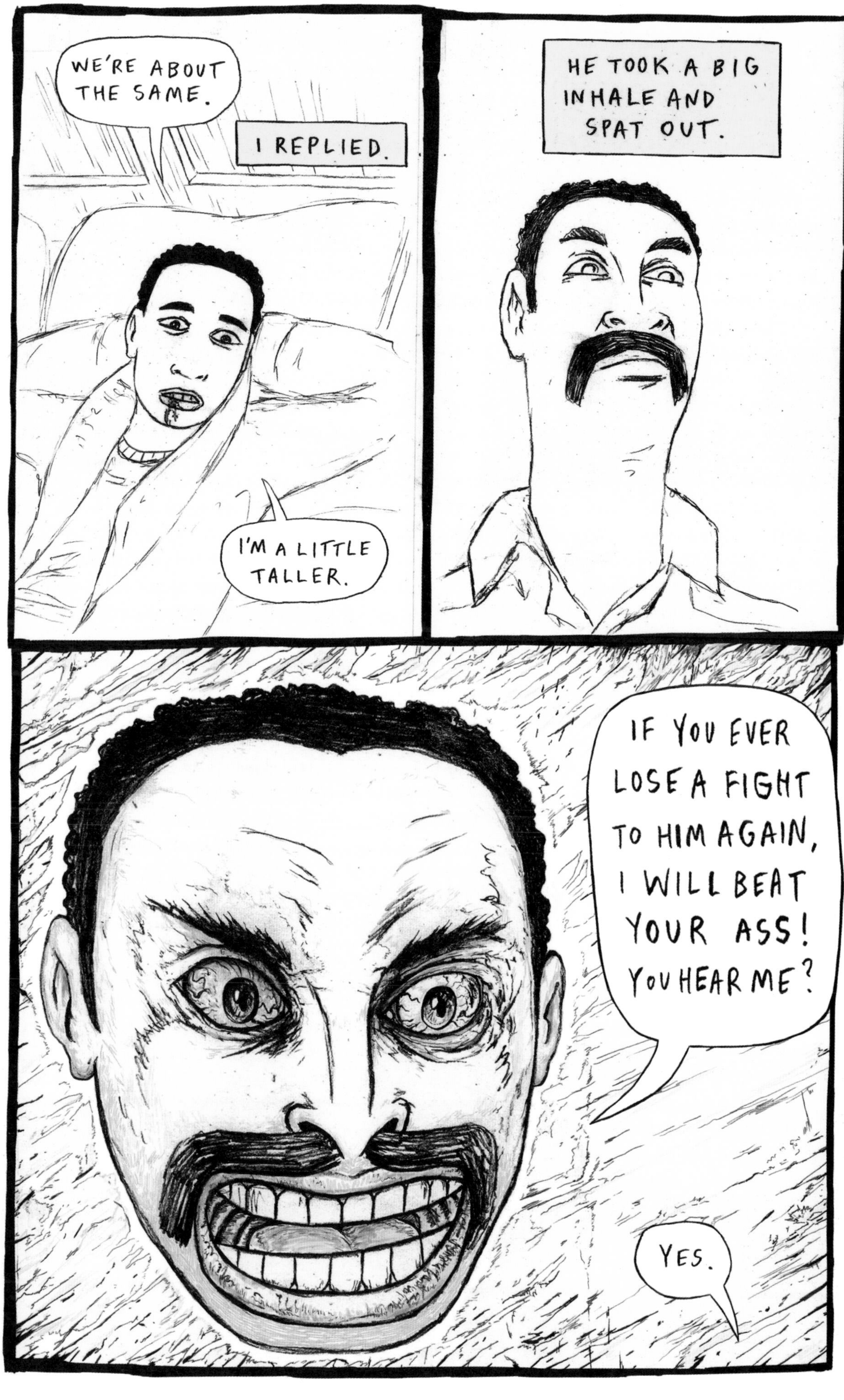
WE'RE ABOUT THE SAME.
I REPLIED.
I'M A LITTLE TALLER.
HE TOOK A BIG INHALE AND SPAT OUT.
IF YOU EVER LOSE A FIGHT TO HIM AGAIN, I WILL BEAT YOUR ASS! YOU HEAR ME?
YES.

I REPLIED. TO WHICH HE TURNED DISGUSTED, FLIPPED OFF THE LIGHT AND LEFT ME IN THE DARKNESS.

I DECIDED TO NEVER AGAIN TELL EITHER OF THEM ABOUT ANY MORE FIGHTS.

I GOT UP AND TURNED ON MY PORTABLE T.V.

THE DICK VAN DYKE SHOW WAS ENDING.

BOY.

SHE SAID.

GET DOWN HERE AND EAT!

MY MOTHER CALLED UPSTAIRS, FOR ME TO COME DOWN FOR DINNER.

I CALLED BACK THAT I WASN'T HUNGRY.

AFTER DINNER I SAT IN MY ROOM TRYING TO ANTICIPATE THE NEXT DAY.

ACCORDING TO SIT-COM LOGIC, SINCE I'D STOOD UP FOR MYSELF I SHOULD HAVE NO MORE PROBLEMS.

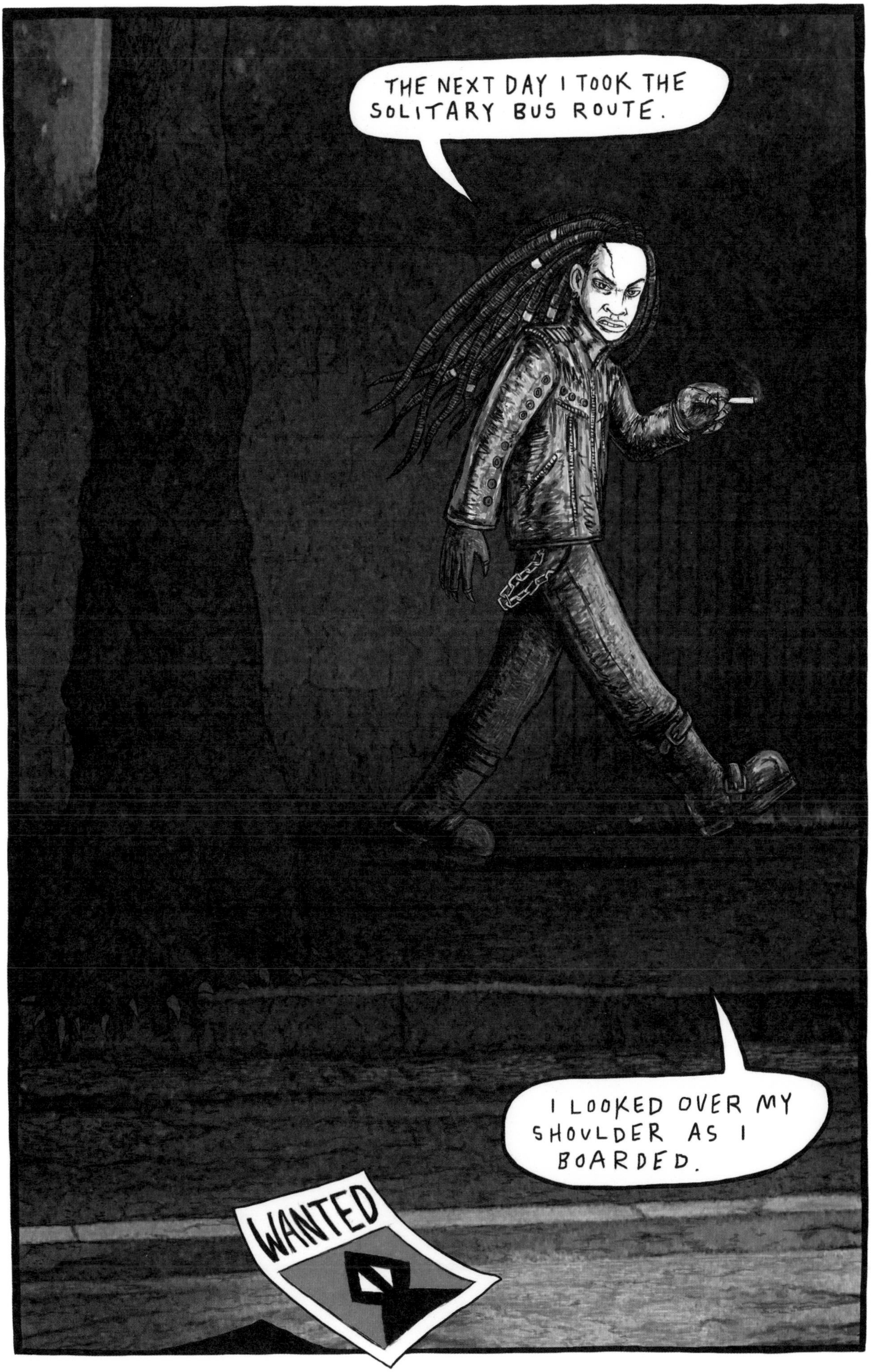
THE NEXT DAY I TOOK THE SOLITARY BUS ROUTE.
I LOOKED OVER MY SHOULDER AS I BOARDED.
WANTED

THE TRIP WAS A BLUR.

IT WAS THE FASTEST THAT BUS HAD EVER GOTTEN ME TO MY DESTINATION.

I WALKED THE LAST TWO BLOCKS TO SCHOOL, SOAKING IN THE QUIET DESOLATION OF THE NEIGHBORHOOD.

IF ONLY I WERE (ACTUALLY) THE LAST MAN ON EARTH.

THE BASEMENT WAS THE STAGING AREA FOR THE STUDENTS. WE GATHERED THERE UNTIL THE BELL RANG IN THE STAIRWELL FOR US TO TRUDGE UP THE STAIRS TO OUR CLASSROOMS.

I WAS STANDING THERE, HOLDING MY BOOK-BAG. I WAS TRYING TO BE NONCHALANT YET WATCHFUL. THE LITTLE KIDS WERE RUNNING AROUND PLAYING. I WAS LOOKING AHEAD AS I HEAR KYLE'S VOICE BEHIND ME SAY.

HEY, PUNK!

I TURN (TRYING NOT TO SPIN TOO QUICKLY) AND THERE WAS KYLE.

HE WAS SITTING ASTRIDE EDSEL PARKS SHOULDERS. HE WAS WAY UP THERE. EDSEL WAS PERHAPS 5', 10" SO KYLE'S FACE HAD TO BE NINE FEET IN THE AIR. HE HAD TO DUCK TO AVOID THE CEILING AS HE BALLED HIS FISTS, SMILED EVILLY AND SAID.

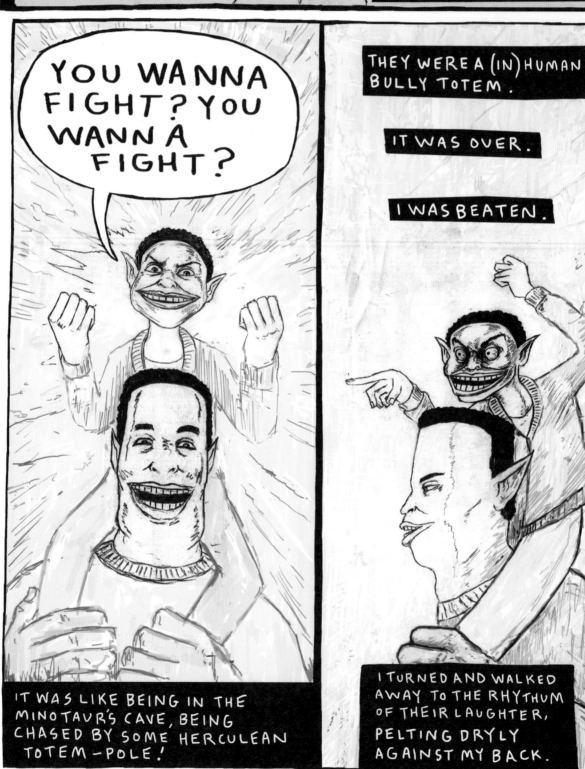

YOU WANNA FIGHT? YOU WANNA FIGHT?

THEY WERE A (IN)HUMAN BULLY TOTEM.

IT WAS OVER.

I WAS BEATEN.

IT WAS LIKE BEING IN THE MINOTAUR'S CAVE, BEING CHASED BY SOME HERCULEAN TOTEM-POLE!

I TURNED AND WALKED AWAY TO THE RHYTHM OF THEIR LAUGHTER, PELTING DRYLY AGAINST MY BACK.

FROM THAT DAY ON THE BULLYING INTENSIFIED AND PERSONALIZED.

PERHAPS IT'S MY IMAGINATION BUT I SEEMED TO TAKE THE HEAT OFF THE OTHER TWO NERDS (FAGS) AND THE ONLY MEXICAN STUDENT WHOM THEY USED TO REFER TO AS "TACO-BENDER."

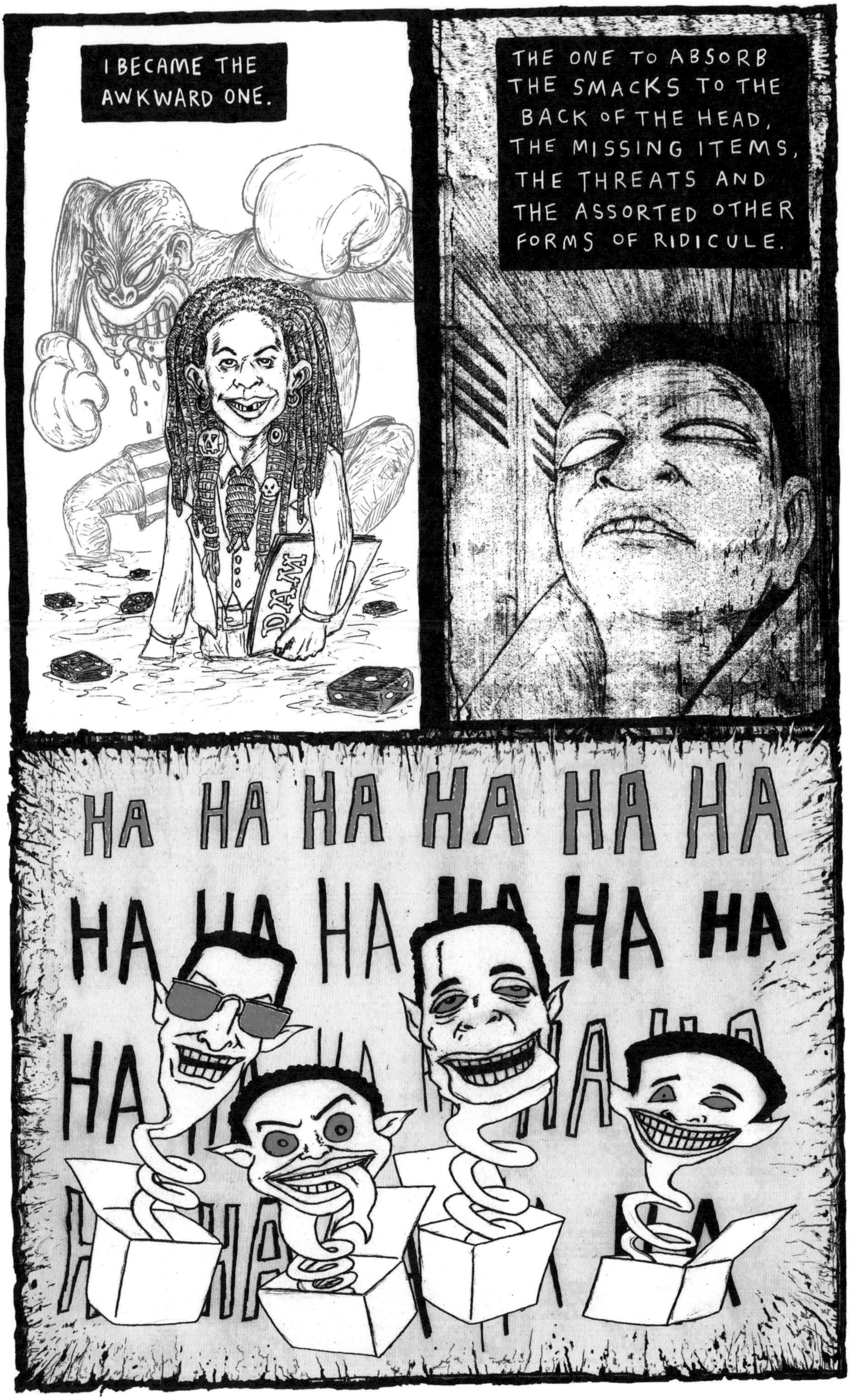
I BECAME THE AWKWARD ONE.
THE ONE TO ABSORB THE SMACKS TO THE BACK OF THE HEAD, THE MISSING ITEMS, THE THREATS AND THE ASSORTED OTHER FORMS OF RIDICULE.
HA HA HA HA HA HA HA
HA HA HA HA HA HA
HA

I SAT IN THE BACK ROW OF THE CLASSROOM, SWEATING FROM THE RADIATOR.

THE BLEAK SLATE-GREY LIGHT COMING THROUGH THE WINDOW, THROUGH WHICH THERE WAS A DANK MONOCHROMATIC VIEW OF GREY WOOD-FRAMED HOUSES WITH BLACK, BROWN AND GREY PATCHED TARRED ROOFS.

THE EMPTY PARKING LOT.

THE DEAD GRASS IN THE TINY BACKYARDS.

I SAT BACK THERE TO AVOID MISSILES. I SAT BACK THERE SO THAT OUR REGULAR TEACHER, MR. FLORENTINO, AND OUR THEOLOGY TEACHER, PASTOR FOLEY, COULD KEEP AN EYE ON WHAT THE OTHERS WERE DOING WITHOUT MY BLOCKING THE VIEW.

I SAT BACK THERE SO THAT I WOULD HAVE THE COURAGE TO ANSWER QUESTIONS IN CLASS AND SO I COULD DRAW IN MY SPIRAL—BINDER UNMOLESTED

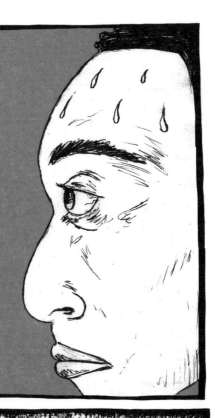

PASTOR FOLEY INSTRUCTED US IN ALL THINGS LUTHERAN. WE MEMORIZED ALL THE TERMINOLOGY, THE NAMES OF THE BOOKS OF THE BIBLE, THE ATHANASIAN AND APOSTLE'S CREED, AND MANY BIBLE-VERSES. I TOOK IT ALL SO SERIOUSLY, THESE MATTERS OF MY ETERNAL SOUL AND THE MINUTIAE OF THE RELIGION. I WONDERED WHY I WAS SUBJECTED TO TORMENT AMONGST SUPPOSED "CHRISTIANS". WAS I NOT PRAYING CORRECTLY? NOT PIOUS ENOUGH?

I SAT IN THE BACK OF THE ROOM PUTTING MY WHOLE HEART INTO READING AND BELIEVING THE WORDS OF THE 22ND (THE BEGGING FOR MERCY) PSALM:

MY GOD, MY GOD, WHY HAVE YOU FORSAKEN ME?

MY GOD, I CRY OUT BY DAY, BUT YOU DO NOT ANSWER, 2 BY NIGHT, BUT I FIND NO REST. YET YOU ARE ENTHRONED AS THE HOLY ONE; 3 YOU ARE THE ONE ISRAEL PRAISES. (C) IN YOU OUR ANCESTORS PUT THEIR TRUST; 4 THEY TRUSTED AND YOU DELIVERED THEM.

TO YOU THEY CRIED OUT AND WERE SAVED; 5 IN YOU THEY TRUSTED AND WERE NOT PUT TO SHAME.

YET GOD DIDN'T SEEM TO BE PAYING ATTENTION.

THIS WAS ABOUT THE TIME THAT I FIRST SAW THE MOVIE MY BODYGUARD.

AS I SAID BEFORE, SINCE EDSEL RESEMBLED THE BODYGUARD IN THE MOVIE I EXPERIENCED SOME COGNITIVE DISSONANCE EVERY TIME I SAW IT.

THE MOVIE WAS A NEW FEATURE ON CHICAGO'S PRIMITIVE PRE-CABLE "ONTV" SERVICE.

I WAS WRAPPED UP IN THAT MOVIE BECAUSE I GOT TO SEE ANOTHER BULLIED BASTARD GO THROUGH THE "I DON'T WANT ANY TROUBLE" BIT.

AFTER WATCHING IT A FEW TIMES IT OCCURRED TO ME THAT PERHAPS IT WOULD BE POSSIBLE FOR ME TO CUT OUT THE MIDDLE-MAN IF I WERE TO DRESS LIKE THE BODYGUARD. IN THE MOVIE HIS POWER CAME FROM THE PERCEPTION THAT HE WAS DANGEROUS, BASED ON HIS QUIET INTENSITY AND OUTSIDER WAY OF DRESSING.

I REALISED THAT I'D BE AT A DISADVANTAGE, CONSIDERING MY CLASSMATES ALREADY KNEW ME, BUT REALLY, WHAT DID I HAVE TO LOSE?

BECAUSE I ASKED MY FATHER FOR AN OLD ARMY FIELD-JACKET HE WAS QUICK TO GIVE ME ONE OF HIS OLD ONES FROM HIS DAYS IN THE NATIONAL GUARD.

HE WAS HAPPY WHENEVER I SHOWED INTEREST IN THE THINGS HE LIKED.

THE JACKET HUNG OFF ME, BUT IT SERVED IT'S PURPOSE.

THE MEAN STREETS

WE WERE STILL IN THE ERA OF THE ANGRY NAM-VET, AND GUYS WEARING OLD ARMY GEAR HAD AN AUTOMATIC EDGE TO THEM.

THEY ALL SEEMED WISE IN VIOLENCE AND READY TO SNAP.

I WENT TO SCHOOL WEARING MY VIETNAM-ERA JACKET AND LOOKING LIKE A DANGROUS YOUNG LONER.

QUIET AND MISUNDERSTOOD, BUT DEEP...

THAT'S WHEN I GOT MY FIRST LESSON IN THE DIFFERENCES OF PERCEPTION BETWEEN WHITE PEOPLE IN THE MOVIES AND URBAN BLACK TEENS. TO MY CLASSMATES I DIDN'T LOOK LIKE A DANGEROUSLY PSYCHOTIC LONER. TO MY CLASSMATES I LOOKED BROKE. BROKE WAS WORSE THAN GAY. IT WAS WORSE THAN BEING HORRIBLE AT SPORTS OR ANSWERING THE TEACHER'S QUESTIONS. BROKE WAS ANATHEMA.

BLACK PEOPLE ARE ALL ABOUT SHINY OBJECTS.

MATERIALISM IS THE MAIN RELIGION OF BLACK PEOPLE.

TRYING TO CONVINCE OTHERS THAT YOU HAVE MONEY IS THE MAIN ART-FORM OF BLACK PEOPLE.

WHATEVER CULTURE BLACK PEOPLE MANAGED TO DEVELOP IN 400 YEARS OF LIFE IN THE AMERICAS WAS WILLINGLY TRADED IN THE LATE-60'S FOR FANCY CARS AND CLOTHING.

IDENTITY AND WORTH
ARE HELD TIGHTLY
WITHIN THE PARAMETERS
OF YOUR POSSESSIONS.

WHATEVER SOUL WAS IN THE HEARTS OF THE PEOPLE HAS BEEN REPLACED BY DESIRE.

WHEREAS PERHAPS, IT MIGHT BE POSSIBLE FOR A PERSON TO FIND INNER-PEACE, THERE IS NEVER AN END TO OUTSIDE THINGS TO JUSTIFY YOUR EXISTENCE.

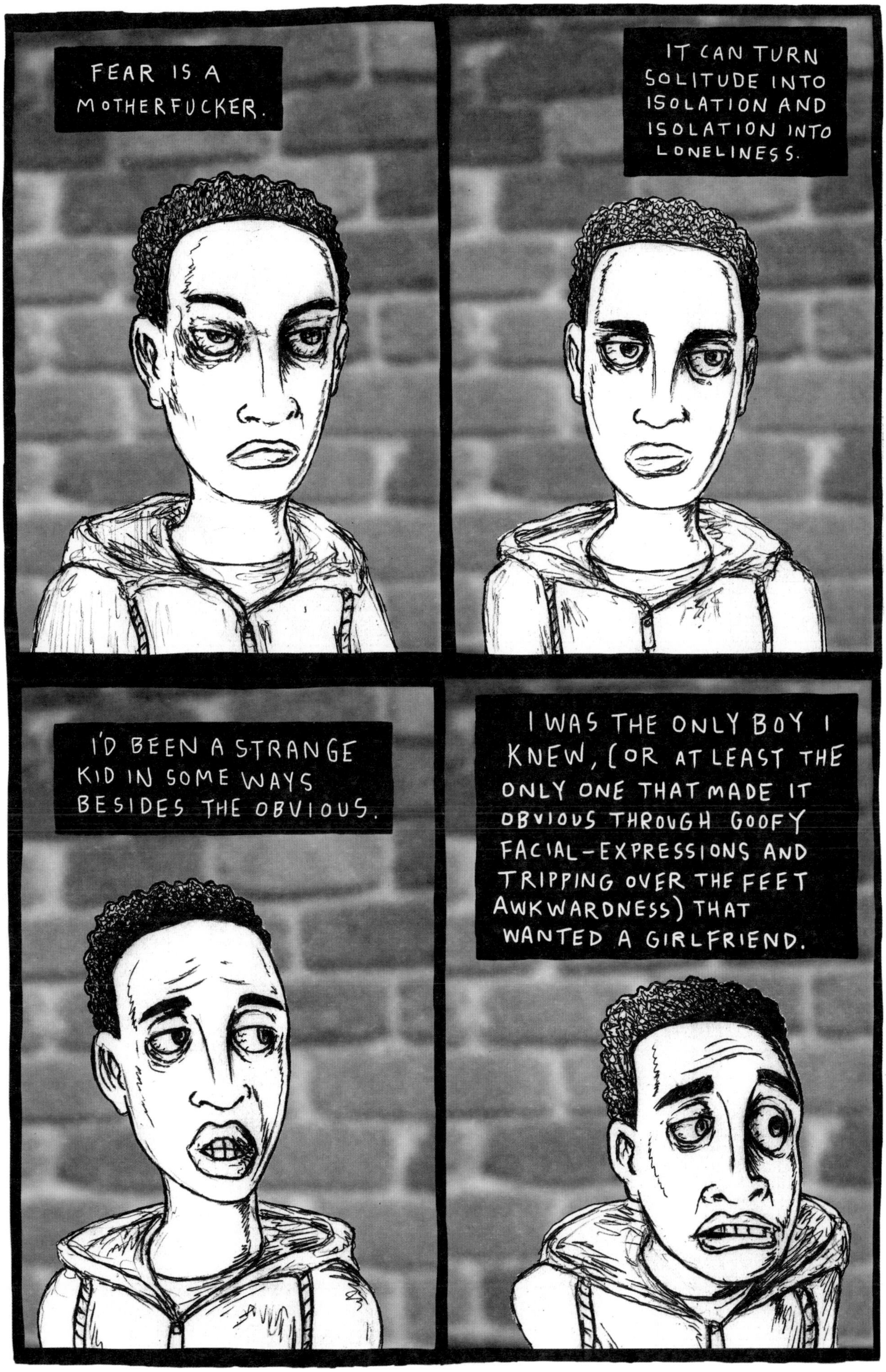
FEAR IS A MOTHERFUCKER.
IT CAN TURN SOLITUDE INTO ISOLATION AND ISOLATION INTO LONELINESS.
I'D BEEN A STRANGE KID IN SOME WAYS BESIDES THE OBVIOUS.
I WAS THE ONLY BOY I KNEW, (OR AT LEAST THE ONLY ONE THAT MADE IT OBVIOUS THROUGH GOOFY FACIAL-EXPRESSIONS AND TRIPPING OVER THE FEET AWKWARDNESS) THAT WANTED A GIRLFRIEND.

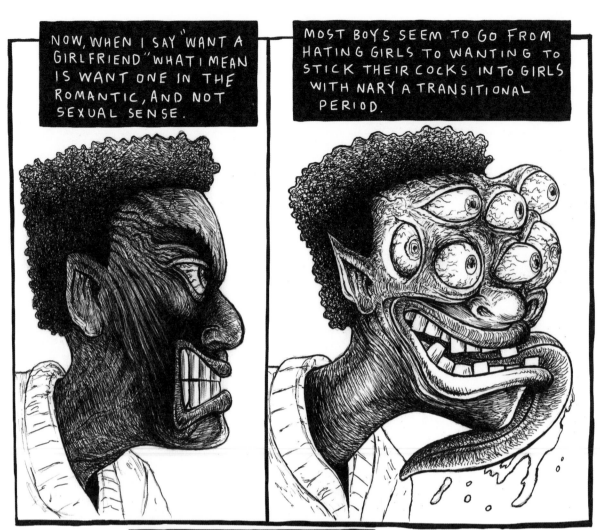

NOW, WHEN I SAY "WANT A GIRLFRIEND" WHAT I MEAN IS WANT ONE IN THE ROMANTIC, AND NOT SEXUAL SENSE.

MOST BOYS SEEM TO GO FROM HATING GIRLS TO WANTING TO STICK THEIR COCKS INTO GIRLS WITH NARY A TRANSITIONAL PERIOD.

I, ON THE OTHER HAND, HAD WANTED TO HOLD HANDS AND KISS VARIOUS GIRLS SINCE I WAS SIX YEARS OLD.

THERE WEREN'T MANY GIRLS FOR ME TO PINE-OVER AT IMMANUEL LUTHERAN SCHOOL.

IT WASN'T THAT THERE WERE NO GIRLS; IT'S JUST THAT THE GIRLS IN MY CLASS WERE JUST AS BAD AS THE BOYS.

THE YEAR BEFORE, WHEN I WAS A SEVENTH-GRADER, I REMEMBER STANDING OUTSIDE OF THE CLASSROOM AT THE HEAD OF THE STAIRS.

IT WAS DURING THE END OF SEMESTER PARTY WHEN I WAS APPROACHED BY A POPULAR EIGHTH-GRADE GIRL NAMED TRISHA.

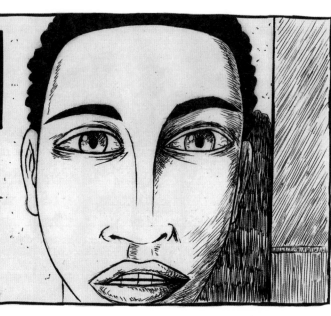

TRISHA WAS A THIN, CHOCOLATE-COLORED GIRL WITH ALMOND-SHAPED EYES.

SHE WAS WEARING SKIN-TIGHT JEANS AND A STRIPED-SWEATER.

SMILING, SHE SAID TO ME.

YOU WANT TO DO IT?

THAT SHOCKED THE HELL OUT OF ME.

WHAT DID I KNOW ABOUT SEX?

NOTHING, IS WHAT I KNEW ABOUT SEX.

I'D HARDLY STARTED TO INCORPORATE MASTURBATION INTO MY LIFE, AS I'D ONLY RECENTLY STARTED PRODUCING SEMEN.

IN A SPLIT-SECOND I PICTURED ME AND HER IN THE CLOAK-ROOM, LYING ON THE DIRTY HARDWOOD FLOOR

I COULD SEE US WITH OUR CLOTHES OFF AND TOGETHER, BUT NOT ACTUALLY FUCKING.

I HAD NO IDEA HOW THE ACTUAL MECHANICS OF SEX WORKED. WHERE WAS THE HOLE?

WHAT DID I DO? I COULDN'T PICTURE US FUCKING, BUT I COULD CLEARLY PICTURE US GETTING CAUGHT FUCKING BY PASTOR FOLEY.

I COULDN'T TELL HER I THOUGHT IT WAS A BAD IDEA. THAT I WAS INEXPERIENCED AND WORRIED ABOUT GETTING CAUGHT.

THAT WOULDN'T BE COOL AT ALL.

I HAD TO TELL HER SOMETHING THAT WOULD SAVE ME FACE.

UNFORTUNATELY I PANICKED AND REPLIED AND PERHAPS THE DUMBEST REPLY POSSIBLE. I SAID,

DO WHAT?

SHE WALKED AWAY FROM ME QUICKLY AND PITYINGLY.

AS THOUGH I WERE A RETARDED KID THAT SHE FELT BAD FOR.

I WAS.

IN RETROSPECT, THAT INCIDENT WAS PROBABLY THE IMPETUS OF MY REPUTATION FOR BEING A "FAGGOT."

THE GIRLS WERE VICTIMS OF HORMONES.

ANY PERSONALITY THEY HAD AS GIRLS HAD BEEN OBSCURED, DENIED AND SWALLOWED UP BY PRETENTION AND EXPECTATIONS OF "MATURITY."

THEY BECAME FALSE, LIKE A WAREHOUSE FILLED WITH MANNEQUINS PLAYING A PERMANENT GAME OF DRESS-UP.

I WAS INTIMIDATED BY THEIR VERY BEING.

BUT, EVEN IN THE MIDST OF A BATTLEFIELD, FLOWERS CAN GROW. THERE WAS A GIRL THAT I LIKED. HER NAME WAS APRIL.

SHE WAS IN THE SIXTH GRADE

SHE WAS LIGHT SKINNED WITH LONG DARK HAIR AND A SLIGHTLY BABY FAT FRAME THAT WOULD PROBABLY IN LATER LIFE TURN TO 30 OR 40 EXTRA lbs

BUT AT THE TIME SHE WAS PERFECTION.

BEING IN THE 8th GRADE HOWEVER I RARELY WAS ABLE TO EVEN CATCH A GLIMPSE OF HER. USUALLY IT WOULD BE FOR A SECOND OR TWO BEFORE SCHOOL STARTED.

SO MY EYES WERE DOUBLY PEELED, FOR BEAUTY OR DANGER. FIGHT OR FLIGHT? HOW ABOUT FIGHT OR FLIGHT OR FINALLY SPEAK TO THE GIRL? NOT VERY LIKELY. IT'S NOT THAT I'D NEVER SAID HELLO TO APRIL. I HAD. BUT BEYOND THAT THERE WAS NOTHING I COULD SAY.

IT WOULD BE BAD ENOUGH IF SHE WERE TO SAY NO WHEN I ASKED HER IF SHE WOULD "GO WITH ME", BUT THE FACT THAT I HAD A PERMANENT AUDIENCE OF HECKLERS WAITING AND WILLING TO HOOT AND YELL AND FALL DOWN LAUGHING AT MY REJECTION WOULD TURN DISAPPOINTMENT INTO TRAUMA.

APRIL WAS, TO ME, AN ETHEREAL BEING. AN ANGEL OF GRACE.

AND LIKE ALL ETHEREAL BEINGS, SHE WAS DESTINED TO REMAIN ON A DIFFERENT PLANE, AND I WAS DESTINED TO WORSHIP HER FROM AFAR.

THERE WAS A TEMPORARY AND CHRONIC RELIEF FROM THE BULLIES THAT I MUST MENTION.

IT IS TIED TO THE IMPORTANCE OF MATERIALISM TO MY TORMENTORS.

IF I WERE TO COME TO SCHOOL WHILE WEARING MY "GOOD CLOTHES" IT MENT A REPRIEVE FROM TORTURE.

IN MY COMMUNITY OF VALUED OUTWARD IMPRESSIONS IT WAS CONSIDERED ALMOST SACRILEGIOUS TO DISRESPECT FANCY CLOTHES.

AND PLEATED SLACKS AND CHURCH SHOES WERE RELIGIOUS VESTMENTS IN THEIR EYES.

ROBERT GRAHAM WAS THE BISHOP OF THE SCHOOL.

HE COULD OFTEN BE FOUND PLAYING "BASKETBALL" IN HIS PIMPY POINTY CHURCH SHOES, BAGGY SLACKS, IRIDESCENT BLOUSE AND SKINNY KNIT-TIE.

SINCE THERE WAS NO HOOP, BASKETBALL WAS PLAYED BY ATTEMPTING TO GET A TENNIS BALL BETWEEN A STEAM PIPE THAT RAN ALONG THE OUTSIDE WALL ABOUT SEVEN FEET UP.

SWIISH

I DISCOVERED "THE "GOOD-CLOTHES" LOOPHOLE ONE DAY AS WE WERE PREPARING TO DO A DRESS-REHEARSAL FOR SOME SORT OF SCHOOL/CHURCH FUNCTION.

I'D COME DRESSED IN MY SUNDAY FINERY.

THE DAY WAS GOING ALONG FINE WHEN QUINTIN BUMPED AGAINST ME AND SAID.

SORRY.

NOW ON THE SURFACE THIS MAY NOT SOUND LIKE A BIG DEAL, BUT WITH THIS YOU HAVE TO TAKE INTO CONSIDERATION THAT MY DAYS WERE ROUTINELY FILLED WITH THESE GUYS RUNNING INTO ME ON PURPOSE AND KNOCKING MY BOOKS TO THE GROUND OR TRIPPING ME.

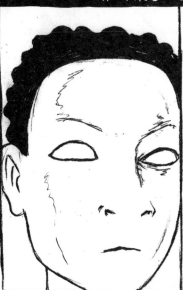

IF ANY OF THEM ACCIDENTALLY BUMPED ME THEIR BOILERPLATE RESPONSE WAS. "GET THE FUCK OUT OF THE WAY!"

LATER THAT DAY ROBERT LOOKED AT ME AND SAID.

THEM SOME NICE SHOES, MAN!

THANKS!

I REPLIED AS COOLLY AS POSSIBLE.

HE NODDED AND WALKED OFF...

THEY'D GIVE A PASS IF I WORE MY "GOOD" CLOTHES, BUT I ONLY HAD A COUPLE OF OUTFITS.

IN TRUTH MY CLOTHING OPTIONS WERE PRETTY LIMITED.

BECAUSE MY PARENTS WERE SO CONSERVATIVE THEIR IDEA OF DRESS CLOTHING WAS A CRESTED BLUE BLAZER, GREY SLACKS AND ROUND TOED BLACK SHOES.

KICK

PICTURE CARLTON FROM THE FRESH PRINCE OF BEL AIRE.

THERE WAS NO LIMIT TO THOSE KINDS OF CLOTHES, HAD I WANTED THEM, WHICH I DIDN'T.

THANKFULLY THROUGH MY GRANDMOTHER I MANAGED TO WHEEDLE A BLACK SHIRT, A LIGHT GREY TIE AND A PAIR OF MORE POINTED-TOED OXBLOOD SHOES. ALONG WITH THE OTHER STUFF I WAS ABLE TO PIECE TOGETHER TWO RESPECTABLE OUTFITS.

UNFORTUNATELY YOU CAN ONLY WEAR THE SAME THING ON A IRREGULAR BASIS. I DIDN'T WANT THEM TO GET USED TO MY DRESS CLOTHES SO I ONLY WORE THEM ONCE A WEEK.

THE CLASS PHOTO THAT YEAR, WAS TAKEN IN DECEMBER.

IF YOU LOOK AT IT YOU CAN TELL ME FROM THE OTHERS BY MY LIGHTER SKIN TONE AND THE LOOK OF NUMB DEPRESSION ON MY FACE. I'M THE ONLY ONE THAT'S NOT EVEN REMOTELY SMILING. THERE'S A STORY BEHIND THE PHOTO.

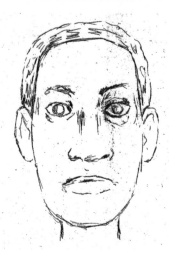

THE CHURCH BASEMENT WAS USED AS A CATCH-ALL AREA. IT SERVED AS EVERYTHING FROM SCHOOL-RECITAL STAGING AREA, TO STUDENT ART CONTEST GALLERY, TO PTA MEETING GROUNDS.

THIS PARTICULAR DAY THE STAGE WAS BEING USED TO SHOOT THE CLASS PHOTOS.

BECAUSE THE 7th AND 8th GRADES WERE HELD IN THE SAME ROOM AND BOTH TAUGHT BY MR. FIORENTINO (WHOM EVERYONE THOUGHT WAS WEARING A BAD WIG) WE WERE INCLUDED IN THE SAME PHOTO.

WE LINED UP IN THREE ROWS.

TALLEST IN BACK, MEDIUM HEIGHT IN THE MIDDLE ROW AND SEATED IN THE FRONT.

I REMEMBER THAT DAY THERE WAS SOME TROUBLE TRYING TO ORGANIZE WHO WOULD BE PLACED WHERE.

THE PHOTOGRAPHER MADE SEVERAL CHANGES THAT FINALLY PLACED ME NEXT TO PASTOR FOLEY.

FOR SOME REASON THE PHOTOGRAPHER HAD TROUBLE GETTING THE PEOPLE BEHIND ME.

WHY DID THINGS HAVE TO FOCUS ON ME?

COULDN'T I JUST BE A FLY ON THE WALL, OR WHITE NOISE?

INSTEAD OF MOVING ME, PASTOR FOLEY SUGGESTED THAT THEY PLACE A FOLDING CHAIR IN FRONT OF ME AND I KNEEL SLIGHTLY AND THE PASTOR WOULD PUT HIS ARM AROUND MY SHOULDER TO STEADY ME.

WHICH THEY DID.

I ALREADY KNEW WHAT THE BOYS WERE THINKING.

I WAS KNEELING BY THE PASTOR.

THIS EQUALS BLOWJOB.

THE FACT HE WAS TOUCHING ME DIDN'T HELP.

IF HE HAD ONLY FLIPPED AND SLICED MY FUCKING HEAD OFF THEN I WOULD HAVE PROBABLY GIVEN HIM A GRATEFUL GHOST BLOWJOB BEFORE MY SOUL DISAPPEARED INTO THE ETHER.

SIGH!

CHOP

THE CHRISTMAS BREAK WAS A WELCOME RESPITE. UNFORTUNATELY IT WAS TAINTED BY THE THOUGHTS OF MY BULLIES. I TRIED TO KEEP POSITIVE THOUGH. PERHAPS THE SEASON WOULD HAVE SOFTENED THEIR SOULS AS VISIONS OF BABY JESUS' AND SILENT NIGHT FILLED THEIR HEARTS.

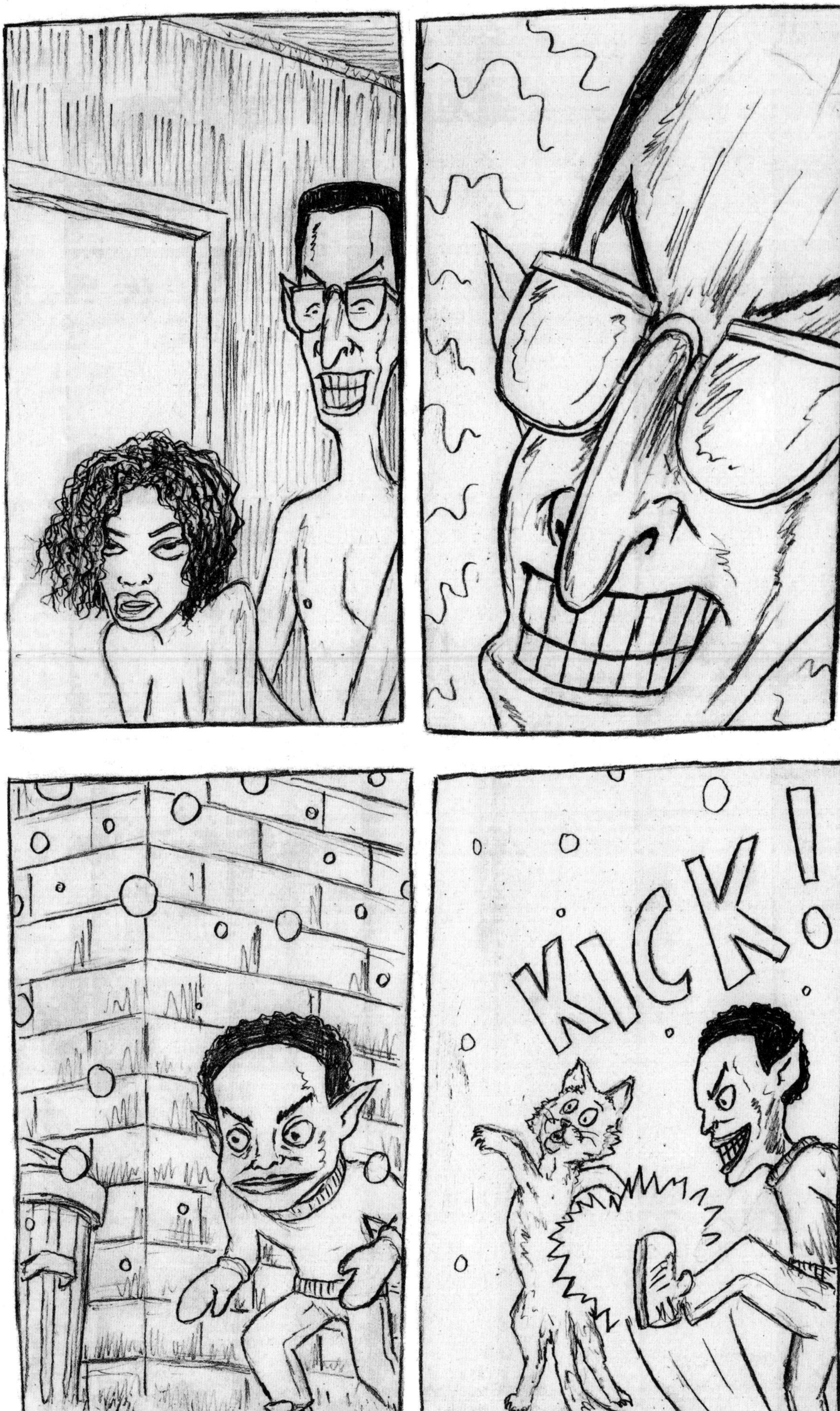
KICK!

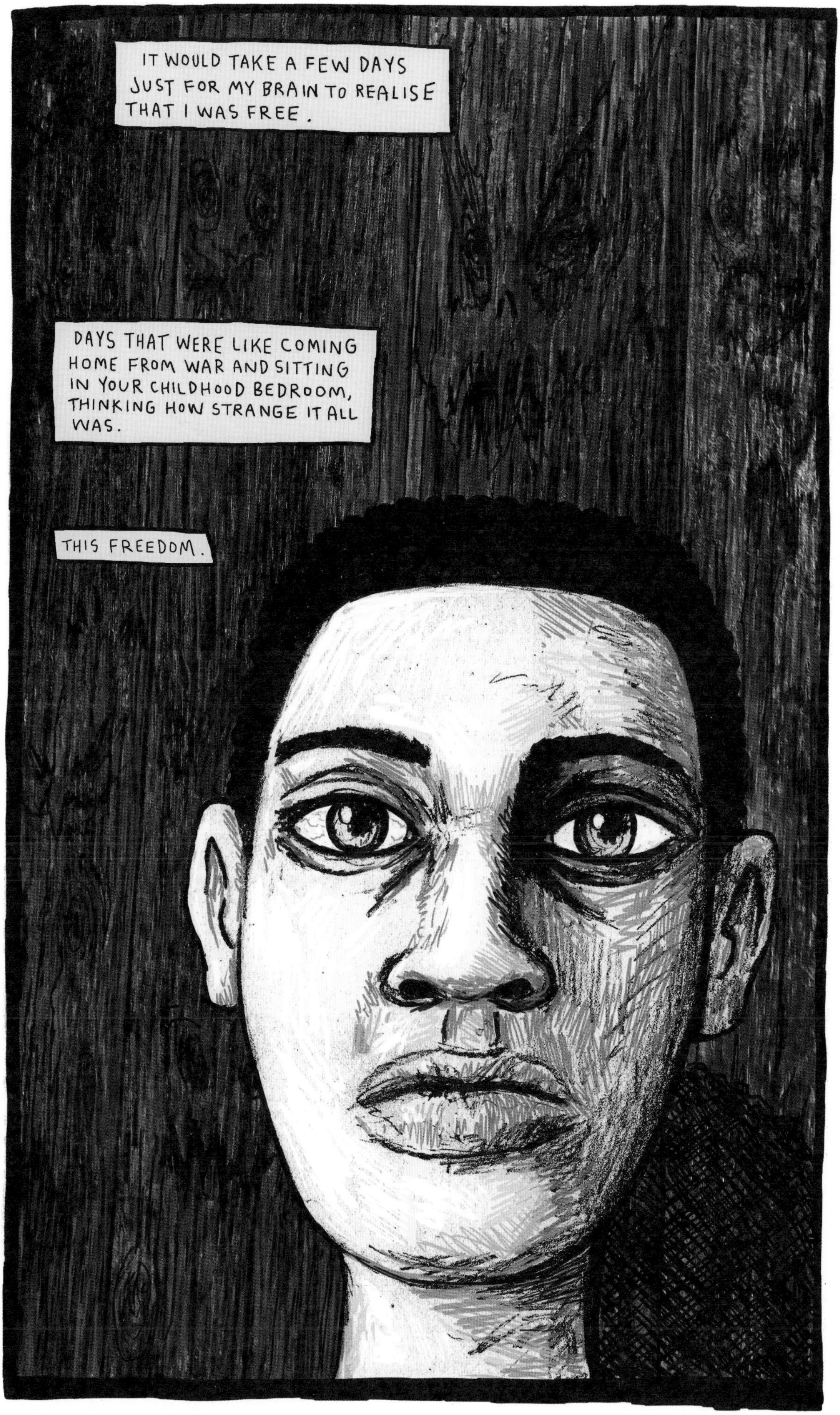
IT WOULD TAKE A FEW DAYS JUST FOR MY BRAIN TO REALISE THAT I WAS FREE.
DAYS THAT WERE LIKE COMING HOME FROM WAR AND SITTING IN YOUR CHILDHOOD BEDROOM, THINKING HOW STRANGE IT ALL WAS.
THIS FREEDOM.

THE DAYS WENT THROUGH THE CYCLE OF CHICAGO WINTER.

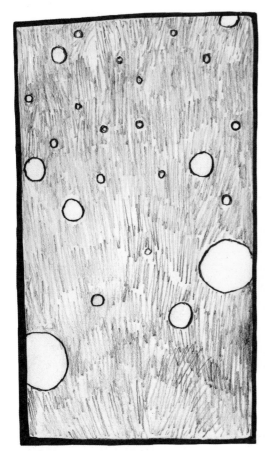

FLUFFY MOUNTAINS OF SNOW FALLING FROM THE STEEL COLORERED SKY.

THE CARS COME ALONG AND PACK IT DOWN INTO SLICK RUTS.

THE SNOWPLOWS THROW CLIFFS OF SNOW ONTO EITHER SIDE OF THE SIDE STREETS.

STORE

LEAVING THE PARKING SPACES UNDER A FOOT OR MORE OF HEAVY, SOOTY, WET COTTON.

IF YOUR CAR IS ALREADY PARKED YOU HAVE TO SHOVEL IT OUT.

IF YOU ARE COMING HOME YOU HAVE TO RAMP YOUR CAR OVER AND INTO THE BANKED SPACE.

GETTING OUT IS A PROBLEM FOR THE NEXT MORNING.

AS THE DAYS PASS THE SNOW GETS PACKED DOWN.

THEN IT GETS PARTIALLY MELTED AND REFROZEN, MAKING A TREACHEROUS RELIEF-MAP OF DIRTY WHITE ICE. OVER THIS ANOTHER BLANKET OF SNOWFALL OR MAYBE FROZEN RAIN. THIS IS REPEATED FROM NOVEMBER UNTIL MARCH OR APRIL.

YOUR NIGHTS (IF YOU ARE PRONE TO DARKNESS) WILL BE FILLED WITH VISIONS OF POWER OUTAGES FROM FROZEN LINES THAT REMOVE THE THIN SECURITY OF HEAT AND PHONE.

YOUR HOME BECOMES A FREEZER SURROUNDED BY IMPASSABLE ROADS.

THE CHRISTMAS BREAK, LIKE ALL EXTENDED BREAKS TEND TO SEND THE ONLY-CHILD DEEPER INTO HIS PRIVATE WORLD.

IT'S ESPECIALLY TRUE FOR WINTER-BREAK THOUGH, WHEN THE DEAD TREES AND UGLY SKIES KEEP YOU INSIDE.

ONCE INSIDE YOU BECOME SO FAMILIAR WITH YOUR SURROUNDINGS THAT THE OUTSIDE BECOMES A MIRAGE.

YOU STARE INTO THE IMPOSSIBLE ETERNITIES IN THE PATTERNS OF YOUR WOOD-GRAIN WALLPAPER.

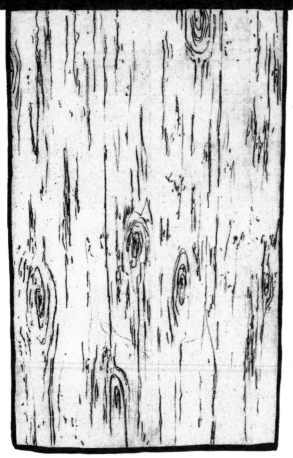

THE SCREAMING FACES IN THE KNOTHOLES.

THE LINES OF THE GARAGES LINING THE ALLEY OUTSIDE YOUR WINDOW.

THE HILLS AND VALLEYS IN A CRUMPLED BLANKET THAT YOUR HOT-WHEELS USE TO RE-CREATE THE SCENES FROM THE MOST DANGEROUS RACE EPISODE OF SPEED RACER.

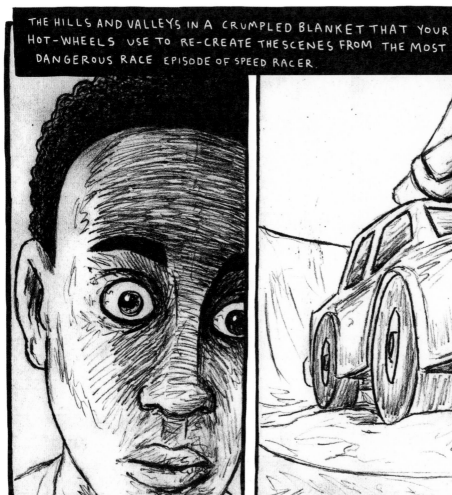

THE KNOBS ON YOUR MOTOROLA PORTABLE TV.

THE INTRICACIES OF THE MOUNDS OF TOYS AND WIRES AND ROCKS AND GAME PIECES IN YOUR BOTTOM DRESSER DRAWER.

LIFE BECOMES THE COMFORTABLE PATTERN OF CARTOONS AND OLD TV SHOWS ON CHANNEL 32 AND CHANNEL 9.

LOST IN SPACE IS SOMETHING YOU LOOK FORWARD TO.

WISHING YOU COULD BE LIKE WILL ROBINSON AND HAVE ADVENTURES WITH A ROBOT AND A BIZARRELY FLAMBOYANT OLD MAN.

THE BRADY'S BECOME YOUR SURROGATE SACCHARINE FAMILY.

THE WISDOM OF MIKE BRADY MORE PERMANENT AND DEEP THAN ANYTHING THAT EVER CAME OUT OF YOUR NATURAL FATHER'S COP-MUSTACHIOED MOUTH.

STARING INTO THE CHRISTMAS TREE LIGHTS UNTIL YOU'VE ALMOST HYPNOTIZED YOURSELF WITH COLORS...

THE PURE PRE-PUBERTY LUST THAT IS FELT ONCE YOU'VE SAID "THANK YOU" AND GATHERED YOUR CHRISTMAS TOYS AROUND YOU BEHIND YOUR BEDROOM DOOR IN AN ORGY OF FRESH IMAGINATION...

THE QUEER EXCITEMENT OF STAYING UP PAST THE NEW YEAR'S MARK AS MARX BROTHER'S MOVIES PLAY ON WGN AND GUNSHOTS RING OUT IN THE CHILL NIGHT.

BANG
BANG

"STAY AWAY FROM THE WINDOWS!" MY MOTHER WOULD YELL FROM THE OTHER ROOM, AS I SAT ON THE FLOOR OF MY BEDROOM WATCHING TV.

WONDERING IF BULLETS WOULD TUMBLE THROUGH MY WINDOW AT AN ANGLE AND GET ME...

IT'S ALWAYS HARD TO GET UP AT SIX IN THE MORNING. ESPECIALLY SO AFTER NOT DOING IT FOR ALMOST TWO WEEKS

MY FATHER HAD BOUGHT ME AN OBNOXIOUS HOWDY DOODY ALARM-CLOCK.

IT WAS NOW 1981.

IF NOT FOR A PARODY IN A COPY OF THE "INSIDE MAD", A PAPERBACK BOOK I'D MEMORIZED LINE FOR LINE, I WOULD'VE HAD ABSOLUTELY NO REFERENCE FOR THE CHARACTER.

I'D BE SOUND ASLEEP WHEN SUDDENLY BUFFALO BOB WOULD SCREAM...

HONK HONK HONK! IT'S HOWDY DOODY TIME, SO PLEASE WAKE UP RISE AND SHINE.

WE ALL HATE GETTING OUT OF BED, AND CLARABELL'S A SLEEPYHEAD, BUT RISING IS EASY FOR ONE AND ALL, WHEN YOU HEAR HOWDY DOODY CALL!...

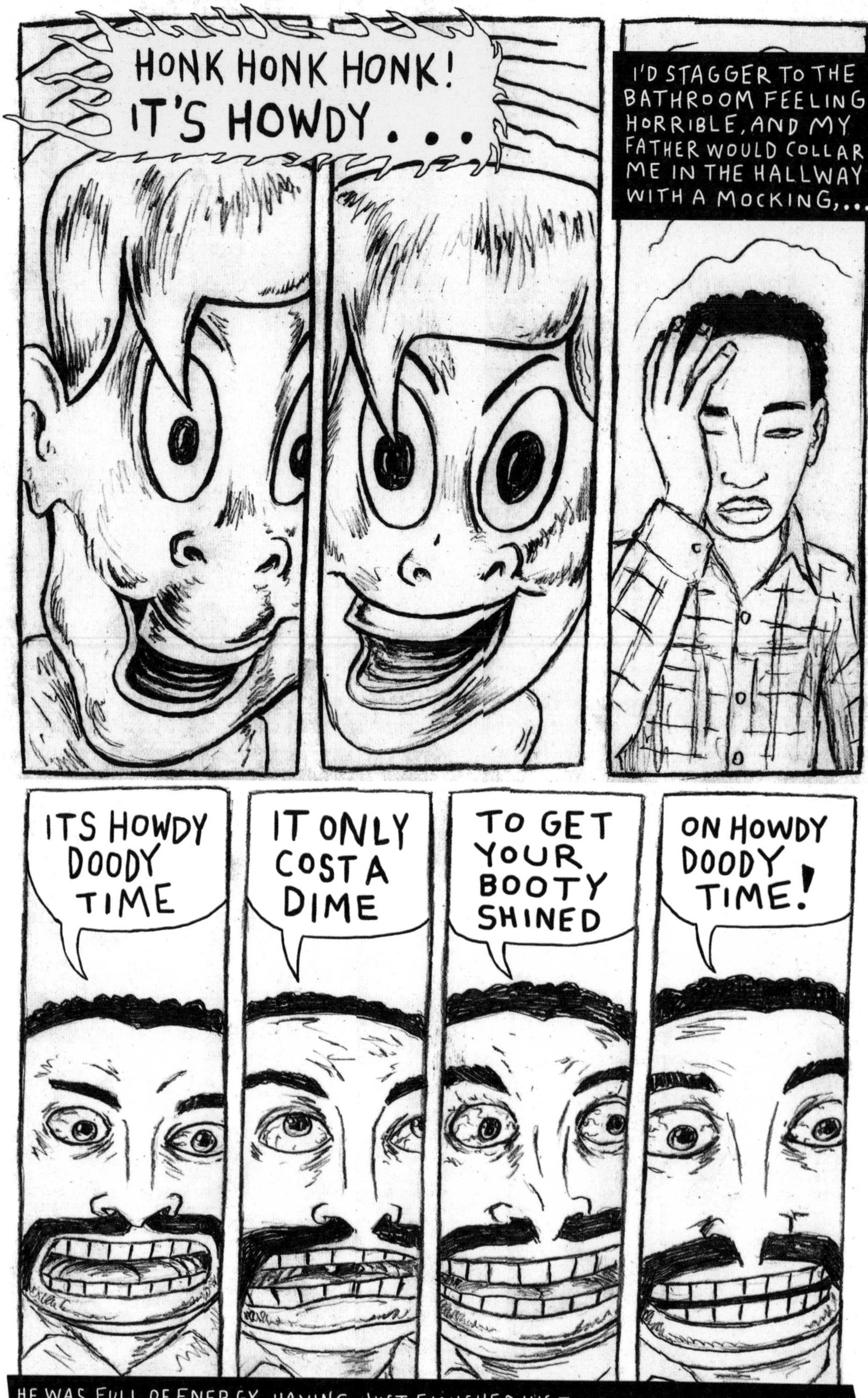
HONK HONK HONK! IT'S HOWDY...
I'D STAGGER TO THE BATHROOM FEELING HORRIBLE, AND MY FATHER WOULD COLLAR ME IN THE HALLWAY WITH A MOCKING,...
ITS HOWDY DOODY TIME
IT ONLY COST A DIME
TO GET YOUR BOOTY SHINED
ON HOWDY DOODY TIME!
HE WAS FULL OF ENERGY, HAVING JUST FINISHED HIS TOUR ON THE NIGHT SHIFT.

I TRIED TO MAKE A FACE THAT CONVEYED MY PAIN, ANGER AND FRUSTRATION, WITHOUT GOADING HIM INTO A REPEAT CHORUS.

THE BATHROOM IS COLD COMPARED TO THE LOVING EMBRACE OF MY BLANKETS.

IN THE MIRROR WAS THE SAME SOFT FACE.

NOT EVEN A HINT OF PEACH-FUZZ.

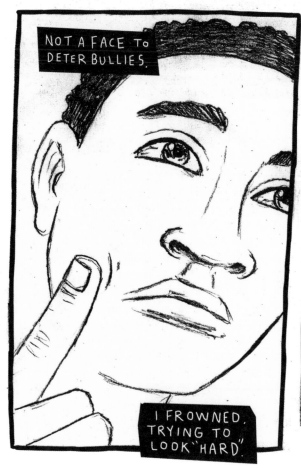

NOT A FACE TO DETER BULLIES.

I FROWNED, TRYING TO LOOK "HARD."

NO LUCK.

MAYBE IN A MOVIE, BUT NOT IN REALITY.

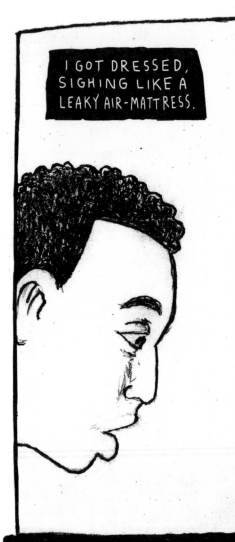

I GOT DRESSED, SIGHING LIKE A LEAKY AIR-MATTRESS.

I WENT DOWNSTAIRS AND TURNED ON THE TELEVISION.

THE FARM REPORT WAS STILL ON.

MAYBE FIVE MINUTES UNTIL THE RAY RAYNOR SHOW. I DIDN'T GET THE FARM REPORT. ALL THAT TALK OF "PORK BELLIES" GOING FOR 50 AND SO DOLLARS. IT WAS CONFUSING. SURELY THERE WERE NO FARMS IN CHICAGO.

112

MY BREAKFAST WAS ON THE STOVE. A SLICE OF CURLED-UP FRIED BALONEY ON A PIECE OF BREAD, TOASTED IN THE OVEN. ONE SIDE DOUGHY, THE OTHER SIDE AS BROWNED AND HARD AS WOOD, EXCEPT FOR THE POOL OF CONGEALED MARGARINE IN THE CENTRE.

I OPENED THE BASEMENT DOOR THAT LED INTO THE KITCHEN AND RELEASED OUR DOBERMAN "DUCHESS".

I OPENED THE BACK DOOR ON THE OTHER SIDE OF THE ROOM AND DUCHESS WENT OUT TO ADD MORE BROWN HEAPS AND YELLOW STAINS TO THE REEKING SNOW.

AFTER SHE FINISHED I LET HER BACK IN AND STUCK HER BACK IN THE BASEMENT.

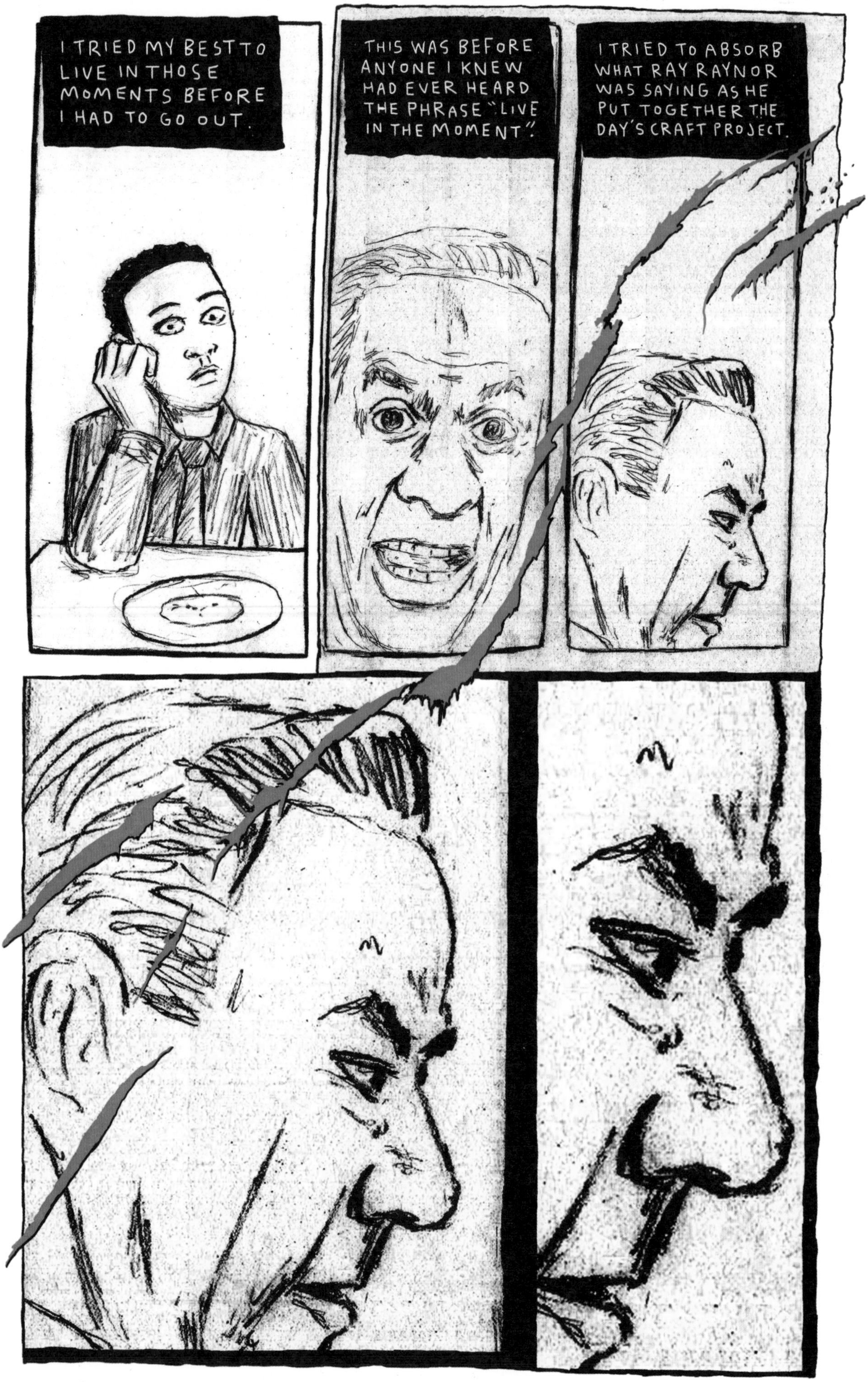
I TRIED MY BEST TO LIVE IN THOSE MOMENTS BEFORE I HAD TO GO OUT.
THIS WAS BEFORE ANYONE I KNEW HAD EVER HEARD THE PHRASE "LIVE IN THE MOMENT".
I TRIED TO ABSORB WHAT RAY RAYNOR WAS SAYING AS HE PUT TOGETHER THE DAY'S CRAFT PROJECT.

AS USUAL HIS ATTEMPT WAS A PALE IMITATION OF THE CRAFT 'PREPARED IN ADVANCE' BY THE EPONYMOUS "CHAUNCEY".

HE AGAIN REMINDED ME TO ALLOW MY ELMER'S GLUE TO GET "TACKY" ON BOTH SURFACES BEFORE I PRESSED THEM TOGETHER.

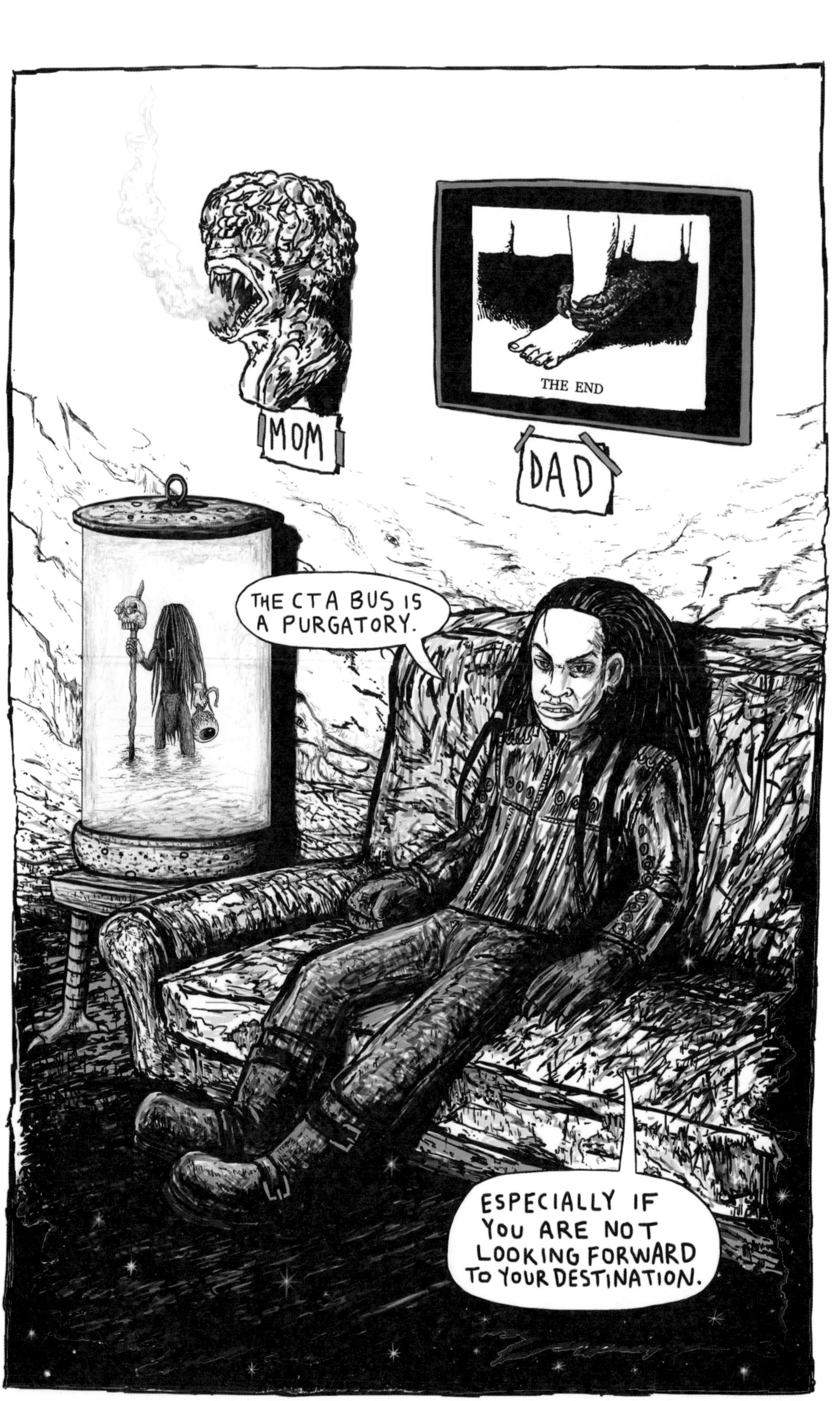
THE END
MOM
DAD
THE CTA BUS IS A PURGATORY.
ESPECIALLY IF YOU ARE NOT LOOKING FORWARD TO YOUR DESTINATION.

IN THE WINTERTIME THEY ARE REMINISCENT OF A MEATPACKING HOUSE ON WHEELS.

NOT FREEZING BUT DEFINITELY COLD AND CLAMMY.

EVERY BUMP IN THE POTHOLE POCK-MARKED SOUTH-SIDE STREETS WOULD RATTLE, LOOSE METAL, LIKE SWINGING MEAT HOOKS IN AN EARTHQUAKE.

CLANK CLUCK TING TING RATTLE!

FACES AROUND YOU, SLEEPY, WAR-WEARY FACES. RUNNY NOSES. BLEARY EYES.

WHEN I GOT OFF THE BUS I NOTED MY SURROUNDINGS AND REMEMBERED WHEN THE BIG BUILDING ON THE CORNER OF HOUSTON WAS A GIANT TOY-STORE.

OR MAYBE IT HAD BEEN GIANT TO LITTLE KIDS ONLY.

TWO STORIES ARE PRETTY BIG. "BARGAIN TOWN" WAS THE NAME.

LATER TO BECOME "TOYS-R-US", WHICH SOMEHOW RUINED EVERYTHING.

I BLAMED THE ANTHROPOMORPHIC GIRAFFE "GEOFFREY", AND LATER HIS WIFE GIGI AND DAUGHTER "LITTLE BABY GI".

THE TERM I WAS FEELING AROUND FOR WAS "SOLD-OUT". AS IN ALL THE MAGIC WAS GONE AFTER BARGAIN TOWN SOLD OUT TO THAT GOOFY GIRAFFE.

THE TWO THINGS THAT POPPED INTO MY HEAD WHEN CONTEMPLATING THE BUILDING WAS THE FACT THAT I'D ONLY BEEN IN THERE ONCE THAT I REMEMBERED.

I WAS WITH MY MOTHER, WHO (LIKE ALL MOTHERS) WAS THERE FOR A PURPOSE THAT HAD NOTHING TO DO WITH MY DESIRE TO BROWSE.

WE WERE ACTUALLY THERE TO GET SOMETHING FOR MY COUSIN'S BIRTHDAY PARTY, SO THERE WASN'T GOING TO BE ANY NEEDLESS FUCKING-AROUND.

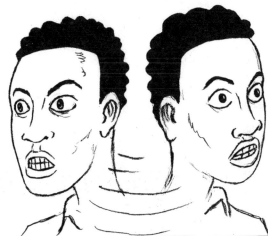

I WAS LIKE A STARVING MAN ATTEMPTING TO STUFF HIMSELF AT A FIVE MINUTE BUFFET.

EXCEPT MY MEAL WAS COLORFUL VISIONS OF TOYS.

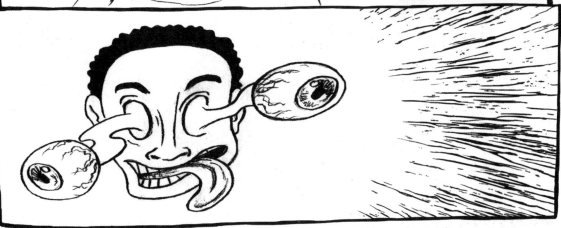

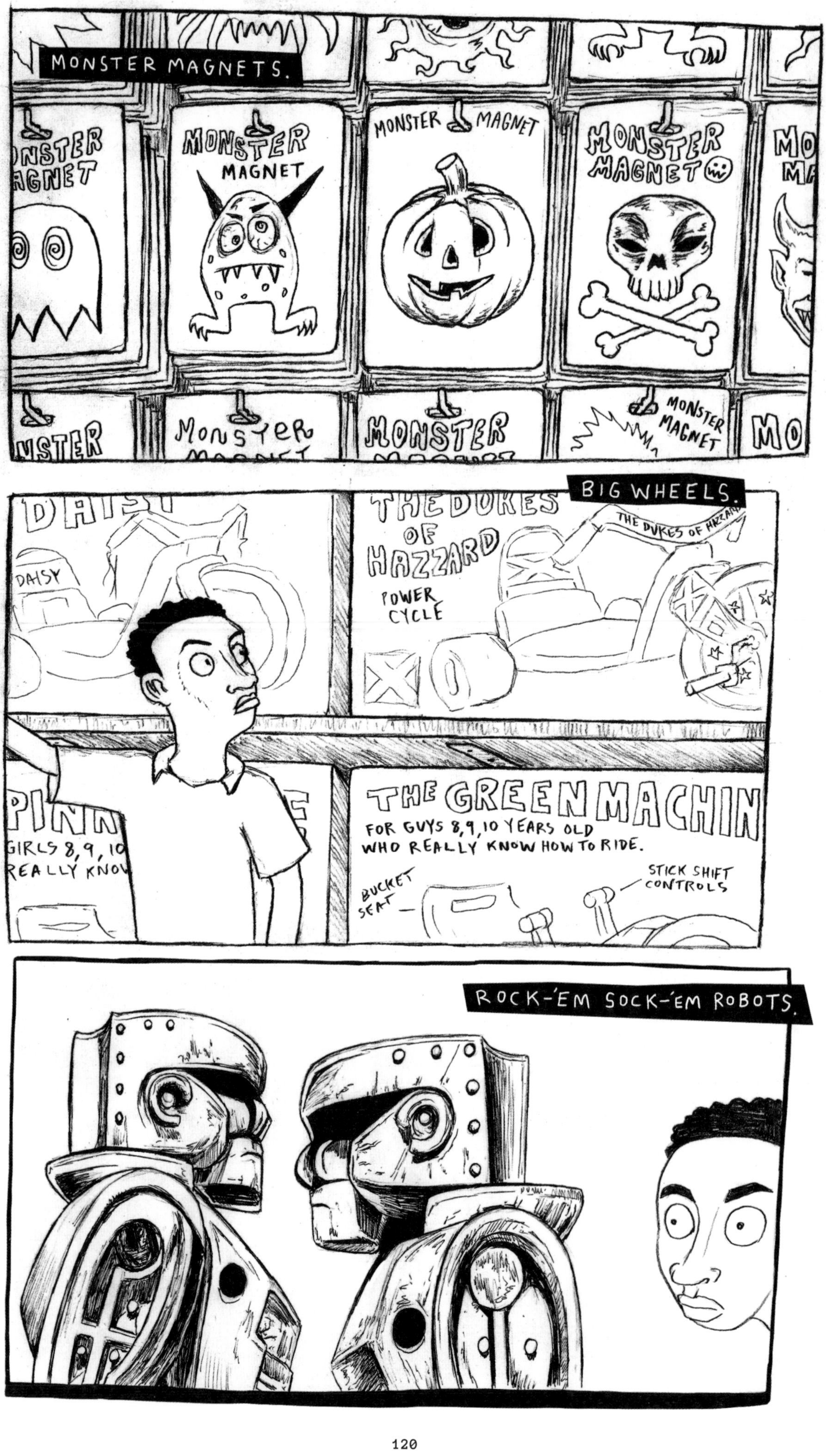
MONSTER MAGNETS.
MONSTER MAGNET
MONSTER MAGNET
MONSTER MAGNET
MONSTER MAGNET
BIG WHEELS.
DAISY
THE DUKES OF HAZZARD
POWER CYCLE
THE DUKES OF HAZZARD
THE GREEN MACHIN
FOR GUYS 8, 9, 10 YEARS OLD WHO REALLY KNOW HOW TO RIDE.
BUCKET SEAT
STICK SHIFT CONTROLS
ROCK-'EM SOCK-'EM ROBOTS.

MILES OF HOT WHEELS TRACK DISPLAY.

AND G.I. JOE'S ENTIRE 1/5 SCALE WORLD.

I SOAKED IT UP AS BEST I COULD WHILE AT THE SAME TIME ATTEMPTING TO FIGURE OUT HOW TO ASK FOR SOMETHING WITHOUT ANNOYING MY MOTHER.

I DIDN'T GET ANYTHING.

AND MY MEMORIES OF WHAT I SAW WERE MUDDIED.

TO CONTINUE THE STARVING MAN METAPHOR, IT WAS LIKE I'D EATEN SO MUCH SO QUICKLY, THAT I JUST THREW UP ON MYSELF.

ADVENTURE TEAM GI JOEEEEE
COILS OF DOOM
AGES 4-12

I DISEMBOWEL YOU FOR CHRIST'S LOVE.

I DO REMEMBER THE SCIENCE TOYS THOUGH.

PROBABLY BECAUSE IT WAS BOTH ODD AND AWESOME THAT A TOY STORE WOULD BE SELLING PRESERVED BIOLOGY SPECIMENS IN JARS OF ALCOHOL.

GUESS WHO CAME HOME ONE DAY TO A WORM, A GRASSHOPPER, AND A FROG?...

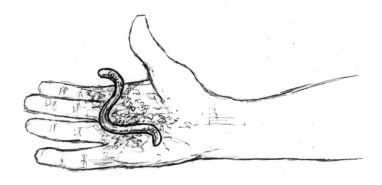

IN ANOTHER BLOCK I WAS PASSING THE YMCA.

I COULD NEVER PASS BY WITHOUT THINKING ABOUT TWO YEARS EARLIER, WHEN MY 5th-GRADE CLASS AT SOUTHEAST LUTHERAN EDUCATIONAL CENTER (SELEC) WAS TAKEN THERE FOR A SERIES OF SWIMMING LESSONS.

I REMEMBER THE GUARD-POST AT THE POOL ENTRANCE WHERE THE GUYS IN THE CAGE WOULD SIGN YOU IN.

THE GUYS IN THE CAGE WERE OLD.

BLACK MEN IN THEIR 50'S OR 60'S.

THE WALLS INSIDE THE CAGE WERE PAPERED WITH GIRLS FROM JET MAGAZINE "BEAUTY OF THE WEEK"

GIRLS WITH HIDEOUS BIKINIS AND AFROS OR RELAXED HAIR SHINING ON THEIR HEADS.

I LIKED THE LIGHT-SKINNED GIRLS ALTHOUGH THEY ALL SEEMED TO HAVE BLEMISHED LEGS AND DARK KNEES. THE OTHER PICTURES WERE FULL NUDES FROM THE BLACK GIRLIE MAGAZINE "PLAYERS"

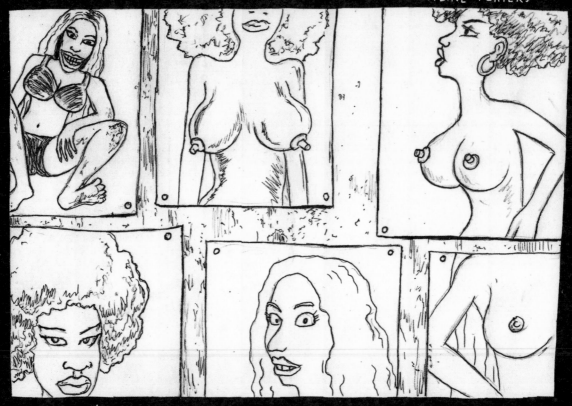

THE GUY IN CHARGE WAS NAMED FRANK. HE HAD A GREYISH BLACK FACE WITH BROAD NOSTRILS AND COTTONY SALT AND PEPPER HAIR. THE FOLLICLES ON HIS FACE WERE AS BIG AS PENCIL-POINTS.

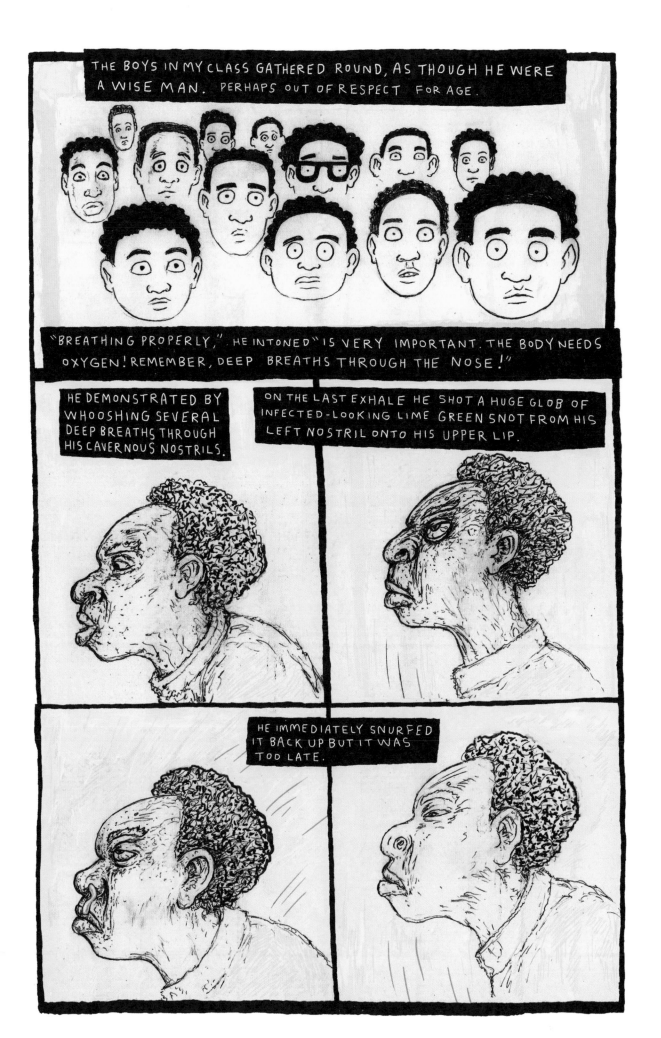

THE BOYS IN MY CLASS GATHERED ROUND, AS THOUGH HE WERE A WISE MAN. PERHAPS OUT OF RESPECT FOR AGE.

"BREATHING PROPERLY," HE INTONED "IS VERY IMPORTANT. THE BODY NEEDS OXYGEN! REMEMBER, DEEP BREATHS THROUGH THE NOSE!"

HE DEMONSTRATED BY WHOOSHING SEVERAL DEEP BREATHS THROUGH HIS CAVERNOUS NOSTRILS.

ON THE LAST EXHALE HE SHOT A HUGE GLOB OF INFECTED-LOOKING LIME GREEN SNOT FROM HIS LEFT NOSTRIL ONTO HIS UPPER LIP.

HE IMMEDIATELY SNURFED IT BACK UP BUT IT WAS TOO LATE.

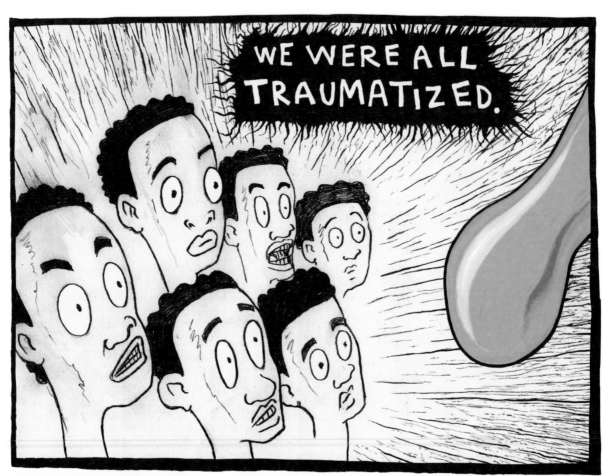

WE WERE ALL TRAUMATIZED.

WE CHANGED INTO OUR TRUNKS IN THE LOCKER ROOM.

THE AIR WAS HOT, STUFFY AND THICK WITH THE SMELL OF CHLORINE.

I WAS HORRIFED TO BE NAKED IN FRONT OF THE OTHER BOYS.

EVEN FOR A SECOND.

THIS WAS PROBABLY AGGRAVATED BY MY LIFE AS AN ONLY-CHILD.

IT SEEMED UNNATURAL.

A GROUP OF BOYS WOULD NEVER BE NAKED AROUND EACH OTHER IN NATURE.

THIS IS A SITUATION THAT HAS TO BE ENGINEERED.

I DON'T KNOW WHAT DISTURBED ME MORE, THE FACT THAT WE WERE FORCED TO BE NAKED TOGETHER, OR THE FACT THAT THE OTHERS DIDN'T SEEM TO BE BOTHERED BY BEING IN A HOT ROOM WITH A GROUP OF NAKED BOYS AND STRANGE NAKED MEN.

THE MEN, BEING STRANGERS, WERE NOT AS DISTURBING, THANKFULLY, OTHERWISE THEIR CASUAL CROTCH DRYING AND HANGING MEAT WOULD HAVE BEEN INTOLERABLE.

STRANGELY ENOUGH, I KNEW THAT IF I WERE TO VOICE THESE FEARS TO THE OTHERS I WOULD BE IMMEDIATELY BRANDED A "GAY".

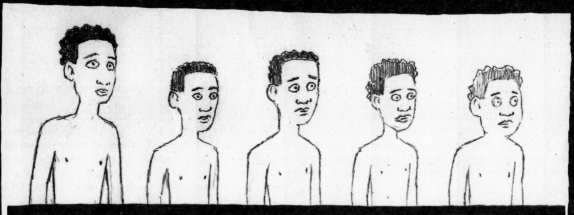

WE STOOD BY THE POOL ON THE WATER-SLICK CONCRETE. OUR LIMBS AS THIN AND FRAGILE AS BIRD WINGS WAITING TO BE SHATTERED.

THE INSTRUCTOR (FRANK) WAS FULLY CLOTHED. A FACT THAT WAS NOT LOST ON ME. BY THE TIME IT WOULD HAVE TAKEN HIM TO SLIP OUT OF HIS SNEAKERS AND KHAKI PANTS, A POTENTIAL DROWNING WOULD HAVE BECOME AN ACTUAL DROWNING.

AS INSTRUCTED, WE LOWERED OURSELVES INTO THE DEEP END OF THE POOL.

HOLDING ON TO THE EDGE WE WENT THROUGH A DRILL OF KICKING AND BLOWING BOUBBLES OUT OF OUR NOSES.

THIS WAS TO PREPARE US IN AN AQUATIC TRAINING-WHEELS WAY FOR THE NEXT STEP: LETTING GO.

THERE WAS A ROW OF US, MAYBE EIGHT, HOLDING ON TO THE EDGE WITH OUR FEET BETWEEN OUR HANDS, PREPARING TO LAUNCH OURSELVES INTO A BACKSTROKE.

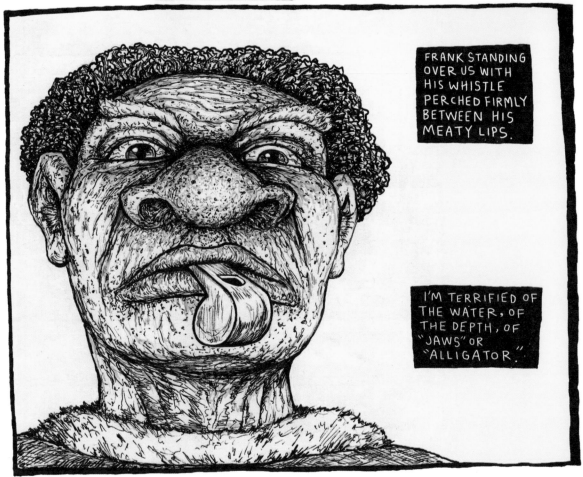

FRANK STANDING OVER US WITH HIS WHISTLE PERCHED FIRMLY BETWEEN HIS MEATY LIPS.

I'M TERRIFIED OF THE WATER, OF THE DEPTH, OF "JAWS" OR "ALLIGATOR."

THE WHISTLE BLASTS AND I PUSHED AWAY FROM THE EDGE. I'M NOT SURE HOW DEEP THE POOL WAS.

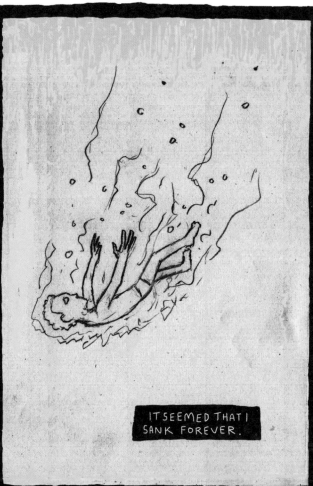

IT SEEMED THAT I SANK FOREVER.

WHEN I HIT THE BOTTOM IT WAS ALL A DARK BLUR. I WAS UPSIDE-DOWN. I WAS UPSIDE-DOWN UNDER WATER IN THE DARKNESS. I HADN'T EXPECTED TO BE DOWN THERE SO I HAD NO BREATH IN MY LUNGS.

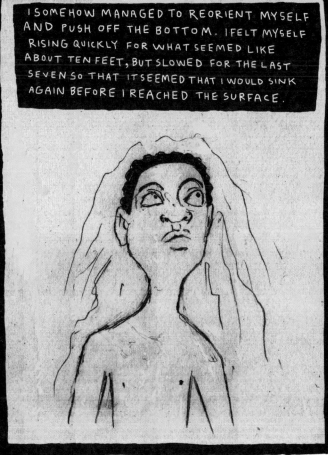

I SOMEHOW MANAGED TO REORIENT MYSELF AND PUSH OFF THE BOTTOM. I FELT MYSELF RISING QUICKLY FOR WHAT SEEMED LIKE ABOUT TEN FEET, BUT SLOWED FOR THE LAST SEVEN SO THAT IT SEEMED THAT I WOULD SINK AGAIN BEFORE I REACHED THE SURFACE.

MY HEAD POPPED OUT OF THE WATER FOR A FRACTION OF A SECOND.

I TOOK A QUICK BREATH AND STARTED GOING UNDER AGAIN.

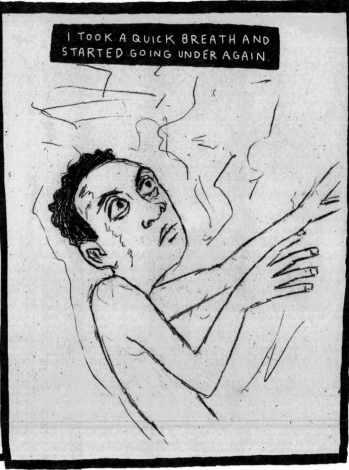

BEFORE I SANK TO CERTAIN DOOM MY ARM SHOT OUT BLINDLY AND MY FINGERS MADE NEBULOUS CONTACT WITH THE EDGE OF THE POOL.

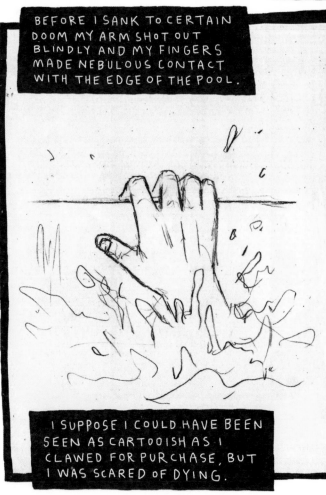

I SUPPOSE I COULD HAVE BEEN SEEN AS CARTOOISH AS I CLAWED FOR PURCHASE, BUT I WAS SCARED OF DYING.

AFTER I GOT A FIRM GRIP, I REFUSED TO GO BACK. I SAT ON THE EDGE UNTIL IT WAS OVER. LOOKING AT THE OTHERS I WAS CONVINCED THAT THEY'D KNOWN HOW TO SWIM BEFORE THE LESSON....

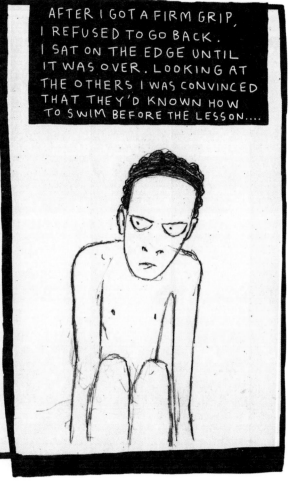

I CROSSED THE STREET AND PASSED THE PUBLIC LIBRARY, WHICH WAS NEXT THE CHURCH. THE LIBRARY ITSELF WAS A PRETTY ORDINARY BRANCH, BUT IT HAD A XEROX MACHINE THAT I WAS FASCINATED WITH. FOR A DIME YOU COULD MAKE A COPY. IT WAS BRAND NEW TECHNOLOGY, AT LEAST TO ME. I'D BEEN EXPERIMENTING WITH COPYING MY SPIRAL-NOTEBOOK COMICS. I WAS THINKING THAT I'D DRAW A FEW ONE PAGE SERIALS, MAKE COPIES AT THE LIBRARY, AND SELL MY CLASSMATES A NEW EPISODE DAILY FOR A QUARTER. I HAD DOLLAR SIGNS IN MY EYES. THERE WAS NO WAY THEY COULD RESIST!...

THE CHURCH WAS ONE OF THOSE HUGE OLD CHICAGO MASTERPIECES WITH ARCHED STAINED-GLASS WINDOWS.

BUILT BY GERMAN SETTLERS IN THE 1860'S, IT WAS TALL AND ORNATE WITH A BELL IN THE STEEPLE AND A HUGE CROSS AT THE PEAK.

WE ALL TOOK TURNS BEING ACOLYTES BUT ONLY A CHOSEN FEW WERE ALLOWED TO BE BELL-RINGERS. ACTUALLY ALL YOU HAD TO DO WAS ASK, BUT I WAS NEVER INTERESTED.

THE RINGERS WOULD HAVE DISCUSSIONS ABOUT HOW COOL IT WAS IF YOU PULLED REAL HARD AND HELD ONTO THE ROPE BECAUSE THE BELL WOULD YANK YOU UPWARDS LIKE A CARNIVAL RIDE.

SEEMED DANGEROUS TO ME.

I WAS WAITING FOR THE DAY THE BELL YANKED ONE OF THE YOUNG DAREDEVILS UP AND INTO THE MECHANISM, CHEWING OFF THEIR HANDS IN THE WORKS.

AT LEAST I HOPED IT WOULD HAPPEN, SO I COULD JUSTIFY MY CONSTANT USE OF COMMON SENSE AND BASIC SAFETY AS SOMETHING OTHER THAN CRAVEN COWARDICE.

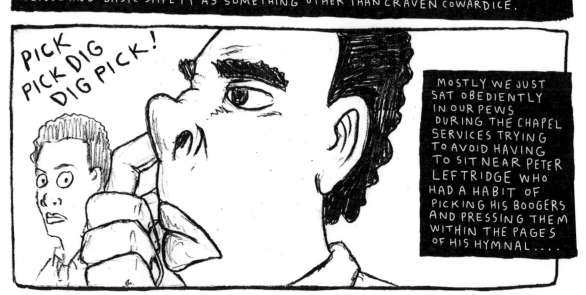

PICK PICK DIG DIG PICK!

MOSTLY WE JUST SAT OBEDIENTLY IN OUR PEWS DURING THE CHAPEL SERVICES TRYING TO AVOID HAVING TO SIT NEAR PETER LEFTRIDGE WHO HAD A HABIT OF PICKING HIS BOOGERS AND PRESSING THEM WITHIN THE PAGES OF HIS HYMNAL....

I WALKED DOWN THE STAIRS BETWEEN THE CHURCH AND SCHOOL BUILDINGS. CHICAGO HAS RAISED STREETS ON THAT SIDE OF TOWN, CLOSE TO THE LAKE. I WAS TOLD THAT THE LAKE USED TO BE AT A HIGHER LEVEL BUT IT WAS LATER DAMMED UP OR SOMEHOW CONTROLLED SO THAT LATER BUILDINGS COULD BE BUILT ON THE RECLAIMED LAND. WHO KNOWS?

I MADE NOTE OF THE PLASTIC-COVERED REFRIGERATOR BOX IN THE SPACE BETWEEN THE STAIRS AND WALL OF THE CHURCH. SANTA CLAUS LIVED IN THE BOX. ACTUALLY HIS NAME WAS ED, BUT HE LOOKED JUST LIKE SANTA WITH HIS LONG WHITE BEARD, BIG BELLY, AND WIRE-RIMMED GLASSES.

HE WAS THE FIRST HOMELESS PERSON THAT MOST OF US HAD EVER SEEN.

I ALWAYS SAW HIM AS SOMEHOW MYSTICAL, AS THOUGH HE MAY REALLY BE SANTA, OR PERHAPS AN UNDERCOVER ANGEL. HOW ELSE COULD HE SURVIVE THE SUB-ZERO WINTERS IN A CARDBOARD BOX?

PASTOR FOLEY INVITED HIM TO STAY IN THE CHURCH ON BAD NIGHTS, BUT ED ALWAYS CHOSE THE BOX.

OF COURSE THE KIDS MADE FUN OF HIM, BUT I ONLY SAW HIM GET MAD ONCE. HE WAS USING ONE OF THE BASEMENT TOILET-STALLS AT THE BEGINNING OF THE DAY AND THE LITTLE KIDS WENT IN TO KNOCK ON THE STALL DOOR AND RUN AWAY LAUGHING.

HE WAS PRETTY ANGRY, BUT THE MOST HE HAD TO SAY AS HE EMERGED FROM THE BATHROOM WAS "STOP KNOCKING ON THE DAMN DOOR!"

I WORRIED, BECAUSE EVEN THAT INNOCENT EXCLAMATION COULD TURN INTO LIES IN THE MOUTH OF KIDS.

"HE SAID 'SHIT'. OR "HE CHASED US!" OR WORSE.

THANKFULLY, NOTHING CAME OF IT....

THE HOLIDAY SEEMED TO HAVE HAD A CALMING EFFECT ON MY SCHOOLMATES. PERHAPS THEY WERE JUST BLUE FROM HAVING TO BE BACK. THE TALK WAS MOSTLY OF WHAT WAS GOTTEN FOR CHRISTMAS. AIR JORDAN'S AND SPORTING GOODS HAD TAKEN THE SPOTS OF TOYS IN THEIR HEARTS.

OR ON THE SURFACE, ANYWAY. I THOUGHT THEY WERE JUST TRYING TO OUT-MATURE EACH OTHER. THAT'S WHAT THE GIRLS WERE STARTING TO WANT: MATURITY.

THE PROBLEM WITH FORCED MATURITY IS THAT ITS AFFECT IS OFTEN CRUELTY.

THE NEUROTIC MIDDLE-CLASS FEEDING ON THE OUTCAST TO TRANSFER THE ATTENTION OF THEIR PEERS.

I'D DONE IT MYSELF, THE PREVIOUS YEAR. DRAWING A HEINOUS CARTOON OF ANOTHER NERDY AND STUDIOUS BOY TO GET IN GOOD WITH THE OTHERS. FOR THOSE FIVE MINUTES OF ATTENTION I WAS THROWN UNDER THE BUS BY ROBERT AND THE BOYS.

MY GRAPHICALLY SCATOLOGICAL AND HOMOPHOBICALLY ONANISTIC MASTERPIECE WINDING UP IN THE HANDS OF PASTOR FOLEY AND THE PRINCIPAL, MS. SMITH.

I COULD HAVE SWEAT BLOOD FROM THE WORRY I EXPERIENCED, AS I SAT IN THAT OFFICE. I WAS HANDED A LETTER TO GIVE TO MY PARENTS, THEN SENT BACK TO CLASS. FOR THE FOLLOWING THREE HOURS I WAS AT MY DESK, IMAGINING.

I WAS THE BAD GUY!

WHAT THE FUCK HAD I BEEN THINKING?

THE ONLY FORESEEABLE OUTCOME (BESIDES A VICIOUS BEATING) WOULD BE A BAN ON MY DRAWING ANY MORE. WHICH WOULD BE WORSE THAN THE BEATING BY A THOUSAND FOLD.

I TRIED TO MAKE EYE CONTACT WITH THE BOY THAT I'D WRONGED, BUT HE KEPT HIS FACE FORWARD.

AS SOON AS 3:00 CAME I RUSHED DOWN TO THE OFFICE.

THE SECRETARY ASKED ME WHAT I WANTED, BUT I BROKE INTO CHOKING SOBS AND THE MOST SINCERE APOLOGY OF MY LIFE.

I BEGGED HER.

I'D NEVER BEEN IN ANY TROUBLE BEFORE! I PROMISED TO BE A QUIET ANGEL FROM THEN ON! SHE TOLD ME TO WAIT THERE AND WENT INTO PASTOR FOLEY'S OFFICE. I SAW HER SPEAKING TO HIM THROUGH THE GLASS.

MOMENTS LATER, THE PRINCIPAL SMITH EMERGED. "DID YOU HAVE SOMETHING TO TELL ME?" SHE ASKED.

I TRIED NOT TO CRY AS I REPEATED MY PROMISES TO BE GOOD. I LIED WHEN I TOLD HER THAT I JUST DIDN'T WANT MY PARENTS TO BE DISAPPOINTED IN ME.

I DIDN'T WANT TO LIE, BUT I FELT THAT VOICING MY FEAR OF BEING BANNED FROM DRAWING WOULD SOUND RIDICULOUS, AND MORE LIKE A LIE THAN THE TRUTH.

"SO," SHE SAID, "YOU'VE LEARNED YOUR LESSON?"

"YES!" I CRIED, "I'LL NEVER DO ANYTHING LIKE THAT AGAIN!"

SHE LOOKED AT ME THOUGHTFULLY, AND THEN ASKED ME FOR THE LETTER, AND I GLADLY HANDED OVER THE ACCURSED PAPER, SWORD OF DAMOCLES.

I THANKED HER AND THEN HER SECRETARY AND RUSHED OUT BEFORE SHE COULD CHANGE HER MIND.

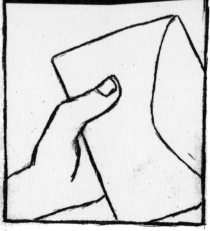

AS I DESCENDED THE FRONT STAIRS I WONDERED IF SHE HAD BEEN PLAYING A TRICK ON ME, AND WOULD SEND THE LETTER IN THE MAIL.

I HAD TO; HOWEVER, REMOVE THAT POSSIBILITY FROM MY MIND AS SOMETHING TOO HORRIBLE TO ACTUALLY OCCUR....

THE BACK-TO-SCHOOL CONVERSATIONS CONTINUED UP THE STAIRS AND INTO THE CLASSROOM.

I STASHED MY BALONEY AND MUSTARD SAND-WICH AND CHIPS UNDER MY CHAIR.

I NEVER KEPT ANYTHING IN THE CLOAK-ROOM. IT WAS TOO EASY FOR ANYONE WHO WANTED TO STEAL OR TAMPER WITH YOUR STUFF. BESIDES, THE NARROW, DRAB, WOOD-FLOORED ROOM REMINDED ME TOO MUCH OF THE PUNISHMENT CLOSET IN THE MOVIE CARRIE.

I MOVED AROUND THE ROOM, COMING INTO THE ORBIT OF THE DIFFERENT TALKERS. I VIVIDLY REALIZED THE STIGMA OF BEING A LONER-WEIRDO/PERFECT VICTIM IF I NEVER LEFT MY DESK. I CAME NEAR THE OTHERS OUT OF A NAIVE HOPE THAT ONE DAY I WOULD BE TOLERATED.

AS I MADE MY ROUNDS I STOPPED AT QUINTON'S DESK, WHERE HE WAS TALKING TO KYLE AND EDSEL. I STOOD QUIETLY BY AS HE TALKED, AND TRIED TO INGRATIATE MYSELF INTO THEIR PRESENCE, SLOWLY, BY A SORT OF NERD-OSMOSIS.

THAT'S WHEN I HEARD ROBERT'S VOICE, BEHIND ME, YELL,...

DANCE FEVER!

138

I FELT THE STING, AND AS I TURNED SAW HIM SMILING, AND FINISHING THE TELEVISION CATCH-PHRASE,...

COMIN' ATCHA LIVE!

BACK THEN THERE WAS A METHOD OF PEER DEGRADATION KNOWN AS THE "JACK-SLAP."

THIS WAS WHEN YOU TOOK YOUR INDEX AND MIDDLE FINGERS, PUT THEM TOGETHER AS YOU FOLDED YOUR OTHER FINGERS INTO A LOOSE FIST.

YOU WOULD THEN LICK THE PALM-SIDE OF YOUR EXTENDED FINGERS, REACH WAY BACK, AND THEN SLAP THE BACK OF ANOTHER PERSON'S NECK WITH THE WET FINGERS.

ROBERT HAD JUST JACK-SLAPPED ME IN FRONT OF EVERYONE ON THE FIRST DAY BACK. SO MUCH FOR THE RESIDUAL HOLIDAY-SPIRIT....

I'VE ALWAYS BEEN AN EXPLORER. NO MATTER HOW OFTEN I'D BEEN BEATEN FOR IT I COULDN'T STOP EXPLORING WHAT WAS IN MY PARENT'S DRESSER-DRAWERS. IN MY DEFENSE, MY PARENTS HAD A LOT OF INTERESTING STUFF.

AT LEAST STUFF THAT WOULD BE INTERESTING TO A KID... OR AT LEAST INTERESTING TO ME. I WOULD, WHEN THEY WERE AWAY FROM HOME, GO ON MY ARCHAELOGICAL DIGS INTO THE STRANGE WORLD OF ADULTS.

MY MOTHER'S STUFF WAS PRETTY UTILITARIAN. A RONCO BUTTON-SETTER, A RONCO STUDSETTER, AN EPILADY, HAIR-ROLLERS, MAKEUP AND ETC.

I DID TRY ALL OF THE ABOVE, INCLUDING THE MAKEUP, BEING VERY CAREFUL TO ENSURE MY FATHER WASN'T COMING UP THE WALKWAY.

IT'S A TRIBUTE TO INDIVIDUAL TASTES, THE DIFFERENCES BETWEEN MY PARENT'S DRAWERS AND CLOSETS.

WHEREAS MY MOTHER'S BELONGINGS WERE STRICTLY ABOVE-BOARD AND USEFUL, MY FATHER'S BELONGINGS WERE LIKE A TRIP INTO THE MIND OF A 1960'S TEENAGE BOY.

TIJUANA BIBLES, A HUGE FAKE DIAMOND NECKLASE THE SIZE OF A DOORKNOB, A SWITCHBLADE, CONDOMS, EROTIC NOVELS, BRASS-KNUCKLES, NOVELTY SQUEEZE TOYS, LEATHER COLD WEATHER MASKS AND ON AND ON, AD INFINITUM.

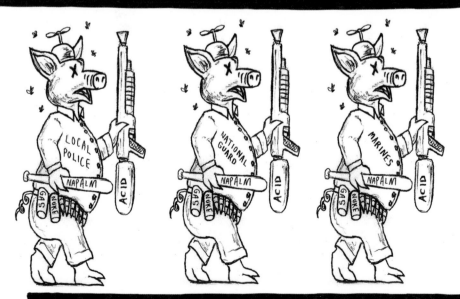

IT WAS BECAUSE OF THIS BOUNTY THAT I WAS ABLE TO START CARRYING WEAPONS TO SCHOOL.

I'M SURE THAT KIDS HAVE BEEN CARRYING WEAPONS TO SCHOOLS SINCE THE BEGINNING OF SCHOOLS. IT WAS JUST THE DEATHS OF A BUNCH OF WHITE HIGH SCHOOL BULLIES THAT MADE THE CARRYING OF WEAPONS A VISIBLE AND HISTRIONIC PHENOMENON.

ACTUALLY I'M QUITE SHOCKED THAT THERE HAVEN'T BEEN MORE BULLY KILLINGS. THE ONLY REASON I CAN IMAGINE THERE AREN'T IS THAT NERDS LACK THE IMPULSIVE AGGRESSION TO KILL THEIR TORMENTORS. WHICH IS PROBABLY SOMETHING BULLIES INSTINCTIVELY UNDERSTAND. WHICH IS THE REAL REASON THAT COLUMBINE WAS SO SHOCKING. THE NERDS WENT OFF SCRIPT.

I MADE AN EDUCATED GUESS CONCERNING WHAT THINGS MY FATHER MIGHT MISS FROM HIS DRESSER DRAWERS. FOR ABOUT THREE WEEKS I WAS ARMED.

I WOULDN'T BE ABLE TO USE ANY OF MY WEAPONS IN SCHOOL. I KNEW THAT.

THERE WOULD BE NO WAY TO PLEAD SELF-DEFENCE IN SUCH A HOSTILE ENVIRONMENT.

IT WOULD BE MY WORD AGAINST THE WORD OF A GROUP.

NO, I SAVED MY WEAPONS FOR THE AFTERSCHOOL TREK UNDER THE VIADUCT TOWARDS HOME.

I PICTURED KYLE, AS ALWAYS TRYING TO FOLLOW ME INTO THE DARKNESS, LIKE SOME SORT OF MONSTROUS BAT.

IN THE LOWER RIGHT POCKET OF MY FIELD-JACKET WAS A LARGE BLACK CAN OF MACE. IN THE LOWER LEFT POCKET, A SET OF BRASS-KNUCKLES. I CARRIED A SWITCHBLADE IN THE UPPER RIGHT POCKET.

MATERIALLY I WAS READY FOR KYLE. IF HE CAME UP BEHIND ME I WOULD SPRAY HIM WITH MACE AND THEN CRUSH HIM WITH MY BRASS KNUCKLES.

THAT WAS THE PLAN.

BUT EVEN HAVING THE UPPER HAND I WAS AFRAID THAT SOMETHING WOULD GO WRONG. THAT THE MACE WOULDN'T SPRAY, OR THAT IT WOULD SPRAY IN THE WRONG DIRECTION.

I WAS TERRIFIED THAT I WOULD FALTER AND THAT KYLE WOULD GET MY KNIFE OR KNUCKLES AWAY FROM ME AND KILL ME.

EVEN ARMED TO THE TEETH, I COULDN'T QUITE PICTURE MYSELF NOT FUCKING UP.

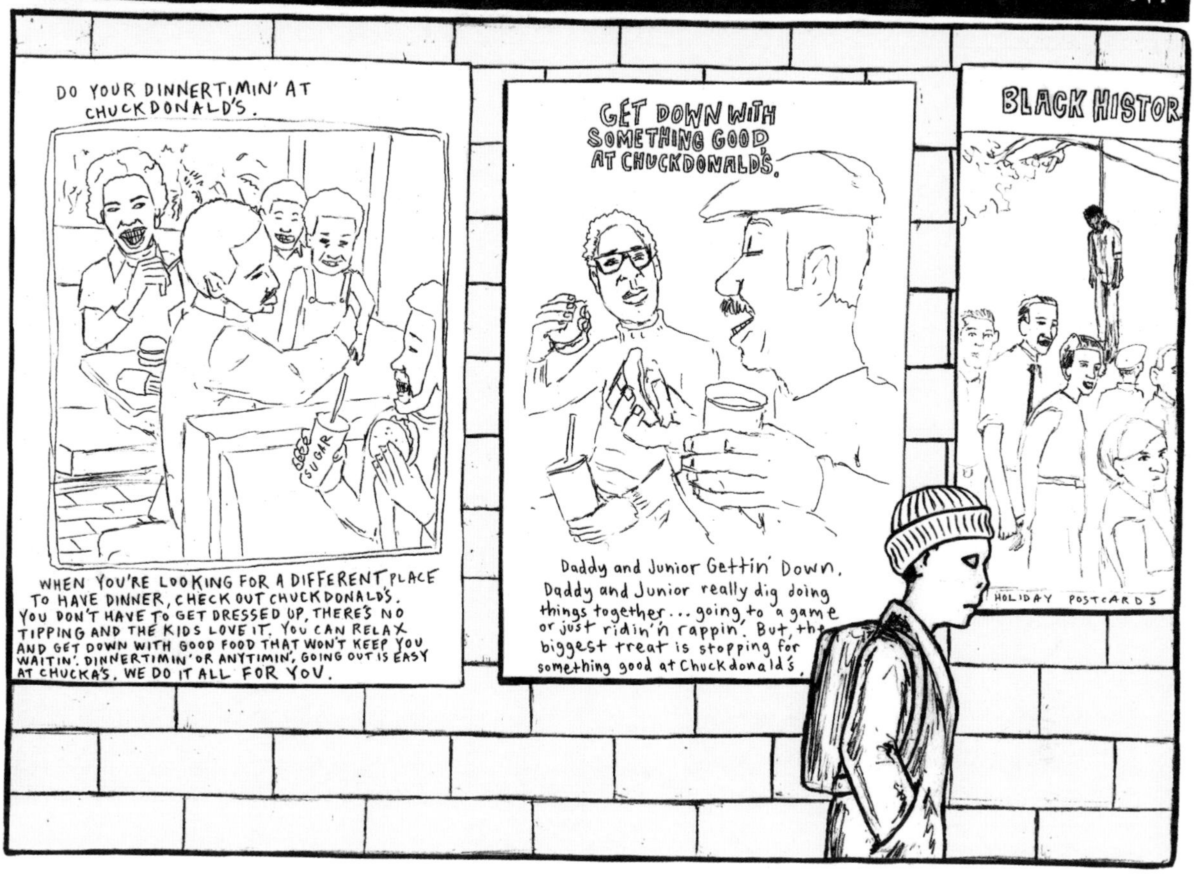

DO YOUR DINNERTIMIN' AT CHUCKDONALD'S.
SUGAR
WHEN YOU'RE LOOKING FOR A DIFFERENT PLACE TO HAVE DINNER, CHECK OUT CHUCKDONALD'S. YOU DON'T HAVE TO GET DRESSED UP, THERE'S NO TIPPING AND THE KIDS LOVE IT. YOU CAN RELAX AND GET DOWN WITH GOOD FOOD THAT WON'T KEEP YOU WAITIN'. DINNERTIMIN' OR ANYTIMIN', GOING OUT IS EASY AT CHUCKA'S. WE DO IT ALL FOR YOU.
GET DOWN WITH SOMETHING GOOD AT CHUCKDONALD'S.
Daddy and Junior Gettin' Down. Daddy and Junior really dig doing things together... going to a game or just ridin' 'n rappin'. But, th biggest treat is stopping for something good at Chuckdonald's
BLACK HISTOR
HOLIDAY POSTCARDS

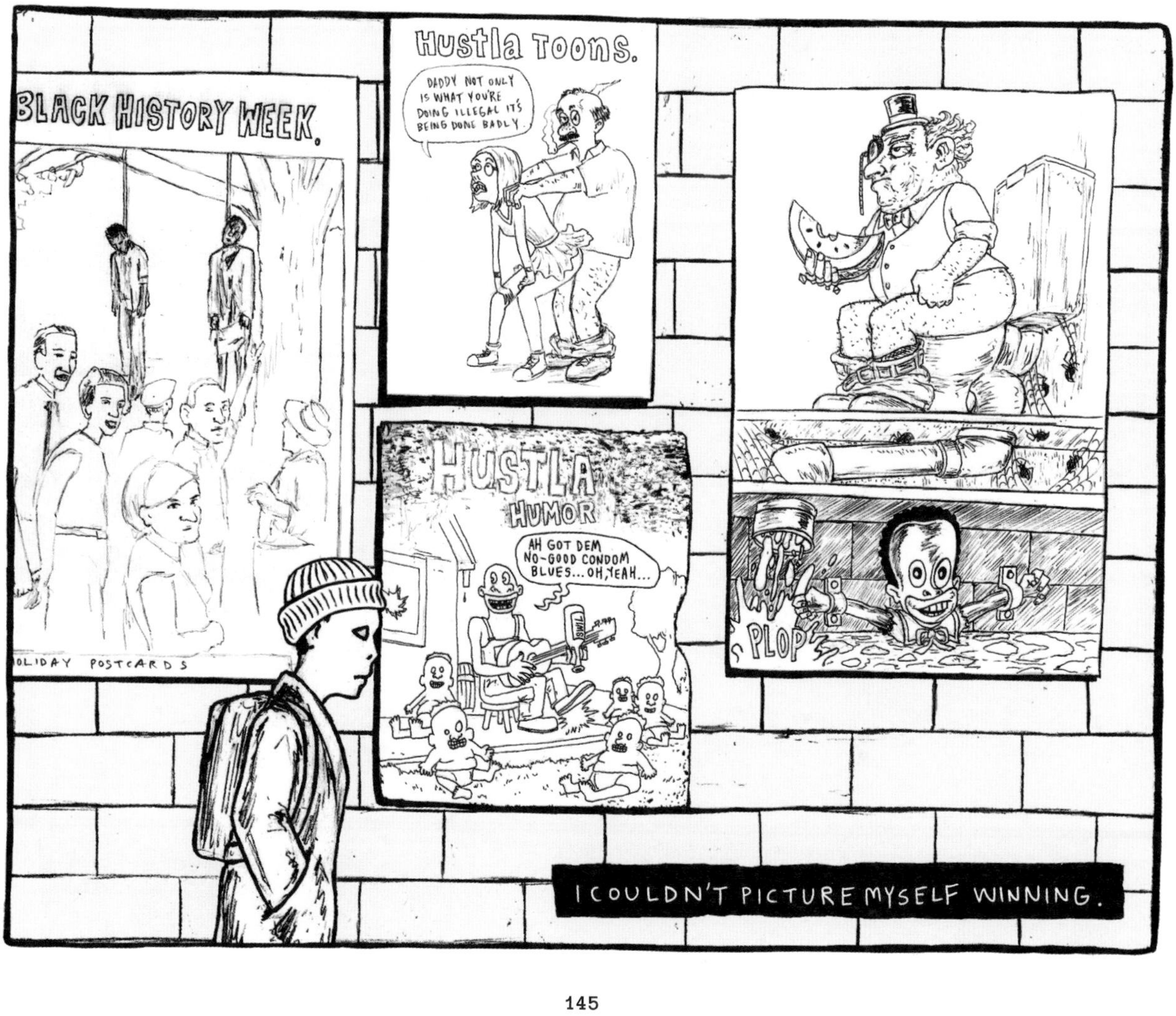

BLACK HISTORY WEEK.
OLIDAY POSTCARDS
Hustla Toons.
DADDY NOT ONLY IS WHAT YOU'RE DOING ILLEGAL IT'S BEING DONE BADLY.
HUSTLA HUMOR
AH GOT DEM NO-GOOD CONDOM BLUES... OH, YEAH...
PLOP
I COULDN'T PICTURE MYSELF WINNING.

CAROLYN BRYANT.

EMMETT LUIS TILL

SO MY DAILY TREK THROUGH THE DARKNESS WAS LITERALLY A NIGHTMARE "KILL OR BE KILLED" SCENERIO.

THERE WAS NO MIDDLE GROUND. MY MOTHER HAD TOLD ME THAT WHEN FACED WITH A FIGHT I SHOULD GET A STICK AND TRY TO "KNOCK THEIR HEAD OFF"

I HAD NO FEAR OF ARREST FOR SOME REASON. PROBABLY BECAUSE I TRUSTED THE WISDOM OF MY PARENT'S HEAD-KNOCKING ADVICE.

POP!

THANKFULLY KYLE NEVER SHOWED.

ONE DAY IN SCHOOL I SHOWED EDSEL THAT I HAD A SET OF NUNCHUCKS. WE WERE (FOR SOME REASON) IN THE ACCURSED CLOAK-ROOM.

EDSEL HAD BEEN TEASING ME SO I QUIETLY OPENED MY JACKET AND SHOWED HIM THE NUN CHUCKS IN THE INSIDE POCKET. I WAS ATTEMPTING TO PUT HIM OFF BY BOTH PROVING THAT I WAS BOTH CRAZY, AND A REGULAR GUY.

HIS EYES GOT WIDE AND A GRIN STOLE ACROSS HIS FACE.

QUINTON CAME INTO THE CLOAK-ROOM JUST ABOUT THEN.

WAS MY HAND BEING FORCED?

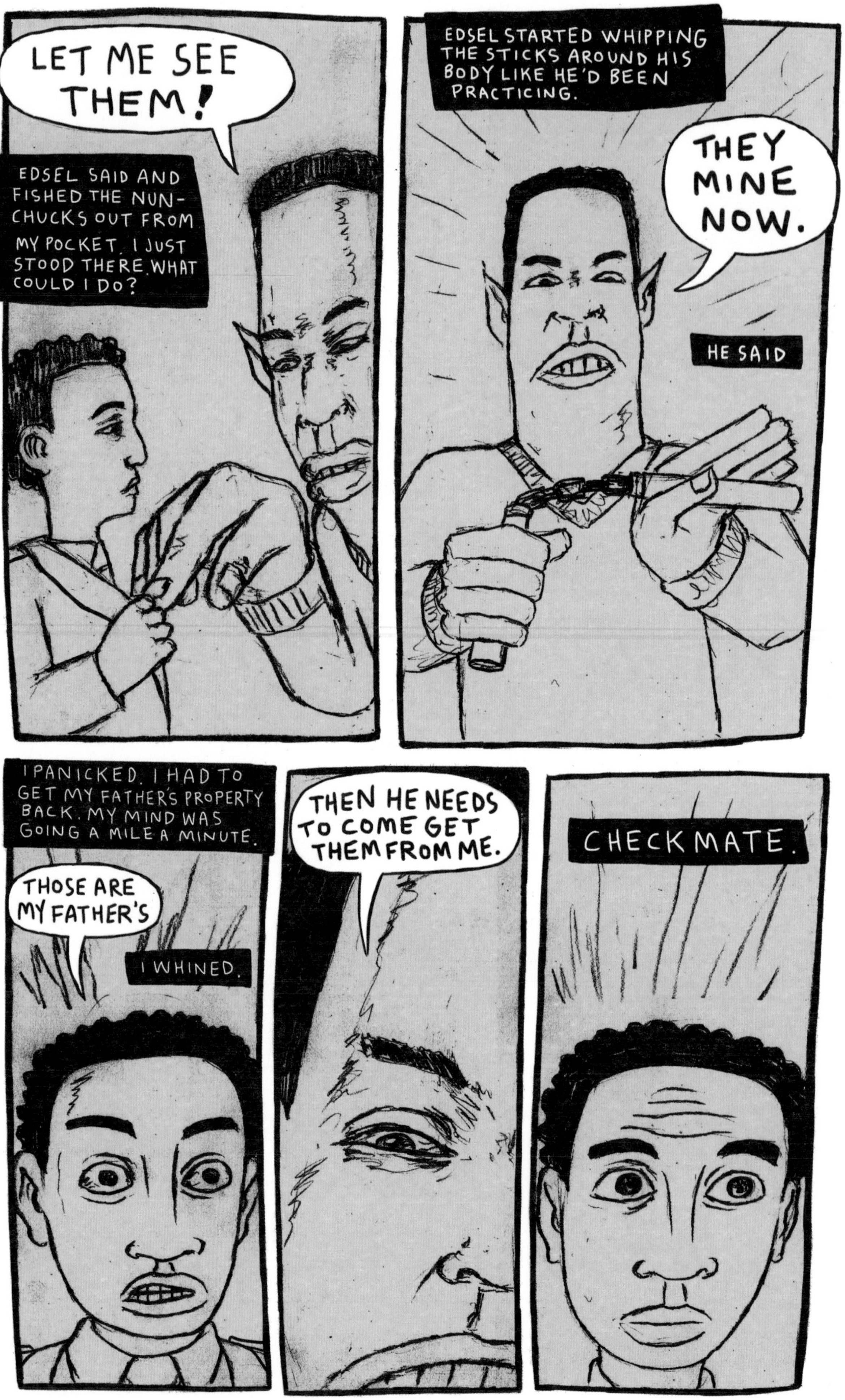
LET ME SEE THEM!
EDSEL SAID AND FISHED THE NUN-CHUCKS OUT FROM MY POCKET. I JUST STOOD THERE. WHAT COULD I DO?
EDSEL STARTED WHIPPING THE STICKS AROUND HIS BODY LIKE HE'D BEEN PRACTICING.
THEY MINE NOW.
HE SAID
I PANICKED. I HAD TO GET MY FATHER'S PROPERTY BACK. MY MIND WAS GOING A MILE A MINUTE.
THOSE ARE MY FATHER'S
I WHINED.
THEN HE NEEDS TO COME GET THEM FROM ME.
CHECKMATE.

MR. FLORENTINO'S VOICE THEN CAME FROM THE CLASSROOM.

FIND YOUR SEATS PEOPLE.

HE SAID.

EDSEL PUT THE NUNCHUCKS UP HIS SLEEVE AND WALKED OUT INTO THE CLASSROOM AND TO HIS DESK.

I SAT AT MY DESK AS THE CLASS PROCEEDED, UNABLE TO LISTEN AND SILENT IN MY REAR-ROW SEAT. I WAS SCANNING EDSEL AND HIS DESK LIKE THE TERMINATOR. WHERE WERE THOSE NUNCHUCKS? IN HIS BAG? INSIDE HIS DESK? MAYBE STILL INSIDE THE CLOAKROOM?

HOW TO TELL?

RADAR

SCAN

BEEP

BEEP

MAYBE I COULD GO ASK MR FLORENTINO TO GO TO THE RESTROOM AND THEN SNEAK INTO THE CLOAKROOM FROM THE OTHER SIDE...

MY HAND HAND WENT UP....

THE ONLY RESTROOMS WERE IN THE BASEMENT SO THEY WERE ACCESSIBLE VIA THE STAIRWELL ON EITHER SIDE OF THE BUILDING.

THE STAIRS WERE GLOOMY IN THE WINTER, LIKE SOME NOIR TENEMENT SET.

149

I MADE MY WAY DOWN THE BACK STAIRS, CROSSED THE BASEMENT, AND MADE MY WAY TO THE FRONT STAIRS, SO THAT WHEN I GOT TO THE THIRD FLOOR, I WOULD BE AT THE CLASS-ROOM ENTRANCE NEXT TO THE CLOAK-ROOM.

THE FRONT STAIRS WERE THE MIRROR OPPOSITE OF THE BACK STAIRS.

NO... THAT'S NOT RIGHT.

THE FRONT STAIRS WERE LIKE A PHOTO NEGATIVE OF THE REAR STAIRWELL.

A PHOTO-EMO NEGATIVE.

WHEREAS THE REAR STAIRS WERE ALWAYS DARK, THE FRONT STAIRS WERE ALWAYS LIGHT.

THE SUN POURED IN THROUGH WINDOWS IN THE FRONT OF THE BUILDING, WHICH WAS THE WEST SIDE, SO THE FRONT STAIRS HAD A WONDERFUL AFTERNOON GLOW.

THIS ALSO MEANT THAT THE FRONT WERE EVENLY LIT FROM THE SIDE, WHEREAS THE REAR STAIRS WERE LIT ONLY BY NORTH/SOUTH LIGHT COMING THROUGH NARROW WINDOWS.

THIS LIGHT HIT THE STEPS RIGHT IN THE FACE.

THIS PUT BOTH SIDES IN GLOOMY HALF-SHADOW/HALF-LIGHT.

THE FRONT STEPS WERE WHERE THE OFFICES AND MAIN DOORS WERE.

WAS THIS SOME SORT OF SUBCONSCIOUS MINDFUCKERY PUT FORTH TOWARD THE STUDENTS TO INSPIRE THEM?

IE: "IF YOU ARE GOOD AND WORK HARD, THEN ONE DAY YOU TOO CAN WALK IN THE SUNLIGHT. ONE DAY YOU TOO CAN WALK THROUGH THE FRONT DOORS, AND WORK IN AN OFFICE."

I MADE IT UP TO THE THIRD FLOOR AND STOOD NEXT TO THE DOORWAY LIKE A DETECTIVE EXPECTING GUNFIRE.

IF I LOOKED AROUND THAT CORNER AND MR. FLORENTINO SAW ME THEN THE ENTIRE JOURNEY WAS IN VAIN.

UNFORTUNATELY, THERE WAS NO WAY TO JUDGE HIS POSITION IN THE ROOM.

IT WAS DO OR DIE, A MATTER OF GUTS AND STEALTH.

I FOCUSED MYSELF, FEELING THE ENERGY OF THE ROOM, MY EARS BAT-LIKE, MY MUSCLES LIKE A CAT.

I CAME AROUND THE CORNER LIKE A SHADOW AND STEPPED ON A FLOORBOARD THAT GROANED LIKE THE THREE STOOGES PRYING OPEN A PACKING CRATE.

MR. FIORENTINO LOOKED RIGHT AT ME WITHOUT BREAKING THE RHYTHM OF HIS LESSON.

CREEEEEEK!

I NODDED AND WALKED INTO THE CLOAK-ROOM.

WITH HIM HAVING SEEN ME I ONLY HAD SECONDS TO MAKE IT THROUGH THE CLOAKROOM, FIND MY NUN-CHUCKS, AND EXIT TO THE DOOR AT THE REAR ROW OF THE CLASSROOM.

I SCURRIED LIKE A COCKROACH, HITTING LOOSE BOARD AFTER LOOSE BOARD LIKE A WOOD-CREAK SAVANT.

WHICH WAS EDSEL'S COAT?

I THOUGHT IT WAS ON THE WEST WALL!

GRAB GRAB GRAB GRAB GRAB

FUCK IT, I WENT FOR BROKE, QUICKLY GROPING EVERY JACKET LIKE A ROW OF DISTENDED TITS... NOTHING.

I EXITED THE ROOM AND FOUND MY DESK.

SO MUCH FOR MY FUTURE AS A BURGULAR.

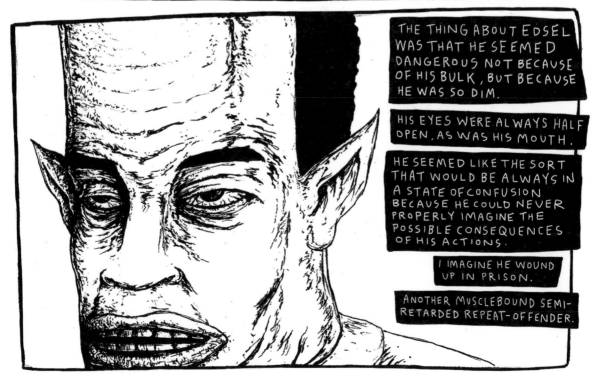

THE THING ABOUT EDSEL WAS THAT HE SEEMED DANGEROUS NOT BECAUSE OF HIS BULK, BUT BECAUSE HE WAS SO DIM.

HIS EYES WERE ALWAYS HALF OPEN, AS WAS HIS MOUTH.

HE SEEMED LIKE THE SORT THAT WOULD BE ALWAYS IN A STATE OF CONFUSION BECAUSE HE COULD NEVER PROPERLY IMAGINE THE POSSIBLE CONSEQUENCES OF HIS ACTIONS.

I IMAGINE HE WOUND UP IN PRISON.

ANOTHER MUSCLEBOUND SEMI-RETARDED REPEAT-OFFENDER.

AFTER CLASS I APPROACHED EDSEL WARILY. IT WOULD HAVE BEEN TRAGICALLY POETIC TO BE SMACKED AROUND WITH THE SAME NUNCHUCKS I'D PACKED IN MY BAG THAT MORNING.

HE WAS STANDING OUTSIDE THE GODDAMED COAT-ROOM. HE HAD HIS COAT ON AND LOOKED LIKE HE WAS READY TO LEAVE.

HEY EDSEL.

I SAID AS I APPROACHED.

I'M GONNA NEED THOSE CHUCKS BACK. THEY BELONG TO MY FATHER.

WHAT?

HE SAID.

THE NUNCHUCKS. I'M A NEED TO GET THEM BACK.

I STIFLED A WINCE AT MY STIFF ATTEMPT AT STREET TALK.

WHAT NUNCHUCKS?

HE SAID WITH DIM EYES. I HONESTLY COULDN'T TELL IF HE'D ALREADY FORGOTTEN OR IF HE WAS TEASING ME.

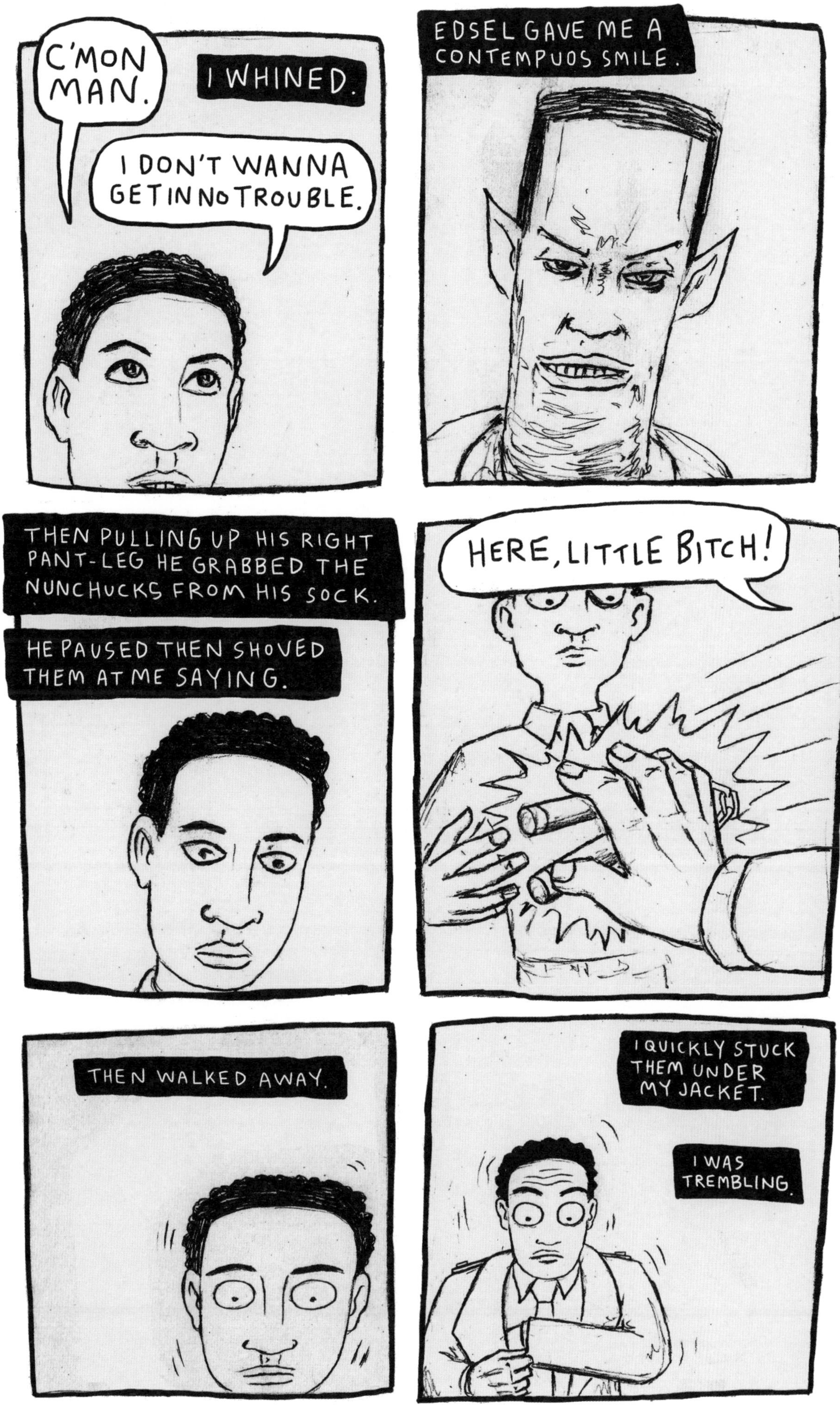
C'MON MAN.
I WHINED.
I DON'T WANNA GETINNOTROUBLE.
EDSEL GAVE ME A CONTEMPUOS SMILE.
THEN PULLING UP HIS RIGHT PANT-LEG HE GRABBED THE NUNCHUCKS FROM HIS SOCK.
HE PAUSED THEN SHOVED THEM AT ME SAYING.
HERE, LITTLE BITCH!
THEN WALKED AWAY.
I QUICKLY STUCK THEM UNDER MY JACKET.
I WAS TREMBLING.

I WAS USELESS WITH OR WITHOUT A WEAPON.

I DIDN'T HAVE THE VIOLENCE IN ME.

I WAS THE LAST ONE OUT OF THE ROOM.

I TOOK THE LONG WALK TO MY PRIVATE BUS STOP.

GIVEN MY BACKGROUND THE CONCEPT OF HOOKY WAS AS TABOO TO ME AS SATANISM.

I WAS A "GOOD" BOY FROM A "GOOD" FAMILY, NOT SOME STREET-NIGGER.

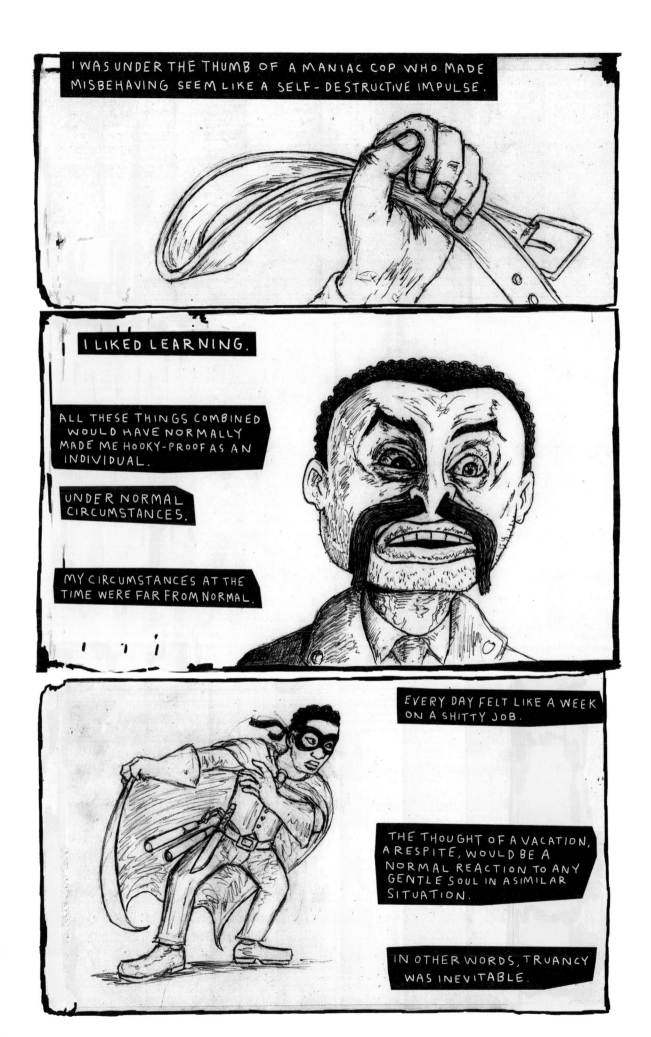

I WAS UNDER THE THUMB OF A MANIAC COP WHO MADE MISBEHAVING SEEM LIKE A SELF-DESTRUCTIVE IMPULSE.

I LIKED LEARNING.

ALL THESE THINGS COMBINED WOULD HAVE NORMALLY MADE ME HOOKY-PROOF AS AN INDIVIDUAL.

UNDER NORMAL CIRCUMSTANCES.

MY CIRCUMSTANCES AT THE TIME WERE FAR FROM NORMAL.

EVERY DAY FELT LIKE A WEEK ON A SHITTY JOB.

THE THOUGHT OF A VACATION, A RESPITE, WOULD BE A NORMAL REACTION TO ANY GENTLE SOUL IN A SIMILAR SITUATION.

IN OTHER WORDS, TRUANCY WAS INEVITABLE.

ITCAME TO ME IN A FLASH, ONE ICY JANUARY MORNING AS THE BUS I WAS ON PASSED 95th STREET.

I HAD A VISION OF THE "PLAZA."

EVERGREEN PLAZA WAS A POPULAR SHOPPING MALL ON THE BORDER THAT CAGED THE BLACK POPULATION AND KEPT US FROM CONTAMINATING THE ALL-WHITE NEIGHBORHOOD OF OAK LAWN WITH OUR DIRTY BLACK SELVES.

DIG DIG

NOTE TO ED. NOT ACTUAL VISION.

THE PLAZA ITSELF BEING AN ANOMALY AS IT'S THREE BLOCK LENGTH WAS ACTUALLY SET ON THE "WHITE" SIDE OF THE BORDER.

Evergreen plaza

Evergreen plaza

DOLLAR VALVE DAYS
SALE
THURS FRI & SAT

DOLLAR VALVE DAYS
SALE
THURS FRI & SAT

IT SEEMED THAT BLACK DOLLARS PROVIDE A CERTAIN AMOUNT OF CUSHION TO RACIST SENSIBILITIES.

I REMEMBER MY GRANDMOTHER TOLD ME THAT IN THE LONG AGO 60's (AT THAT PRESENT POINT JUST 10 YEARS GONE) IF A BLACK WOMAN WANTED TO TRY ON A HAT AT THE EVERGREEN PLAZA STORES

SHE WOULD HAVE BEEN REQUIRED TO FIRST COVER HER HEAD WITH A HANDKERCHIEF.

WE HAD OVERCOME!

MY VISION WAS OF WALKING THE HALLS OF THE PLAZA DURING SCHOOL HOURS.

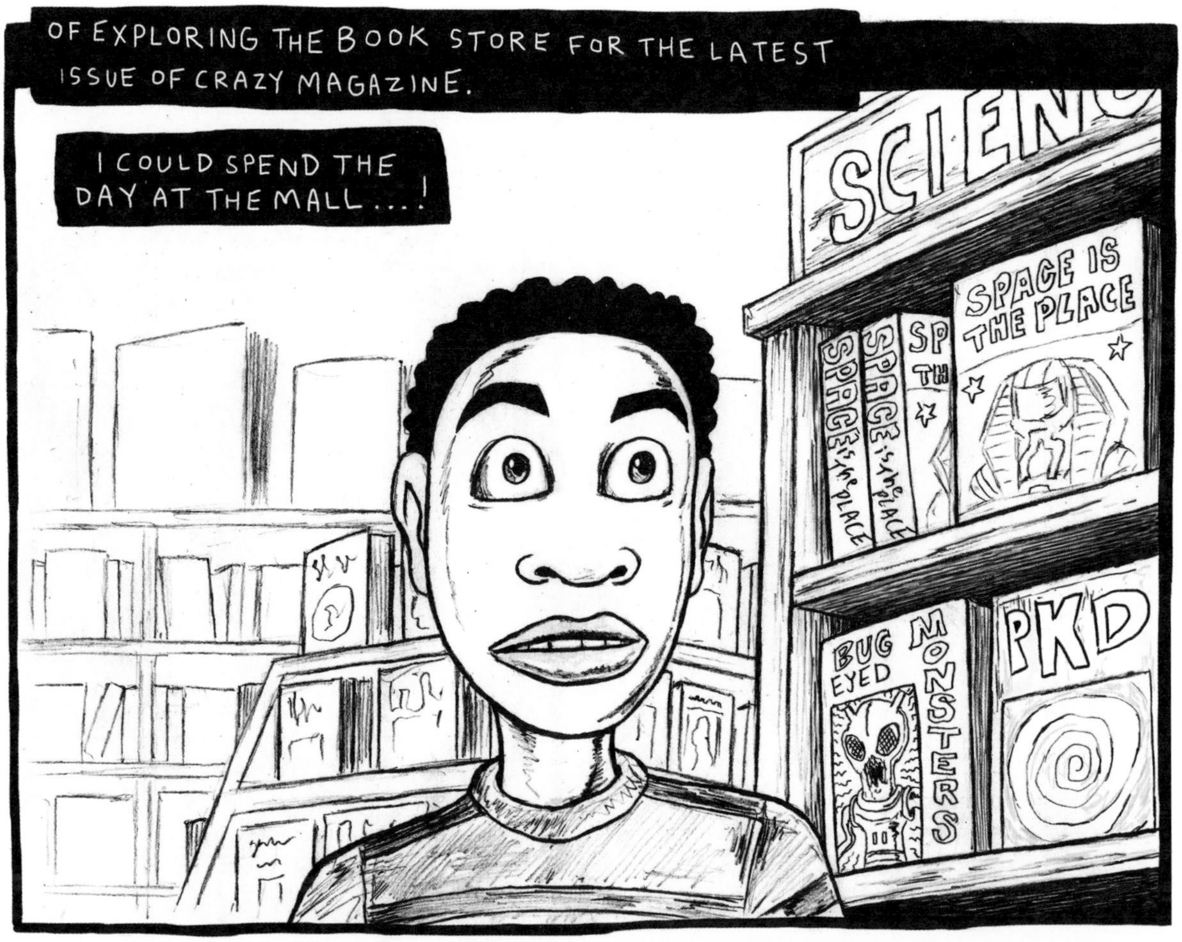
OF EXPLORING THE BOOK STORE FOR THE LATEST ISSUE OF CRAZY MAGAZINE.
I COULD SPEND THE DAY AT THE MALL....!
SCIENC
SPACE IS THE PLACE
BUG EYED MONSTERS
PKD

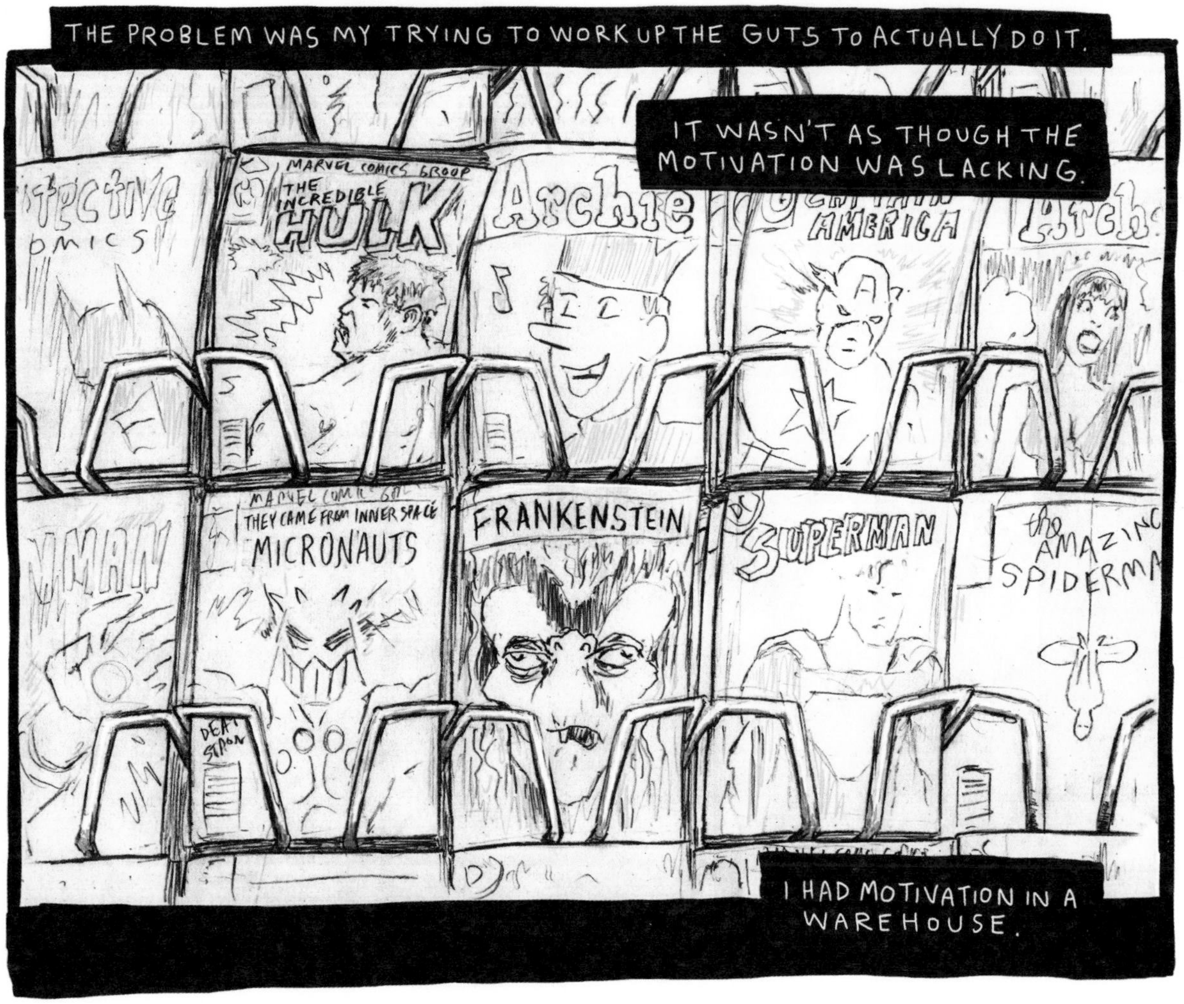
THE PROBLEM WAS MY TRYING TO WORK UP THE GUTS TO ACTUALLY DO IT.
IT WASN'T AS THOUGH THE MOTIVATION WAS LACKING.
MARVEL COMICS GROUP
THE INCREDIBLE HULK
Archie
AMERICA
THEY CAME FROM INNER SPACE
MICRONAUTS
FRANKENSTEIN
SUPERMAN
I HAD MOTIVATION IN A WAREHOUSE.

It came down to anticipation of pain on both sides, which was what eventually decided me.

I WAS HEADING TO SCHOOL ONE DAY ON MY PRIVATE BUS-ROUTE WHEN IT OCCURRED TO ME THAT THERE WOULD BE PAIN UNDER ANY CIRCUMSTANCE, SO WHY SHOULDN'T I DEFER IT UNTIL A LATER TIME?

[OF COURSE I REALISE NOW THAT THERE IS NO SUCH THING AS DEFERRAL OF PAIN IF YOU ARE AFRAID. ANTICIPATION OF PAIN, ITSELF IS PAIN.]

I REMEMBER THINKING
THAT IT MIGHT BE POSSIBLE
TO RIDE THE BUS ALL DAY LONG.
All I NEEDED WAS A PLAN.

I SPENT THAT DAY
TRYING TO FIGURE
THE INS AND OUTS OF
SOMETHING I'D NEVER
TRIED BEFORE.

CERTAIN THINGS WERE
OBVIOUS.

I'D HAVE TO WEAR MY
GOOD CLOTHES.

THIS WOULD BE EXTREMELY
UNCOMFORTABLE TO DO,
CONSIDERING THE FRIGID
WEATHER, BUT THE GOOD
CLOTHES SERVED A DUAL
PURPOSE.

THE SUIT ALSO SERVED ITS USUAL PURPOSE
OF KEEPING THE BULLIES OFF MY NECK
IN CASE I LOST MY NERVE AND DECIDED
TO GO TO SCHOOL AFTER ALL. I ALSO
NEEDED A LOOSE ITINERARY. I FIGURED
THAT RIDING THE BUS WOULD TAKE UP
MOST OF THE DAY.

I FIGURED THAT IF I WAS OUT ALL DAY
THAT I'D LOOK LESS LIKE A TRUANT
AND MORE LIKE A KID THAT'S COME
FROM A FUNERAL OR GOING TO A
MAGNET-SCHOOL INTERVIEW, OR
SOME OTHER SUCH IMPORTANT,
SUIT-WEARING HULLABALOO.

THEN THE PLAZA WOULD TAKE UP A CHUNK.
BUT THAT'S WHERE MY MIND WENT
BLANK.

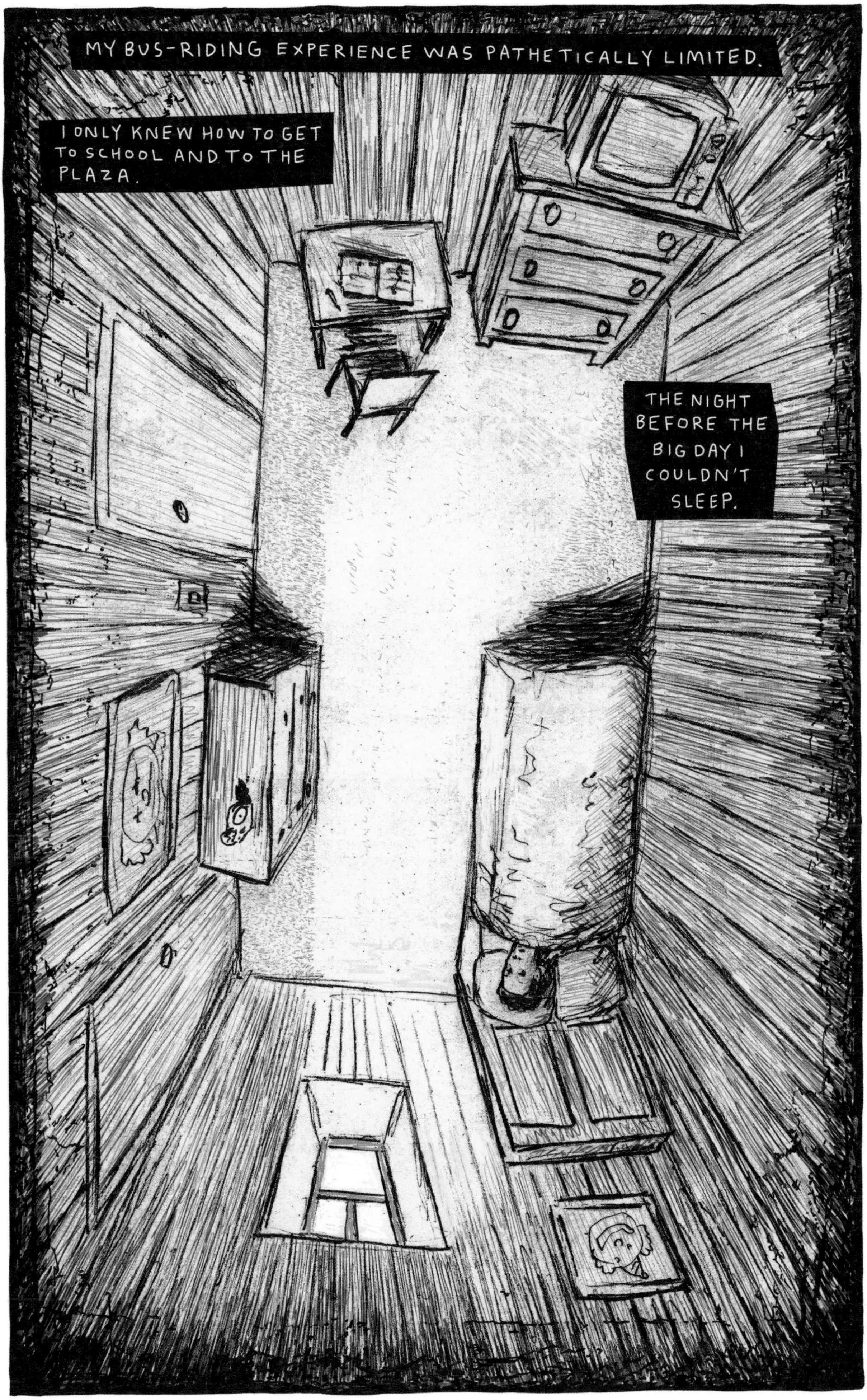
MY BUS-RIDING EXPERIENCE WAS PATHETICALLY LIMITED.
I ONLY KNEW HOW TO GET TO SCHOOL AND TO THE PLAZA.
THE NIGHT BEFORE THE BIG DAY I COULDN'T SLEEP.

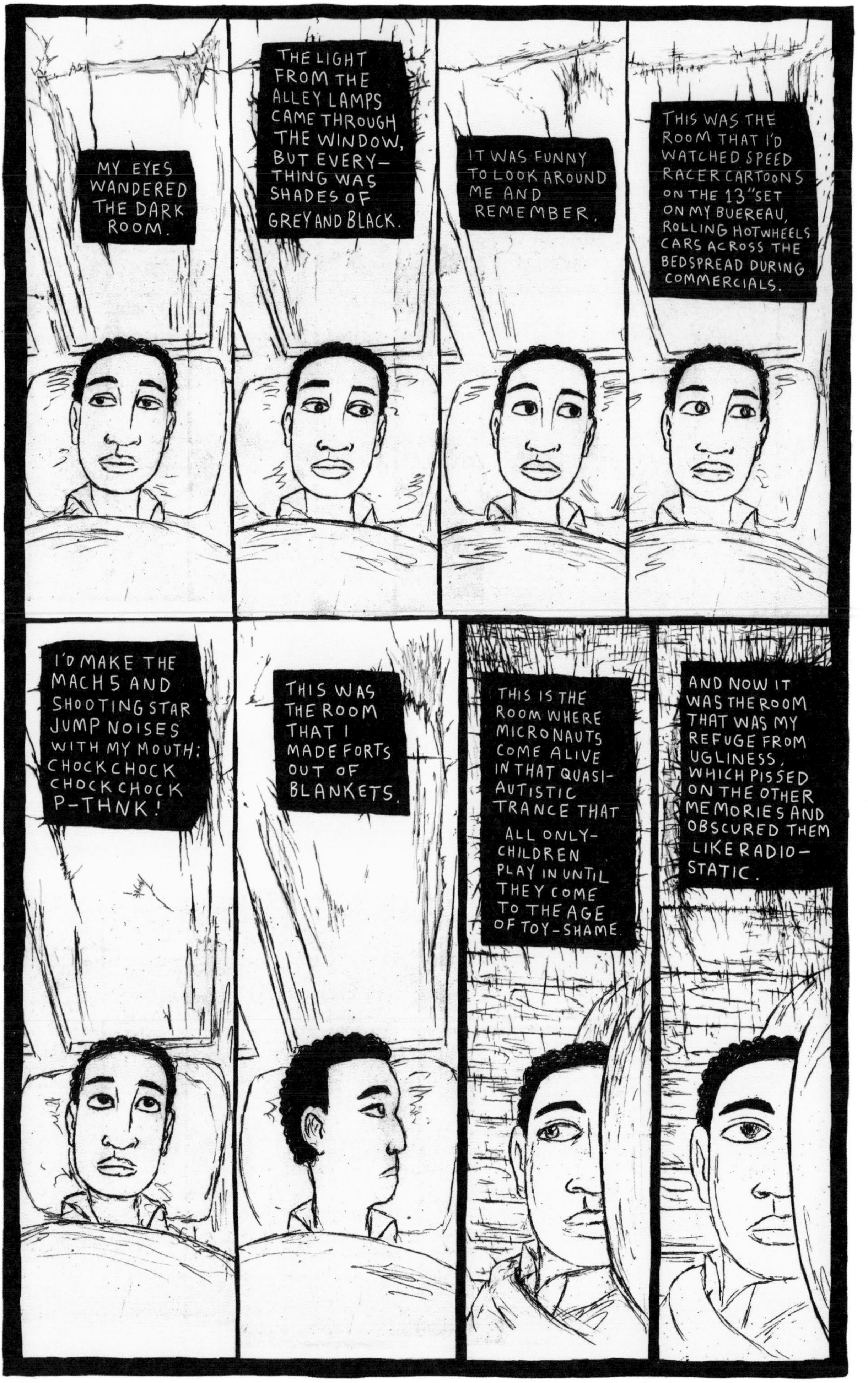
MY EYES WANDERED THE DARK ROOM.
THE LIGHT FROM THE ALLEY LAMPS CAME THROUGH THE WINDOW, BUT EVERY-THING WAS SHADES OF GREY AND BLACK.
IT WAS FUNNY TO LOOK AROUND ME AND REMEMBER.
THIS WAS THE ROOM THAT I'D WATCHED SPEED RACER CARTOONS ON THE 13" SET ON MY BUEREAU, ROLLING HOTWHEELS CARS ACROSS THE BEDSPREAD DURING COMMERCIALS.
I'D MAKE THE MACH 5 AND SHOOTING STAR JUMP NOISES WITH MY MOUTH: CHOCK CHOCK CHOCK CHOCK P-THNK!
THIS WAS THE ROOM THAT I MADE FORTS OUT OF BLANKETS.
THIS IS THE ROOM WHERE MICRONAUTS COME ALIVE IN THAT QUASI-AUTISTIC TRANCE THAT ALL ONLY-CHILDREN PLAY IN UNTIL THEY COME TO THE AGE OF TOY-SHAME.
AND NOW IT WAS THE ROOM THAT WAS MY REFUGE FROM UGLINESS, WHICH PISSED ON THE OTHER MEMORIES AND OBSCURED THEM LIKE RADIO-STATIC.

I CLOSED MY EYES THEN OPENED THEM.

DARKNESS THEN THE GREY SWIRLING WALLPAPER.

DARKNESS THEN THE FRAMED CLOWN PAINTINGS.

DARKNESS THEN THE CLOSED BEDROOM DOOR.

DARKNESS THEN DARKNESS THEN DARKNESS...

THE GODDAMNED HOWDY DOODY CLOCK WENT OFF BUT FOR ONCE IT DIDN'T ANNOY ME.

THAT MORNING I WAS A MAN WITH A MISSION. I WENT TO THE BATHROOM, PISSED, BRUSHED MY TEETH AND WASHED MY FACE LIKE A GOOD BOY.

I WENT BACK TO MY BEDROOM AND TURNED ON THE JAUNDICED CEILING LIGHT.

I OPENED THE DRESSER AND PULLED OUT A FRESH THERMAL UNDERSHIRT, LONG DRAWERS AND SOCKS.

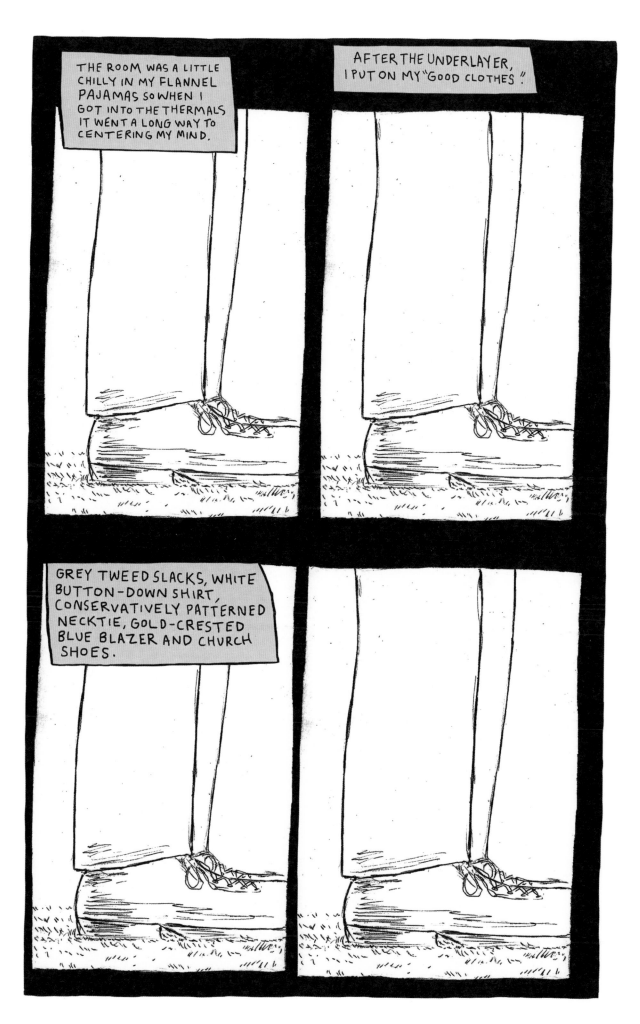

THE ROOM WAS A LITTLE CHILLY IN MY FLANNEL PAJAMAS SO WHEN I GOT INTO THE THERMALS IT WENT A LONG WAY TO CENTERING MY MIND.

AFTER THE UNDERLAYER, I PUT ON MY "GOOD CLOTHES."

GREY TWEED SLACKS, WHITE BUTTON-DOWN SHIRT, CONSERVATIVELY PATTERNED NECKTIE, GOLD-CRESTED BLUE BLAZER AND CHURCH SHOES.

I HEAD DOWNSTAIRS AND TOSS MY BOOK-BAG, PEA COAT, SCARF, GLOVES AND NAVY BLUE SKI-CAP ONTO THE PLASTIC COVERED CHAIR IN THE LIVING ROOM.

WE HAVE TWO CHAIRS AND A COUCH IN SHOWROOM-NEW CONDITION, WRAPPED IN PLASTIC FOR A MISTY FUTURE WHEN PEOPLE NO LONGER ENJOY LOUNGING STIFFLY ON SWEATY CRINKLING PLASTIC.

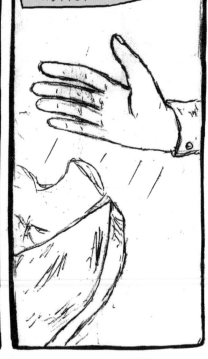

I ENTER THE KITCHEN THROUGH THE TINY DINING ROOM. IN THE KITCHEN THERE IS A SMALL LEAF-TABLE, SURROUNDED BY FOUR CHAIRS, ONE OF WHICH IS JAMMED AGAINST THE BACK WALL TO MAKE ENOUGH ROOM TO WALK AROUND THE TABLE.

THERE IS A TOASTER OVEN IN THE CORNER ON A TV TABLE.

A SMALL TELEVISION SITS ON THE KITCHEN TABLE IN THE EMPTY SPOT, LIKE AN HONORED GUEST.

NEXT TO IT IS A STACK OF COMIC BOOKS, MY FATHER HAS BROUGHT UP FROM THE BASEMENT.

FEATURING THE HAUNTED TANK

THE BASEMENT DOOR IS HELD SHUT BY AN EYE HOOK.

THE HOOK CLATTERS IN THE EYE AS THE DOOR IS RATTLED.

CLATTER CLATTER

I POP THE HOOK AND THE FAMILY DOG, DUTCHESS THE DOBERMAN, BURSTS INTO THE KITCHEN WITH THE FRENTIC ENERGY OF AN ANIMAL THAT'S BEEN LOCKED IN A COLD BASEMENT ALL NIGHT.

SHE DANCED WHILE I UNLOCKED THE DOOR THAT LED TO THE BACKYARD, HER NAILS BEARING STACATTO ON THE LINOLEUM.

THE DOOR OPENED, SHE SCATTERED ACROSS THE BACK PORCH AND INTO THE FILTHY MOUNDS OF SHIT-STAINED SNOW.

I CLOSED THE DOOR.

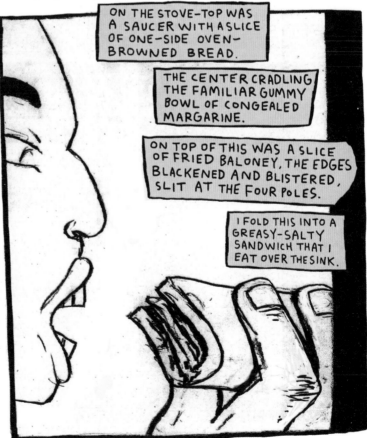

ON THE STOVE-TOP WAS A SAUCER WITH A SLICE OF ONE-SIDE OVEN-BROWNED BREAD.

THE CENTER CRADLING THE FAMILIAR GUMMY BOWL OF CONGEALED MARGARINE.

ON TOP OF THIS WAS A SLICE OF FRIED BALONEY, THE EDGES BLACKENED AND BLISTERED, SLIT AT THE FOUR POLES.

I FOLD THIS INTO A GREASY-SALTY SANDWICH THAT I EAT OVER THE SINK.

OUTSIDE, DUTCHESS HAS ADDED SOME FRESH COLOR TO HER SCATOLOGICAL MASTERPIECE.

WHEN SHE'S HAD THE CHANCE TO RUN AROUND FOR A FEW MINUTES, I LET HER BACK INSIDE.

USUALLY I'D LET HER PAL AROUND WITH ME FOR A BIT, BUT THIS WAS THE BIG DAY, SO BACK DOWN INTO THE DUNGEON SHE WENT.

WGN WAS THE ONLY STATION WITH ANYTHING GOOD ON AT 7 IN THE MORNING.

CHICAGO WOULDN'T GET CABLE FOR ANOTHER FEW YEARS.

WE HAD THE "ON-TV" PAY SERVICE, BUT THAT WAS UPSTAIRS IN MY PARENT'S BEDROOM.

EVEN IF WE HAD A BOX DOWNSTAIRS IT WAS ONLY MOVIES, SPORTS AND NEWS.

NOT A CARTOON OR OLD SITCOM ANYWHERE TO BE SEEN.

RAY RAYNOR WAS A MORNING STAPLE TO US 70'S KIDS.

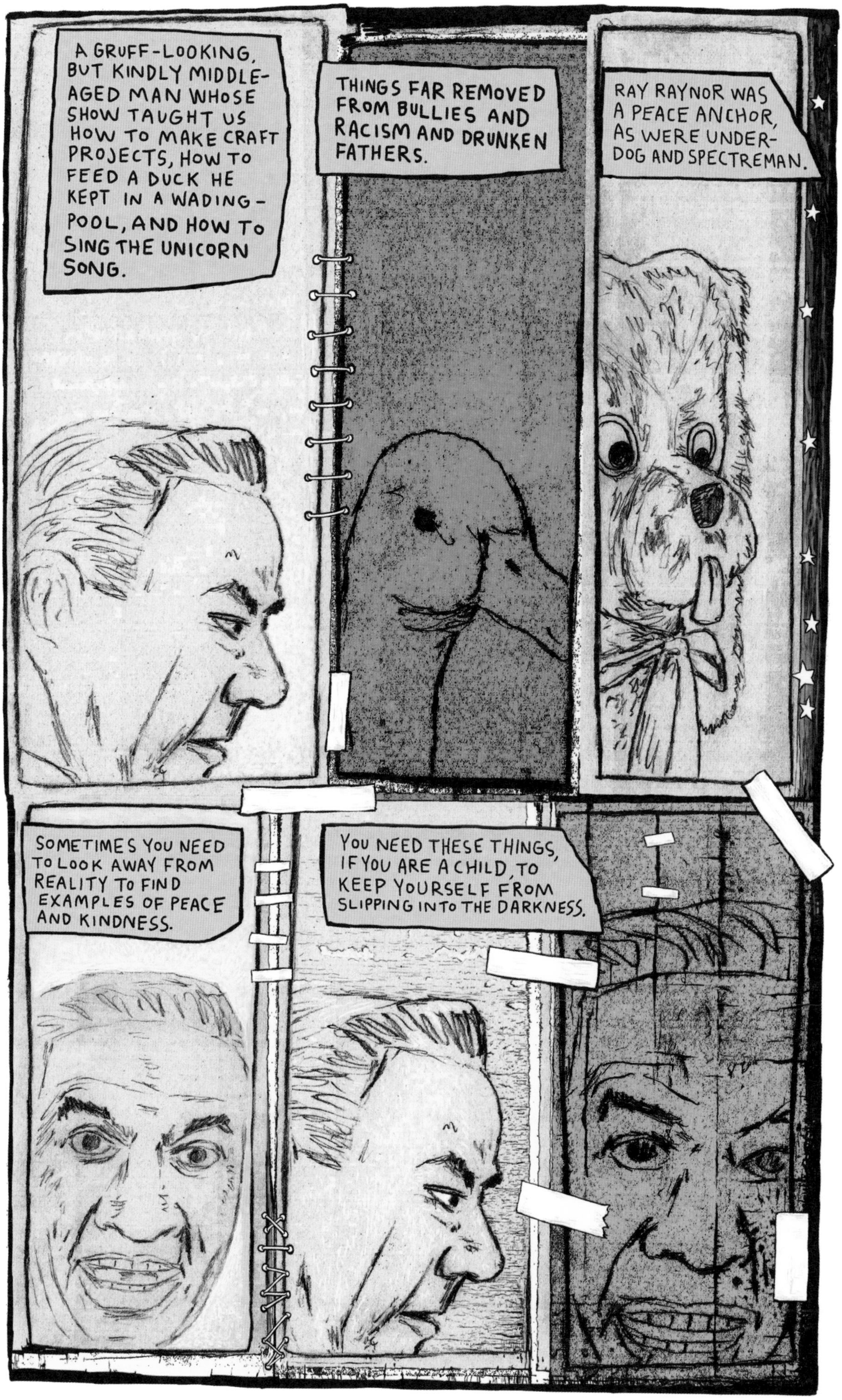
A GRUFF-LOOKING, BUT KINDLY MIDDLE-AGED MAN WHOSE SHOW TAUGHT US HOW TO MAKE CRAFT PROJECTS, HOW TO FEED A DUCK HE KEPT IN A WADING-POOL, AND HOW TO SING THE UNICORN SONG.
THINGS FAR REMOVED FROM BULLIES AND RACISM AND DRUNKEN FATHERS.
RAY RAYNOR WAS A PEACE ANCHOR, AS WERE UNDERDOG AND SPECTREMAN.
SOMETIMES YOU NEED TO LOOK AWAY FROM REALITY TO FIND EXAMPLES OF PEACE AND KINDNESS.
YOU NEED THESE THINGS, IF YOU ARE A CHILD, TO KEEP YOURSELF FROM SLIPPING INTO THE DARKNESS.

AFTER RAY RAYNOR'S SHOW WAS BOZO'S CIRCUS. I WAS ABLE TO CATCH THE FIRST FEW MINUTES BEFORE I HAD TO GO. WHEN I WAS SIX YEARS OLD MY 1st GRADE CLASS WENT TO WGN STUDIOS TO WATCH AN EPISODE BEING TAPED. I WOUND UP BEING ON CAMERA IN ONE OF THE PRIZE-GAMES. IT WAS A SCOOTER RACE. MY TEAM CAME IN SECOND-PLACE AND WE EACH RECEIVED A HALF-GALLON CARTON OF MALTED-MILK BALLS. THAT HAD BEEN A GOOD DAY.

BUT THAT WAS A WORLD AWAY FOR ME AS I PUT ON MY PEA-COAT, SCARF, GLOVES AND HAT.

LOCKING THE DOOR BEHIND ME, I STEPPED OUT INTO THE FRIGID WORLD.

IT WAS REALLY COLD, SOMEWHERE UNDER 20 DEGREES.

ON THOSE DAYS THE WORLD FOR ME WAS A YINYANG OF SKY BLUE AND SLAT GREY.

THE HORRIBLE CRYSTALLINE WIND WOULD BLEACH THE COLORS RIGHT FROM MY EYES. AS I WALKED DOWN THE BLOCK I COULD FEEL THE FRIGD WORLD ATTEMPTING TO MOLEST ME BY CRAWLING UP MY PANTS-LEGS AND SLEEVES, WRAPPING AROUND MY WRISTS AND ANKLES, FORARMS AND SHINS, LIKE A FREON-PYTHON, SLOWLY CORK SCREWING IT'S WAY ALONG...

BACK THEN BUS-FARE WAS LESS THAN A DOLLAR.

I WOULD KEEP THE COINS AND AFTERWARDS, THE TRANSFER, INSIDE THE PALM OF MY LEFT GLOVE.

THAT WAY I WOULDN'T HAVE TO TRY AND USE MY NUMB LIFELESS FINGERS TO DIG THROUGH MY POCKETS FOR CHANGE.

WHEN THE BUS CAME I PAID MY FARE AND SAT NEAR THE FRONT.

I LEFT MUCH LATER THAN I USUALLY DID. I'D PURPOSEFULLY TIMED IT SO THAT IF I CHICKENED OUT I WOULD BE FORCED TO WALK INTO CLASS LATE.

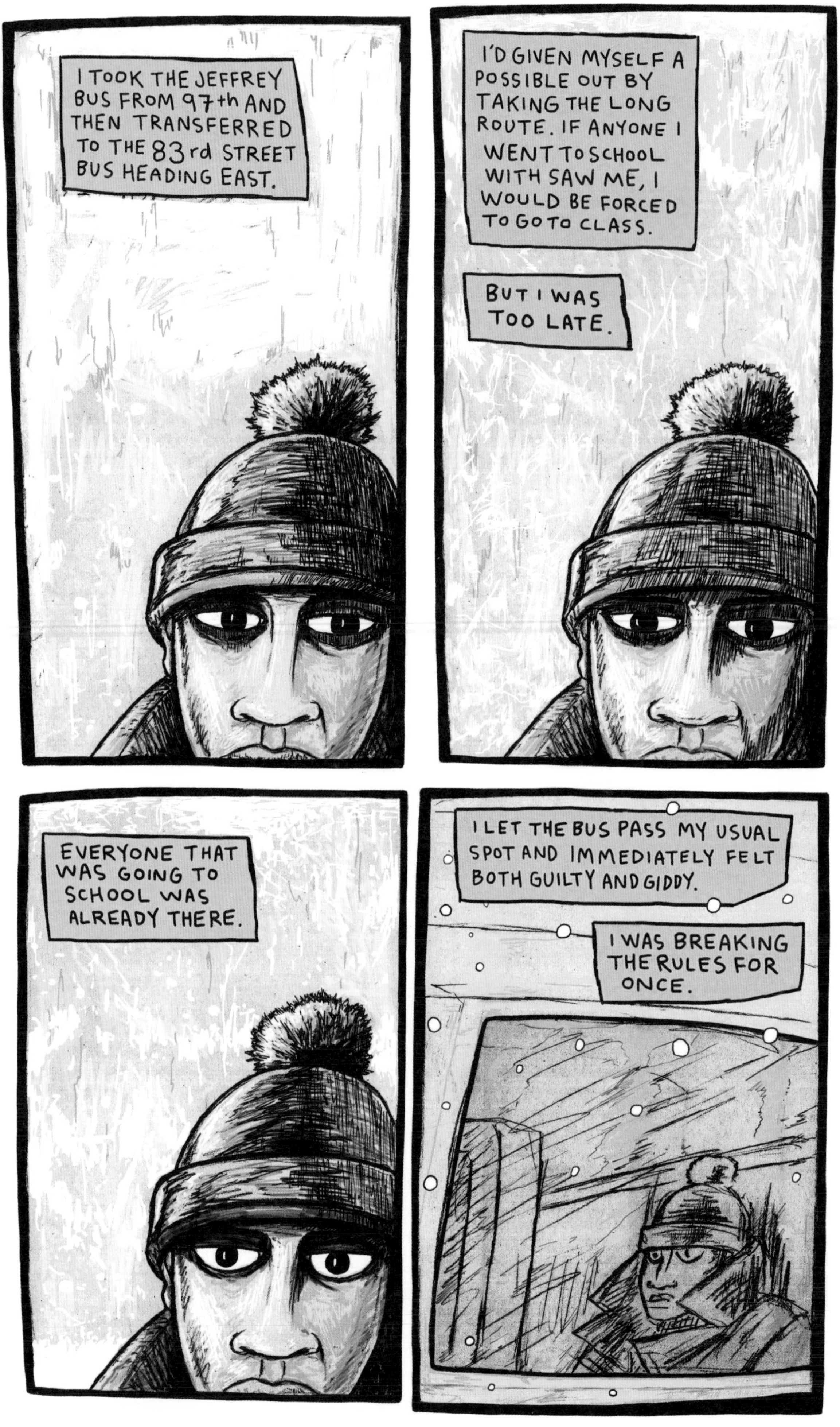

I TOOK THE JEFFREY BUS FROM 97th AND THEN TRANSFERRED TO THE 83rd STREET BUS HEADING EAST.
I'D GIVEN MYSELF A POSSIBLE OUT BY TAKING THE LONG ROUTE. IF ANYONE I WENT TO SCHOOL WITH SAW ME, I WOULD BE FORCED TO GO TO CLASS.
BUT I WAS TOO LATE.
EVERYONE THAT WAS GOING TO SCHOOL WAS ALREADY THERE.
I LET THE BUS PASS MY USUAL SPOT AND IMMEDIATELY FELT BOTH GUILTY AND GIDDY.
I WAS BREAKING THE RULES FOR ONCE.

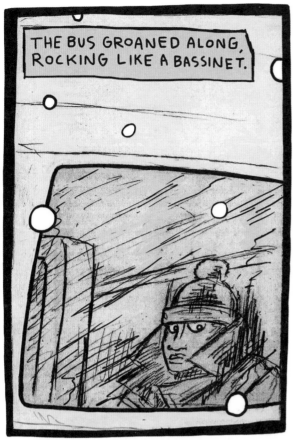

THE BUS GROANED ALONG, ROCKING LIKE A BASSINET.

I WAS SITTING IN THE VERY LAST SEAT ON THE LEFT REAR.

I DUCKED DOWN TO MAKE MYSELF LESS OBVIOUS TO THE DRIVER.

I'D BEEN STARING AT THE BACK OF HIS HEAD FOR A WHILE.

HE WAS DEFORMED.

WHETHER BY ACCIDENT OR NATURE I COULDN'T TELL. HE WAS WEARING A DRIVER'S CAP BUT HIS BALD-HEAD WAS OBVIOUS. HE HAD DEEP DARK CHOCOLATE SKIN AND HIS EARS LOOKED LIKE MELTED WAX, ONLY POINTED IDENTICALLY.

HE LOOKED FOR ALL THE WORLD LIKE A BLACK NOSFERATU, OR MORE PRECISELY: KURT BARLOW.

THE BUS HEADED FURTHER EAST UNTIL IT HIT LAKESIDE. IT RAN ON THE STREET PARALLEL TO THE WATER, SLOWED AND THEN STOPPED.

THE DRIVER STRETCHED.

HE OPENED HIS WINDOW AND LIT A CIGARETTE.

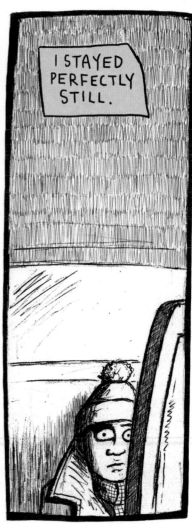

I STAYED PERFECTLY STILL.

HIS EYES RAISED TO THE REARVIEW AND THEIR REFLECTION CAUGHT MINE.

END OF THE LINE FOR YOU.

HE SAID OMINOUSLY.

...WHAT?

I STAMMERED OUT.

END OF THE LINE FOR YOU.

HE REPEATED, THEN OPENED THE REAR DOORS.

YOU HAVE TO GET OFF.

BUT...CAN'T I RIDE BACK THE OTHER WAY?

I ASKED, TRYING TO SOUND PITIFUL.

NOT ON THIS BUS.

HE SAD.

THEN HE SAID SOMETHING UNDER HIS BREATH, AS HIS EYES SEEMED TO LOSE INTEREST AND FELL OFF ME.

I GRABBED MY BAG AND WALKED TO THE REAR EXIT, TRYING TO LOOK PITIFUL.

I STEPPED DOWN ONTO THE STREET AND THE PNEUMATIC DOORS CLUNKED CLOSED BEHIND ME.

I TURNED TO LOOK AT THE BUS AS HE GASSED IT AND DROVE OFF, LEAVING ME STARING AT A NIGHTMARE OF FROZEN GREY AND WHITE WATER AS FAR AS I COULD SEE.

SOME BLOT OF FACTORY OR SOMETHING CUTTING BLACKLY IN ON THE RIGHT.

IT WAS LIKE THE BIZARRO VERSION OF THE SUNNY PEOPLED BEACH ON THE THREES COMPANY INTRO.

I DIDN'T KNOW WHAT TO DO, BUT THE COLD MADE MY BRAIN RUSH THROUGH POSSIBILITIES.

I HAD NO IDEA WHEN OR IF OTHER BUSSES WOULD COME ALONG SO MAYBE WALKING WOULD BE GOOD.

BUT I HAD NO IDEA WHERE THE NEXT BUS-STOP MIGHT BE AND IF THERE WERE A NEXT BUS IT WOULD PASS ME BY AS I WAS WALKING.

BUT THE FROZEN EXPANSE IN FRONT OF ME WAS SO OPPRESSIVELY HUGE AND DISHEARTENING THAT I FELT LIKE I WAS SOMEHOW FADING FROM EXISTENCE.

I MADE THREE FALSE STARTS DOWN THE STREET BEFORE ANOTHER BUS CAME BY AND PICKED ME UP.

I TRANSFERRED TO THE 95th STREET BUS AND HEADED WEST.

I WAS DOING FINE UNTIL THE BUS TURNED INTO THE TRANSFER HUB ON STATE STREET.

I FREAKED OUT A LITTLE BECAUSE I THOUGHT AT FIRST THAT THE BUS WAS GOING TO GO DOWN THE DAN RYAN EXPRESS-WAY, BUT THE BUS STOPPED, AND EVERYONE ELSE DISEMBARKED, SO I DID LIKEWISE.

I WANDERED INTO THE GLASS-ENCLOSED STATION AND STARED AT THE UNHAPPY, DEAD-EYED PASSENGERS.

ALL SCARVES, AND TWEED, AND EARMUFFS; THEY REMINDED ME OF MY MOTHER, WHO MADE THE DAILY TREK FROM SOUTH-SIDE HOME TO DOWNTOWN OFFICE.

I TWIRLED AROUND IN A CIRCLE AND WANDERED BACK AND FORTH FOR A FEW MINUTES, BEFORE I WORKED UP THE COURAGE TO ASK A RANDOM MAN, WHICH BUS WAS GOING WEST ON 95th.

HE LOOKED AT ME WITH WHAT I TOOK TO BE A MIX OF ASTONISHMENT AND PITY, THEN POINTED TO A BUS STANDING IN FRONT OF THE ONE I'D JUST DISEMBARKED.

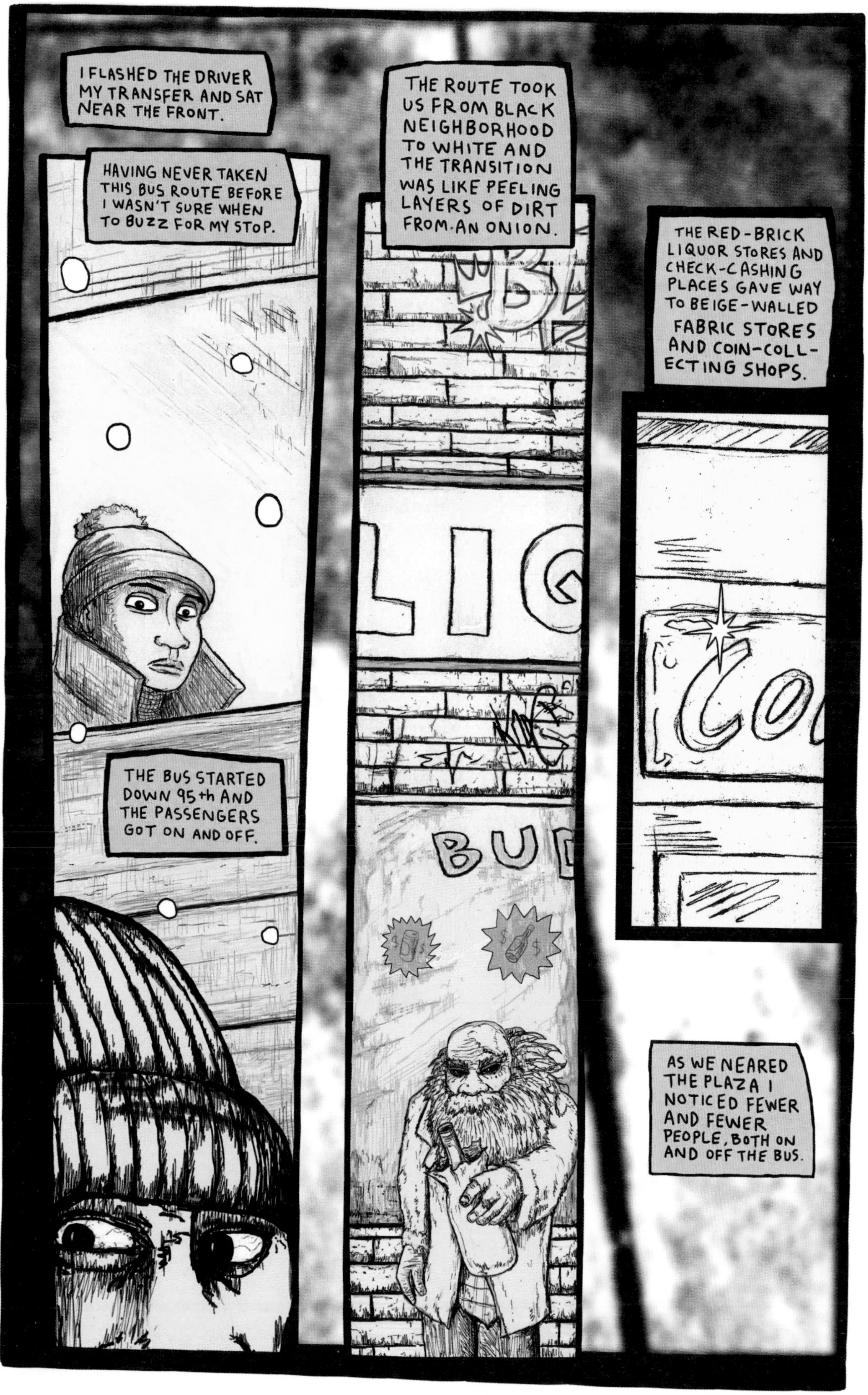
I FLASHED THE DRIVER MY TRANSFER AND SAT NEAR THE FRONT.
HAVING NEVER TAKEN THIS BUS ROUTE BEFORE I WASN'T SURE WHEN TO BUZZ FOR MY STOP.
THE BUS STARTED DOWN 95th AND THE PASSENGERS GOT ON AND OFF.
THE ROUTE TOOK US FROM BLACK NEIGHBORHOOD TO WHITE AND THE TRANSITION WAS LIKE PEELING LAYERS OF DIRT FROM AN ONION.
LIQ
BUD
THE RED-BRICK LIQUOR STORES AND CHECK-CASHING PLACES GAVE WAY TO BEIGE-WALLED FABRIC STORES AND COIN-COLLECTING SHOPS.
AS WE NEARED THE PLAZA I NOTICED FEWER AND FEWER PEOPLE, BOTH ON AND OFF THE BUS.

I EXITED AT THE PLAZA WEST SIDE, AND ENTERED AN INTERNAL HALLWAY THROUGH A SET OF GLASS DOUBLE-DOORS.

I NOTICED THAT IT WAS PRETTY QUIET.

WHEN I GOT TO THE END OF THE HALLWAY I HAD A GOOD VIEW OF BOTH LEVELS OF THE SOUTHERN WING.

I WOULDN'T SEE DAWN OF THE DEAD FOR ANOTHER 5 YEARS SO I HAD NO IDEA HOW SIMILAR WAS WHAT I WAS SEEING TO THE ZOMBIE-MALL IN THE FILM.

THERE WERE VERY FEW PEOPLE, AND THEY ALL SEEMED TO BE WANDERING AIMLESSLY.

THEN I REALISED THAT THE SHUTTERS WERE STILL DOWN ON THE SHOPS.

I HAD GOTTEN THERE BEFORE THE PLACE WAS OPEN FOR BUSINESS.

ONLY A COUPLE OF PLACES THAT SERVED COFFEE AND PASTRIES WERE ACTIVE.

I ASKED A LADY BEHIND THE COUNTER AT ONE OF THE FOOD COUNTERS WHAT TIME THE STORES OPENED.

SHE TOLD ME THEY OPENED AT 9:00.

I CHECKED MY WATCH. IT WAS 8:40. I WEIGHED MY OPTIONS.

I COULD WANDER BACK AND FORTH IN THE MALL FOR THE NEX 20 MINUTES, BUT I RAN THE RISK OF STICKING OUT AND I DIDN'T KNOW IF THERE WERE REALLY TRUANT-OFFICERS LIKE THE ONES I'D SEEN ON THE LITTLE RASCALS, OR (IF THERE WERE) WHETHER THEY WERE LOOKING FOR ALL KIDS OR ONLY FOR PUBLIC-SCHOOL KIDS.

I ALSO HAD THE OPTION OF GETTING BACK ON THE BUS, AND RIDING IT FOR A WHILE, BUT THAT SEEMED SO, BLEAK... AND COLD.

I DECIDED TO RISK THE SPECTRE OF MALL-BOUND TRUANT OFFICERS.

I HAD NO IDEA WHAT THEY LOOKED LIKE.

OLD HOLLYWOOD TAUGHT ME THAT THEY WORE 3-PIECE SUITS WITH FEDORAS AND BADGES PINNED TO THE VESTS.

I'D NEVER SEEN SUCH IN REAL LIFE AND DEDUCED THAT THE REALITY WAS PROBABLY JUST A GUY IN A REGULAR CHURCH-SUIT.

HATS

A CHILL RAN ALL THROUGH ME WHEN I REALIZED THAT THEY MIGHT JUST BE COPS.

I HADN'T THOUGHT OF THAT.

COPS SPELLED "FATHER" AND I DESPERATELY NEEDED TO AVOID THAT.

I HUSTLED THE HORRIBLE THOUGHT OUT OF MY MIND AS MUCH AS I COULD, REMINDING MYSELF THAT I WAS, AFTER ALL, WEARING A SUIT.

AS NONCHALANTLY AS POSSIBLE, I BLENDED INTO THE SEAMS.

I WAS LONGING FOR HOME.

THAT MOSTLY-WARM GINGERBREAD TOWNHOUSE OF BLOOD AND CANDY.

THE PLACE WITH THE THIN WALLS AND DEAD FLIES IN THE SCREEN-WINDOW GUTTERS.

IT WAS CALLING ME.

I WALKED ALONG THE GREEN-TILED FLOOR WITH MY PEA-COAT HEM STIFF AND WOOLY AGAINST MY THIGHS.

NOT AT ALL LIKE THE SERRATED EDGE OF ADAM WEST'S CAPE, BUT THEN AGAIN, SOMEHOW MORE IMPORTANT.

THE CAPTAIN ON THE SHOW STARBLAZERS ALWAYS WORE A PEA-COAT, BUT SOMEHOW THE GRIZZLED OLD MAN DIDN'T RESONATE WITH ME AS WELL.

I NOTICED THAT THE WALDEN BOOK-STORE'S GATE WAS MOSTLY UP AND THAT AT THE BOTTOM OF A PYRAMIDAL DISPLAY RACK WAS A BOOK WITH SPIDER-MAN ON THE COVER.

Walden Books

NEW RELEASES

SO OF COURSE I HURRIED RIGHT OVER TO SEE WHAT IT WAS.

THE BOOK WAS CALLED: HOW TO DRAW COMICS THE MARVEL WAY, AND I NEEDED IT.

I NEEDED THAT BOOK BEFORE I EVEN CRACKED THE COVER.

THE ONLY THING I'D EVER BEEN GOOD AT, BETTER THAN ANYONE THAT I'D KNOWN, WAS DRAWING.

GRRR!

AND THIS ... BOOK, WOULD BE THE TREASURE-CHEST OF TRICKS AND GIMMICKS AND HALF-ASSING THAT WOULD LAUNCH MY COMICS-CAREER!

INK

OR SO I HOPED, AT THE TIME.

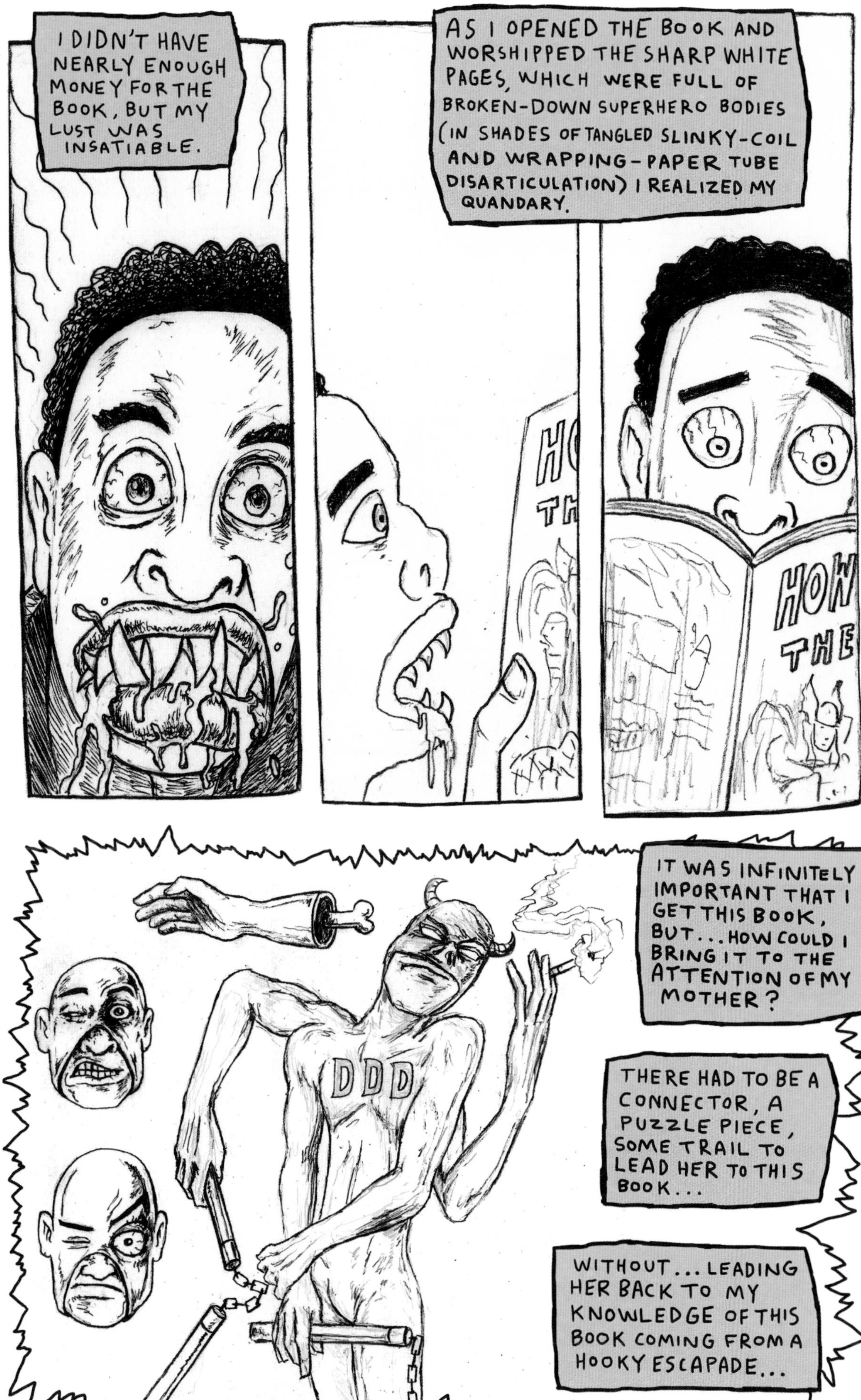
I DIDN'T HAVE NEARLY ENOUGH MONEY FOR THE BOOK, BUT MY LUST WAS INSATIABLE.
AS I OPENED THE BOOK AND WORSHIPPED THE SHARP WHITE PAGES, WHICH WERE FULL OF BROKEN-DOWN SUPERHERO BODIES (IN SHADES OF TANGLED SLINKY-COIL AND WRAPPING-PAPER TUBE DISARTICULATION) I REALIZED MY QUANDARY.
HOW
THE
IT WAS INFINITELY IMPORTANT THAT I GET THIS BOOK, BUT... HOW COULD I BRING IT TO THE ATTENTION OF MY MOTHER?
DDD
THERE HAD TO BE A CONNECTOR, A PUZZLE PIECE, SOME TRAIL TO LEAD HER TO THIS BOOK...
WITHOUT... LEADING HER BACK TO MY KNOWLEDGE OF THIS BOOK COMING FROM A HOOKY ESCAPADE...

I FANNED THROUGH THE PAGES, BROUGHT IT UP TO MY NOSE, INHALED IT'S EXOTIC FRAGRANCE AND (MAYBE) KISSED IT SACREMENTALLY, BEFORE WHISPERING TO IT THAT ONE DAY IT WOULD BE MINE.

PUTTING IT BACK ON IT'S PLACE ON THE SHELF SEEMED AS DOOMED AND SACRED AN ACT AS THE ROMEO AND JULIET REFERENCES I WATCHED IN THE CARTOONS WOULD CALL ME TO COMPREHEND.

I MADE MY WAY TOWARDS THE MALL-EXIT IN WALGREENS.

MY BRAIN SPINNING, FLIPPING AND AUDIBLY CLICKING WITH THE EARNEST EFFORT OF TRYING TO TIE MY POOR MOTHER TO THIS BOOK.

THIS BOOK.

IT WOULD BE HER GRAVESTONE IF SHE DIDN'T GET IT FOR ME... HOW I NEEDED THAT BOOK...

THE 95th STREET BUS WAS WAITING OUTSIDE.

TWO OF THEM ACTUALLY, BACK TO BACK LIKE THEY WANTED TO START A GHETTO WAGON-TRAIN.

THE SETTLERS WERE SLOWLY LOADING THEMSELVES INTO THE CATTLE-CARS.

I PREPARED MYSELF FROM BEHIND THE SHEILD OF THE WALGREENS EXIT-DOOR.

STANDING IN A PUDDLE OF FILTHY, SALT-HEAVY, MELTED SNOW, I PULLED ON MY SKI-CAP, WRAPPED MY NECK WITH MY SCARF (WHICH I THEN TUCKED INTO MY COAT.

I BUTTONED THE COAT-COLLAR AND PULLED ON MY GLOVES AND STEPPED INTO THE COLD.

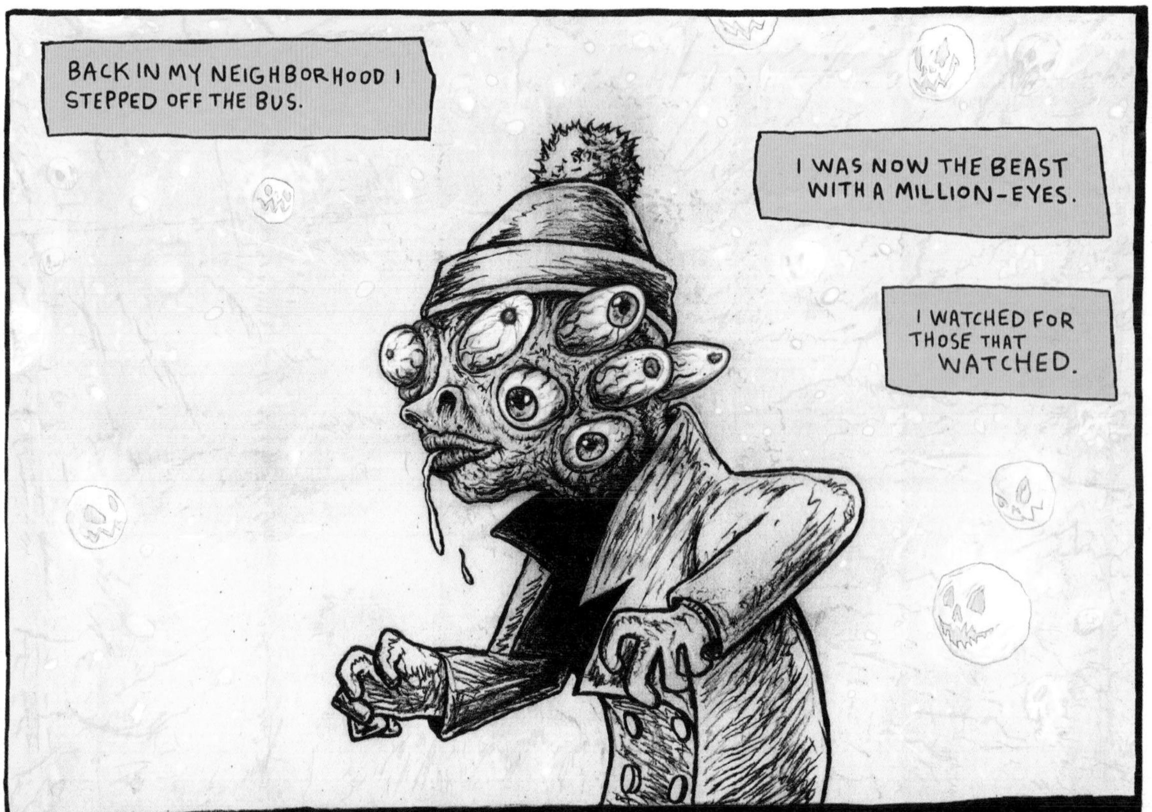
BACK IN MY NEIGHBORHOOD I STEPPED OFF THE BUS.
I WAS NOW THE BEAST WITH A MILLION-EYES.
I WATCHED FOR THOSE THAT WATCHED.

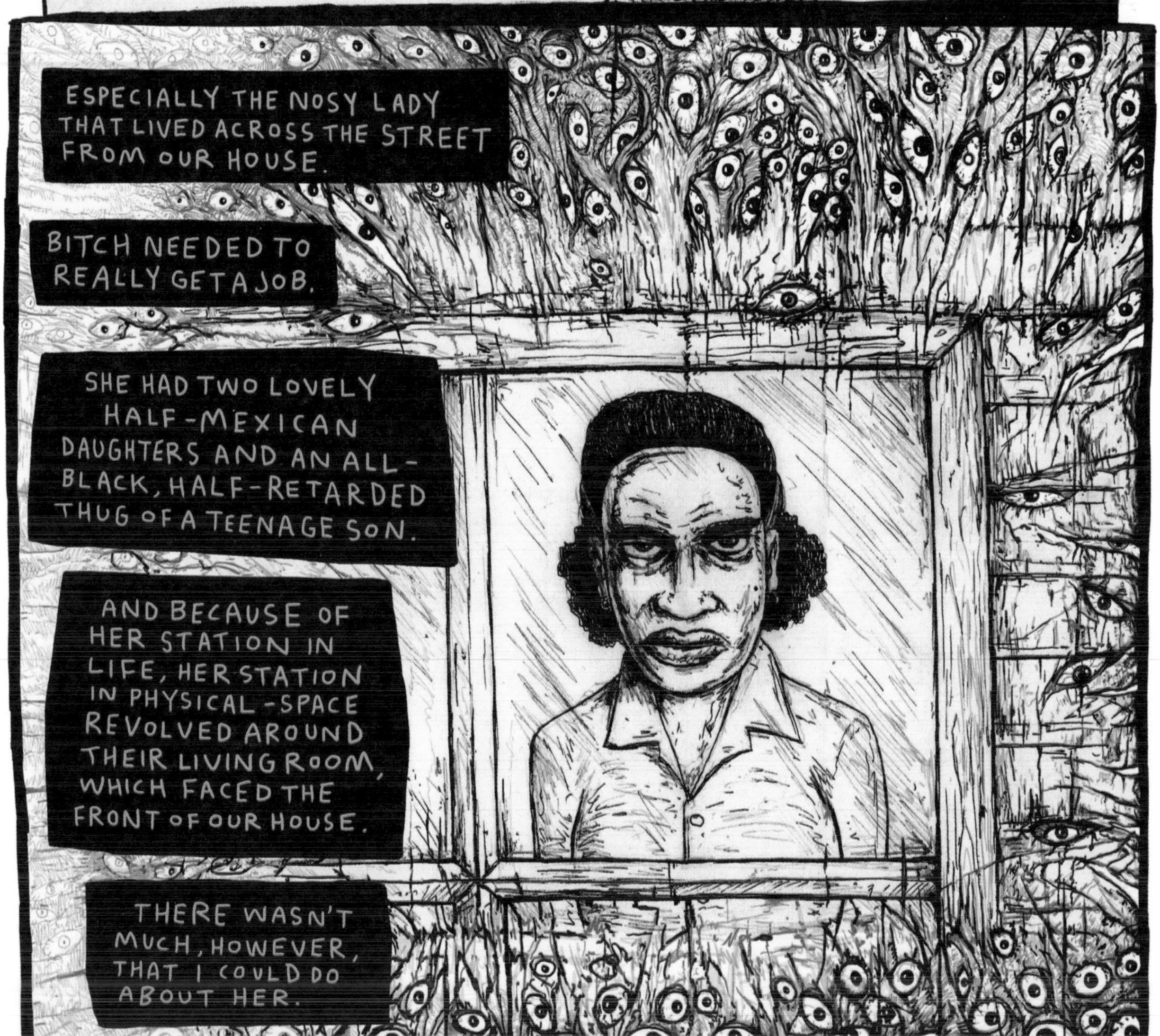
ESPECIALLY THE NOSY LADY THAT LIVED ACROSS THE STREET FROM OUR HOUSE.
BITCH NEEDED TO REALLY GET A JOB.
SHE HAD TWO LOVELY HALF-MEXICAN DAUGHTERS AND AN ALL-BLACK, HALF-RETARDED THUG OF A TEENAGE SON.
AND BECAUSE OF HER STATION IN LIFE, HER STATION IN PHYSICAL-SPACE REVOLVED AROUND THEIR LIVING ROOM, WHICH FACED THE FRONT OF OUR HOUSE.
THERE WASN'T MUCH, HOWEVER, THAT I COULD DO ABOUT HER.

ALL I COULD THINK OF WOULD BE TO MAKE UP THE EXCUSE OF COMING HOME SICK, IF SHE MENTIONED MY QUESTIONABLE DAYLIGHT PRESENCE TO MY MOTHER.

I TURNED THE KEY IN THE LOCK AND PUSHED INTO WHAT SHOULD HAVE BEEN MY COMFORTING HOME.

BUT IT WASN'T.

I MEAN, I'D GOTTEN THE ADDRESS RIGHT, BUT THE JOINT (IF I MAY BE ALLOWED THE SLIP INTO 3 STOOGES VERNACULAR) WAS FAR FROM COMFORTING.

THE EMPTY HOUSE WAS LIKE A CLOSED STORE THAT I HAD BROKEN INTO.

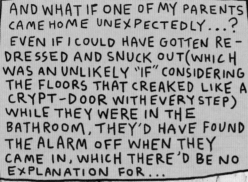

AND WHAT IF ONE OF MY PARENTS CAME HOME UNEXPECTEDLY...? EVEN IF I COULD HAVE GOTTEN RE-DRESSED AND SNUCK OUT (WHICH WAS AN UNLIKELY "IF" CONSIDERING THE FLOORS THAT CREAKED LIKE A CRYPT-DOOR WITH EVERY STEP) WHILE THEY WERE IN THE BATHROOM, THEY'D HAVE FOUND THE ALARM OFF WHEN THEY CAME IN, WHICH THERE'D BE NO EXPLANATION FOR...

I TRIED TO PUT THOSE RACING THOUGHTS AWAY AS I SLIPPED OFF MY SALT-COATED SHOES.

I ASCENDED THE STAIRS TO THE SECOND FLOOR.

I WALKED INTO THE BEDROOM THEN SAT ON THE BED, FULLY CLOTHED (SANS SHOES) AND STARED AT THE WALL.

THE ROOM WAS MURKY WITH ONLY AN ANEMIC LIGHT COMING THROUGH MY EAST-FACING BED-ROOM WINDOW.

THE HOUSE WAS CHILLY AS THE HEAT WAS TURNED DOWN DURING THE DAY.

I SPENT THE NEXT COUPLE OF HOURS TENSELY WATCHING CARTOONS AND SWEATING BLOOD EVERY TIME THE PHONE RANG OR THE HOUSE SETTLED.

SHAKE
SHAKE
SHAKE
SHAKE

I WENT BACK INTO THE COLD AT 1 PM.

BETWEEN THE FEAR, GUILT AND COLD, THIS HAD BEEN ONE OF THE MOST MISERABLE DAYS OF MY LIFE.

YET I KNEW THAT IF I COULD JUST COME UP WITH A PLAN, I COULD MORE COMFORTABLY AVOID SCHOOL.

BETWEEN RIDING THE BUS AND WANDERING AIM- LESSLY I MANAGED TO FILL THE NEXT TWO HOURS, THEN I MADE MY WAY BACK HOME.

I TURNED ON THE TV IN MY ROOM AND LISTENED TO IT FLAVORLESSLY WHILE I WAITED FOR MY FATHER TO GET HOME.

HEY HEY HE

THERE WERE 3 SCENARIOS THAT PLAYED OUT IN MY HEAD: 1) HE KNOWS I PLAYED HOOKY SO HE OPENS THE FRONT DOOR, CALLS MY NAME, BULLS HIS WAY NOISILY UP THE STAIRS AND BEATS THE SHIT OUT OF ME.

2) HE KNOWS I PLAYED HOOKY SO HE COMES IN QUIETLY STEWING, MAKES HIS WAY TO HIS BEDROOM, GRABS HIS WHIPPIN-BELT, COMES TO MY ROOM AND BEATS THE SHIT OUT OF ME WHILE QUICKLY ESCALATING AND DE-ESCALATING HIS RAGE IN THE PROCESS.

3) HE DOESN'T KNOW I'D PLAYED HOOKY SO HE DOES NOTHING, WHILE I STEW IN FIGHT OR FLIGHT STRESS WAITING FOR THE OTHER SHOE TO DROP.

BY SIX O'CLOCK I WAS REASONABLY COMFORTABLE THAT THE THIRD OPTION HAD TRANSPIRED, HOWEVER FOR THE REST OF THE EVENING, I KEPT A FORTH OPTION ON THE PERIPHERY OF MY CONSCIOUSNESS: THAT THEY WERE BOTH WAITING TO SPRING UPON ME IN SOME LATE NIGHT AMBUSH.

NOBODY SAID ANYTHING ABOUT MY ABSENCE THE NEXT DAY AT SCHOOL.

BY LUNCH TIME I WAS COMFORTABLE THAT I'D GOTTEN AWAY CLEAN AND THAT IF I DID IT ONCE, I COULD DO IT AGAIN.

THE ONLY TARNISH ON THE THOUGHT WAS THE FACT THAT I HADN'T ENJOYED MY TIME AWAY.

TRYING TO STAY INVISIBLE WAS HARD WORK.

NOTE TO ED. INDISTINCT CHATTER IN THE BACKGROUND.

ALSO THE TIME SPENT PLAYING HOOKY WASN'T LIKE REGULAR TIME.

IT WAS STRETCHED AND AND SLOWED DOWN.

ONE MINUTE WAS FIVE OR MAYBE TEN.

EVERYTHING; TELEVISION, COMIC BOOKS, TOYS, WAS HORRIBLY BORING.

NERVOUSNESS AND GUILT BLEACHED ALL OF THE JOY OUT OF HOOKY AND MADE IT FEEL LIKE A JOB.

HOW WAS I SUPPOSED TO BALANCE IT OUT?

FEEL TERRIBLE AT SCHOOL OR FEEL TERRIBLE AWAY FROM SCHOOL?

THE CHOICE WAS MINE.

THE NEXT EXPERIMENT WITH HOOKY WASN'T QUITE SO MUCH FUN.

I WAITED A COUPLE OF DAYS BEFORE I ATTEMPTED TO DIVE AGAIN INTO THE RIVER OF TRUANCY.

I MIGHT NEVER HAVE DONE IT MORE THAN ONCE IF...IT HADN'T WORKED, AND IF THE PEOPLE THAT I WENT TO SCHOOL WITH WOULD EVER GET TIRED OF BEING PIECES OF SHIT.

IF, IF, IF...

I DECIDED TO STICK CLOSE TO HOME ON MY NEXT ATTEMPT, SO I STAYED AT HOME.

THAT WAS THE MOST RISKY GAMBIT THAT I COULD HAVE PLAYED.

IF I HADN'T, I NEVER WOULD'VE SET MYSELF UP IN MY BEDROOM, LIKE SOME KIND OF COURAGE-CHALLENGED HUNTER IN A SISSY DEER-BLIND, TO PASS THE SCHOOL DAY.

BUT I DID.

I THINK, IN A WAY, THAT I WANTED TO GET CAUGHT.

I DID AND IT WASN'T ALL THAT BAD.

I HAD MY COMICS (HONESTLY JUST ILLUSTRATED HUMOR MAGAZINES BY THIS TIME), MY TOYS (MICRONAUTS: THE ADVENTURE CONTINUES ON THE EDGE OF THE DRESSER!) AND MY FATHER.

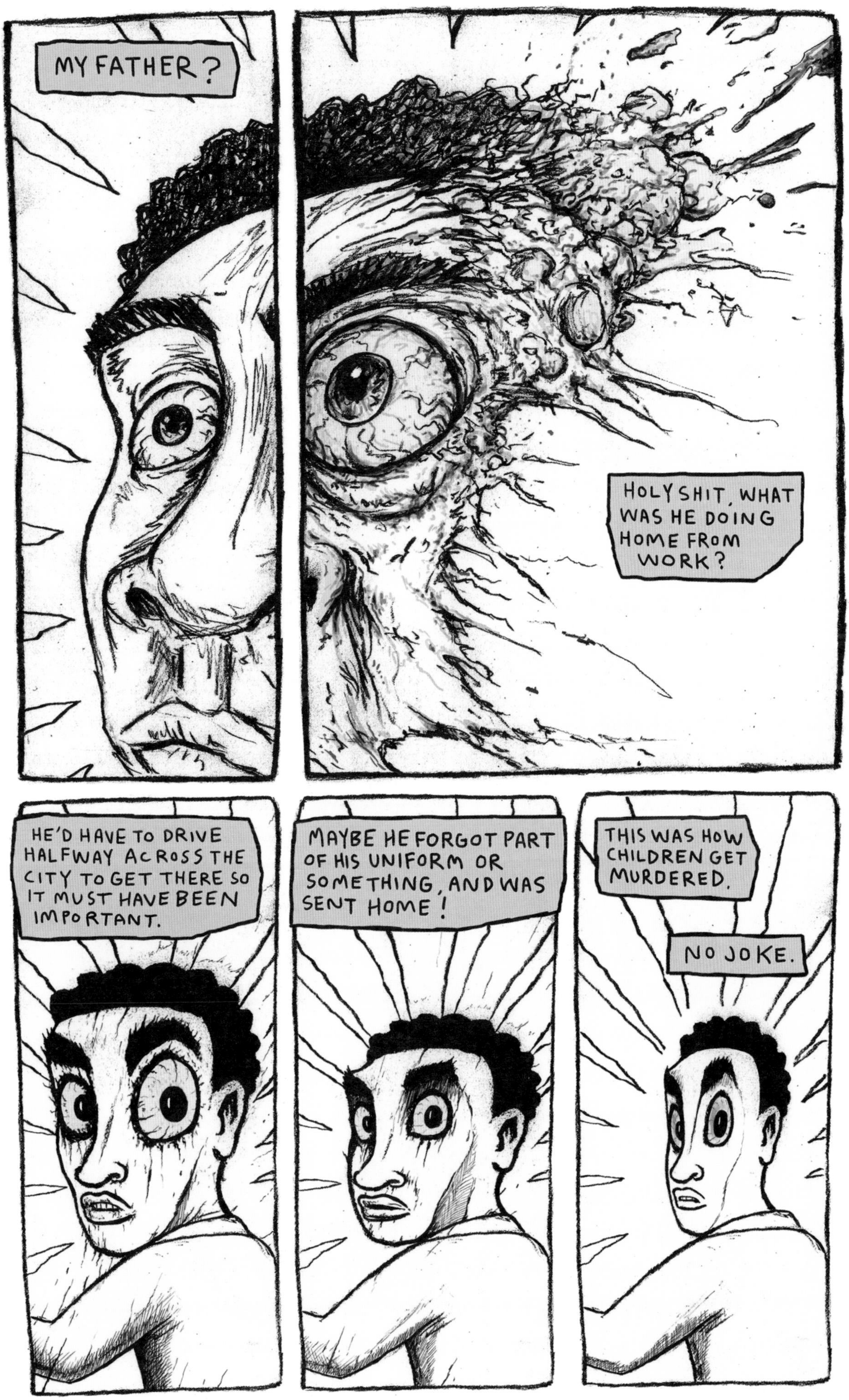
MY FATHER?
HOLY SHIT, WHAT WAS HE DOING HOME FROM WORK?
HE'D HAVE TO DRIVE HALFWAY ACROSS THE CITY TO GET THERE SO IT MUST HAVE BEEN IMPORTANT.
MAYBE HE FORGOT PART OF HIS UNIFORM OR SOMETHING, AND WAS SENT HOME!
THIS WAS HOW CHILDREN GET MURDERED.
NO JOKE.

I WAS HONESTLY AFRAID THAT HE WOULD KILL ME IF HE CAUGHT ME UP THERE.

LUCKILY I'D LEFT MY BEDROOM DOOR CLOSED, BUT THE LIGHT STREAMING UNDERNEATH IT WAS A DEAD SON GIVEAWAY!

I COULD HEAR HIS FOOTSTEPS CREAKING UP THE STAIRS.

THE SAME STAIRS THAT I'D TRIPPED ON A COUPLE OF TIMES BEFORE, BOTH CAUSING ME TO SEND MY HUGE ADULT-SIZED FRONT-TEETH THROUGH THE BAG OF BLOOD THAT WAS MY BOTTOM LIP.

CHOMP!

WHY WAS I THINKING ABOUT BLOODY TEETH?

I HAD TO GET TO THAT LIGHT SWITCH!

BUT THE SAME CREAKING WOOD THAT WAS ON THOSE STAIRS WAS UNDER MY ASS AS I SAT WAITING FOR MY BEDROOM DOOR TO EXPLODE OPEN.

I'LL HAVE TO PULL THE GOD CARD HERE.

202

THAT COULD HAVE BEEN THE ONLY THING THAT KEPT THOSE FEW FLOORBOARDS FROM CREAKING AS I MADE A HEROIC STRETCH, TURNING OFF THE LIGHT BEFORE HE GOT TO THE TOP.

AND I STOOD THERE, DRESSED FOR SCHOOL (A LAST DITCH ATTEMPT AT PRETENDING THAT I WANTED TO GO TO SCHOOL IN CASE I WAS CAUGHT), WITH ONE HAND ON THE LIGHT-SWITCH, THE OTHER HAND STEADYING MYSELF AGAINST THE DRESSER, AND BOTH FEET TRYING NOT TO PUT ANY WEIGHT ON THE FLOOR.

IF HE HAD OPENED THE DOOR AT THAT POINT, I WOULD HAVE SHATTERED.

LUCKILLY HE JUST WENT IN AND TOOK A PISS. I LISTENED TO THE SOUNDS.

THAT WAS ALL I HAD.

I WAS LIKE ZATOICHI THE BLIND SWORDSMAN, HAD HE BEEN A UNIMPRESSIVE SMALL CHILD.

THE SOUND OF THE FLUSH, THE FAUCET, THE SOAP, THE WATER, THE FAUCET, THE TOWEL, THE TWO THUNDERING STEPS TO HIS BEDROOM, THE OPENING OF A DRESSER DRAWER, AND ANOTHER, THE SOUND OF BEDSPRINGS...

...AND THEN THE SOUND OF FOOTSTEPS, ACROSS THE BEDROOM FLOOR, OUT THE DOOR AND DOWN THE STAIRS.

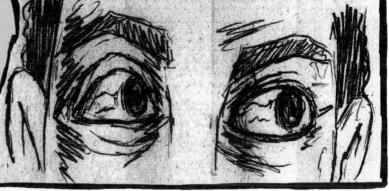

JESUS FUCKING CHRIST... THE SOUND OF HIM PUNCHING IN THE CODE BUTTONS ON THE SECURITY SYSTEM WAS A SYMPHONY.

OBVIOUSLY AFTER THAT I COULDN'T BE TRUANT AT HOME AGAIN.

YET THINGS HAD NOT MIRACULOUSLY CHANGED AT IMMANUEL LUTHERAN.

I'D HAVE TO FIND OTHER SHELTER, AND THAT SHELTER FELL POETICALLY INTO MY HANDS IN THE FORM OF A GOLDEN KEY.

THE GOLDEN COLOR BEING PROBABLY BRASS OR SOMETHING, THIS KEY SAT IN A WHITE TEACUP IN THE CHINA CABINET THAT MY MOTHER HAD PUT TOGETHER.

CHINA CABINET?

SUCH RARIFIED TASTE!

THE KEY BELONGED TO THE FRONT DOOR LOCK OF MY COUSIN CHARLENE (WHOM WE REFERRED TO AS "TOOTSIE") WHO LEFT THE KEY WITH MY PARENTS IN CASE OF EMERGENCY BECAUSE EVIDENTLY BLACK PEOPLE ARE WORRIED ABOUT EVERY GOD-DAMNED THING THERE IS POSSIBLE TO WORRY ABOUT.

I TOOK THAT KEY, AND ON THE FIRST TRY HORRIFIED MYSELF BY OPENING TOOTSIE'S FRONT DOOR AND HEARING THE VOICE OF HER HUSBAND KENNY ASKING, "WHO IS THAT?" FROM UP THE STAIRS.

"I JUST WANTED TO SEE IF THIS KEY WORKED" I HEARD MYSELF SAY FROM SOME-WHERE FAR AWAY.

THE NEXT ATTEMPT WAS MADE WITH ALL MENTAL-CYLINDERS FIRING.

I WAS WILE E. COYOTE.

I FIRST MADE SURE THAT KENNEY'S CADILLAC HAD BEEN MOVED FROM ITS SNOW-COVERED SPOT, FROM THE COMFORT OF MY LIVING ROOM.

THEN, STILL IN PAJAMAS, I STUCK MY FEET INTO MY SNOW BOOTS AND WALKED OUT THE FRONT DOOR A FEW STEPS.

ENOUGH TO GET A GOOD LOOK UP AND DOWN THE STREET FOR SELF-SAME KENNY CADILLAC.

TOOTSIE AND KENNY'S PLACE WAS TWO DOORS DOWN FROM US IN THE TOWNHOUSE.

THEIR FLOOR PLAN WAS SIMILAR, BUT WHEREAS MY PARENTS WERE SUBDUED AND CONSERVATIVE, KENNY AND TOOTSIE HAD FUNKY STYLE!

THEIR LIVING ROOM WALLS WERE LINED WITH GOLD PATTERNED MIRRORS.

WHITE ELEPHANT STATUES WITH GOLDEN HIGHLIGHTS RINGED A SHAG CARPETED LIVING-ROOM THAT I'M SURE WAS NO STRANGER TO COCAINE.

I STEPPED INTO THEIR HOME AND TURNED OFF THEIR ALARM BY PUNCHING IN THE CODE THAT I KNEW BECAUSE JESUS FUCKING CHRIST, MOTHERFUCKERS ARE BREAKING INTO HOUSES IN THIS NEIGHBORHOOD!

PARDON ME, BUT THAT NEEDED TO BE SAID.

I CLOSED THEIR FRONT DOOR BEHIND ME.

"BREAKING AND ENTERING" I HEARD IN MY HEAD, IN MY FATHER'S VOICE FOR SOME REASON.

I WAS ACTUALLY A CRIMINAL AT THIS POINT.

I TRIED TO BALANCE THE WEIGHT BETWEEN MY BREAKING AND ENTERING, VS. THE ASSAULTS I HAD TO ABSORB AT SCHOOL/HOME, AND THE SCALE IN MY HEAD SAID, "FUCK IT!"

TOOTSIE AND KENNY HAD A HUGE KING-SIZED BED IN THEIR BEDROOM.

NOT THE SALT AND PEPPER MISSIONARY-POSITION DOUBLE BED OF MY PARENTS, BUT AN HONEST TO GOD PEOPLE ARE FUCKING IN THIS BED, BED.

I TRIED NOT TO COVER TOO MUCH SPACE AS I REACHED FOR THE TV REMOTE.

CHICAGO WAS LATE TO THE CABLE TV PARTY.

TO MUCH POLITICS AND NOT ENOUGH PALM GREASE MEANT THAT THE SECOND LARGEST CITY IN THE UNITED STATES HAD TO USE THE SAME PAY TV SERVICE AS KOKOMO INDIANA.

ONTV WAS THE SERVICE THAT CHICAGOANS USED IN THE EARLY 80s.

CLICK

MY PARENTS HAD IT AND THANKFULLY TOOTSIE HAD IT.

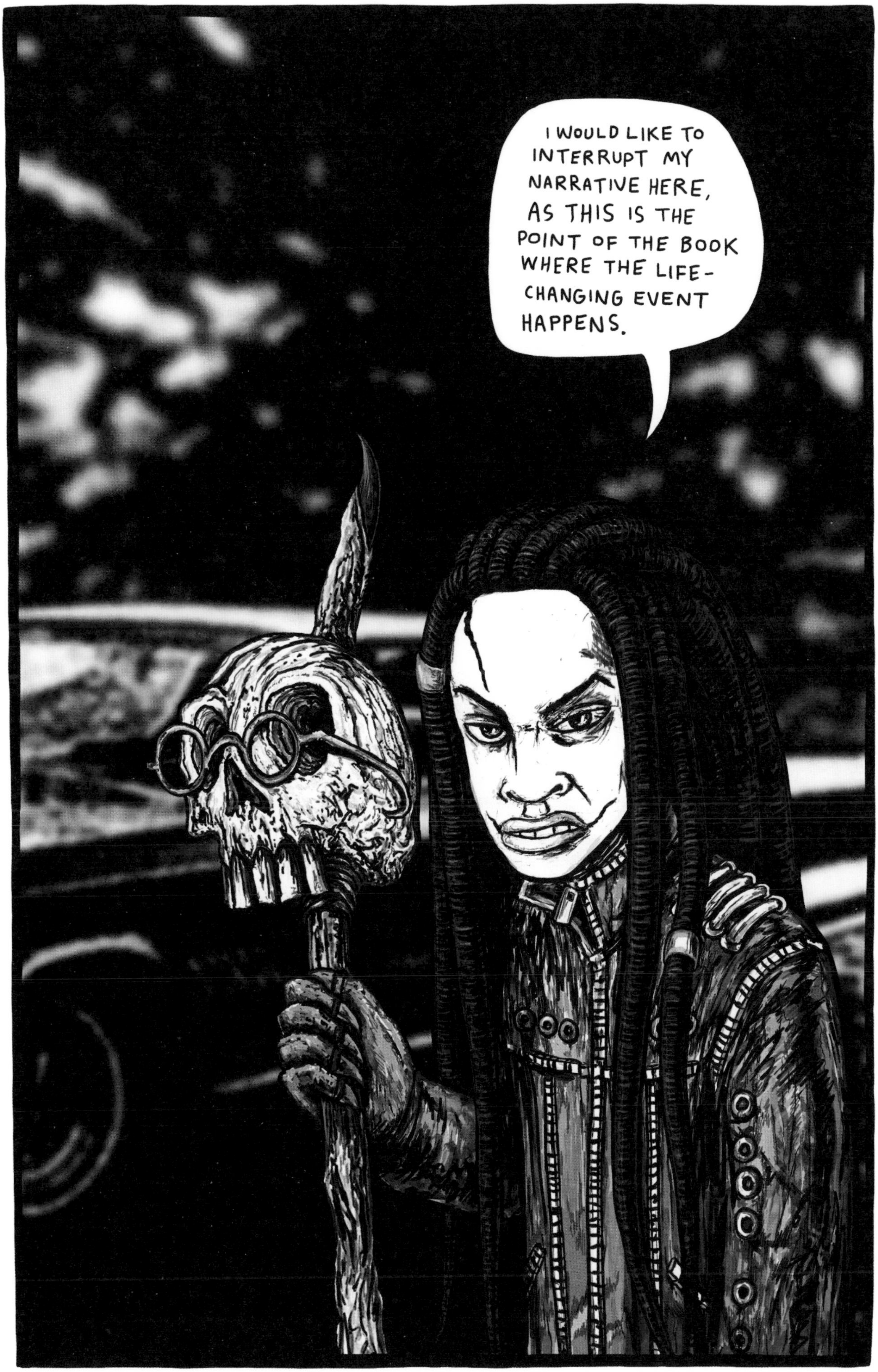
I WOULD LIKE TO INTERRUPT MY NARRATIVE HERE, AS THIS IS THE POINT OF THE BOOK WHERE THE LIFE-CHANGING EVENT HAPPENS.

I WOULD LIKE TO SAY WITH ABSOLUTELY NO HYPERBOLE, THAT MIRACLES HAPPEN AT THE STRANGEST GOD-DAMNED TIMES.

THAT COLD, SNOWY DAY, AS I SAT ON MY COUSIN'S BED, TRYING TO THINK OF NOTHING, I TURNED ON TV AND GOD MIRACLED ME UP, "URGH, A MUSIC WAR!"

1981, I WAS A SKINNY, SLIGHTLY EFFEMINATE, ARTIST KID LIVING ON CHICAGO'S BLACKASSED SOUTH-SIDE.

IT WAS 17 DEGREES OUTSIDE, I WAS PLAYING HOOKY IN MY COUSIN'S HOME TO AVOID THE RAINMAN-LIKE GIFTS OF STRESS THAT MY CLASSMATES WERE SO HOT ON GIVING ME.

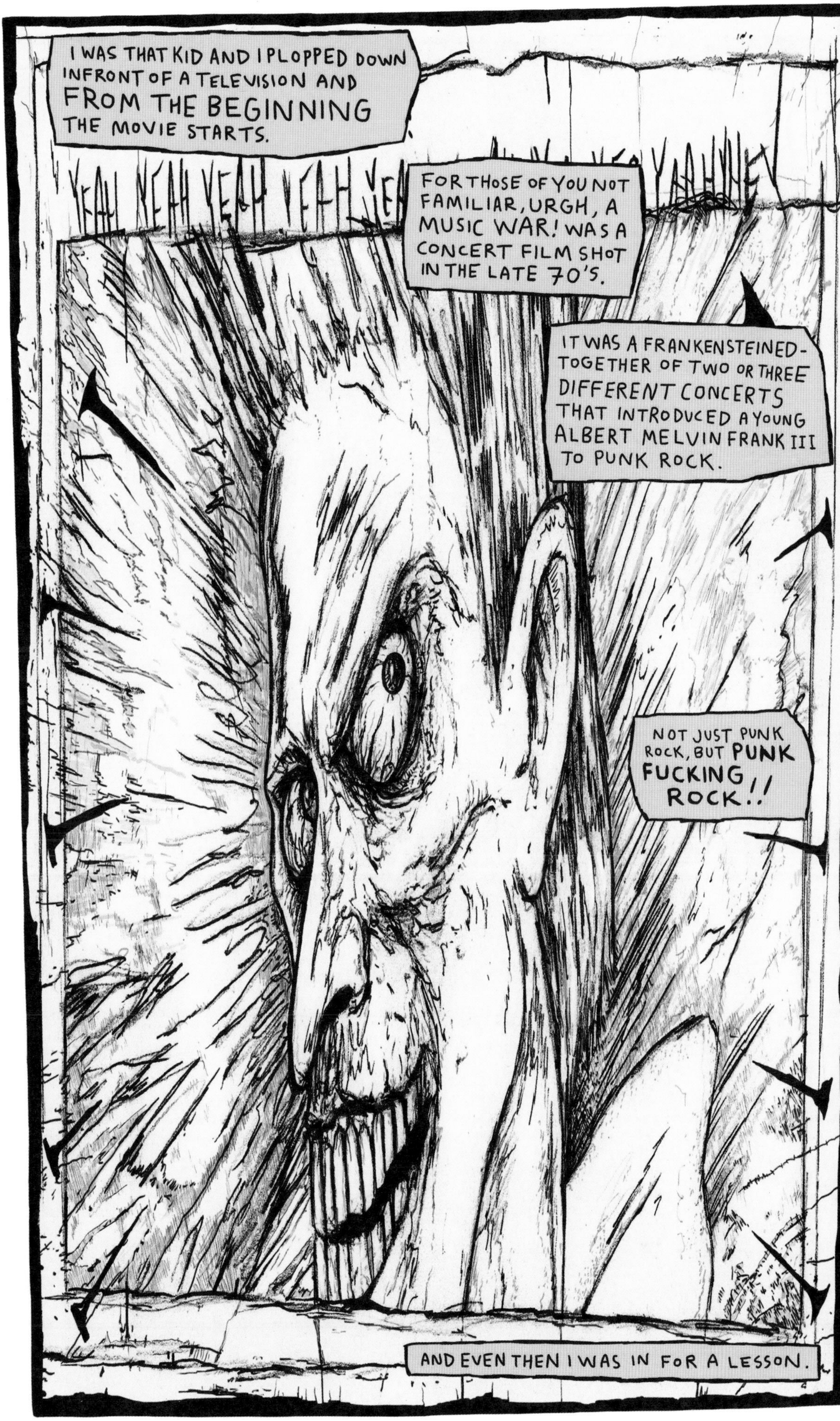
I WAS THAT KID AND I PLOPPED DOWN INFRONT OF A TELEVISION AND FROM THE BEGINNING THE MOVIE STARTS.
FOR THOSE OF YOU NOT FAMILIAR, URGH, A MUSIC WAR! WAS A CONCERT FILM SHOT IN THE LATE 70'S.
IT WAS A FRANKENSTEINED-TOGETHER OF TWO OR THREE DIFFERENT CONCERTS THAT INTRODUCED A YOUNG ALBERT MELVIN FRANK III TO PUNK ROCK.
NOT JUST PUNK ROCK, BUT PUNK FUCKING ROCK!!
AND EVEN THEN I WAS IN FOR A LESSON.

URGH, WAS A CRASH-COURSE OF SORTS, FOR ME.

I'D HEARD OF A FEW OF THE BANDS LIKE THE GO-GO'S, DEVO, AND OF COURSE, GARY NUMAN, BUT URGH MANAGED TO STITCH TOGETHER THE DESPERATE LEATHER BAT-WINGS OF UK PUNK AND NY PUNK AND CALIFORNIA PUNK.

WHILE IT WAS FREEZING OUTSIDE IT WAS FUCKIN ROASTY TOASTY AS CHELSEA PLAYED "I'M ON FIRE" AND LUX INTERIOR DESTROYED ANY LINGERING SCRAPS OF SANITY THAT I MAY HAVE HAD WHEN HE (ALONG WITH THE REST OF THE CRAMPS) MADE A GOD-DAMNEED PIECE OF ART WHEN THEY PERFORMED "TEAR IT UP"!

I WAS WATCHING THIS AND ALL OF A SUDDEN IT OCCURRED TO ME THAT: THESE PEOPLE ARE JUST LIKE ME... THEY EXIST.... SOMEWHERE IN THE WORLD THESE PEOPLE EXISTED, AND THAT MENT, WELL...THAT THE WORLD WASN'T ALL ABOUT GANG-BANGERS, OR CHINA CABINETS, OR SUBURBAN BICYCLES, OR POPPA COPS.

214

SOMEWHERE IN THE WORLD THERE WERE PEOPLE WHO WERE CREATING THEIR OWN REALITY, A BEAUTIFUL REALITY, AND I HAD TO FIND THEM, ONE WAY OR ANOTHER.

MY REVERIE WAS SHORT-LIVED HOWEVER.

I HEARD A KEY TURN IN THE LOCK OF THE FRONT DOOR.

I WAS IN THE CLOSET BEFORE I HEARD THE FIRST WORD.

MY GRANDMOTHER AND HER SISTER (TOOTSIE'S MOTHER) WERE THERE.

DID YOU HEAR SOMETHING UPSTAIRS?

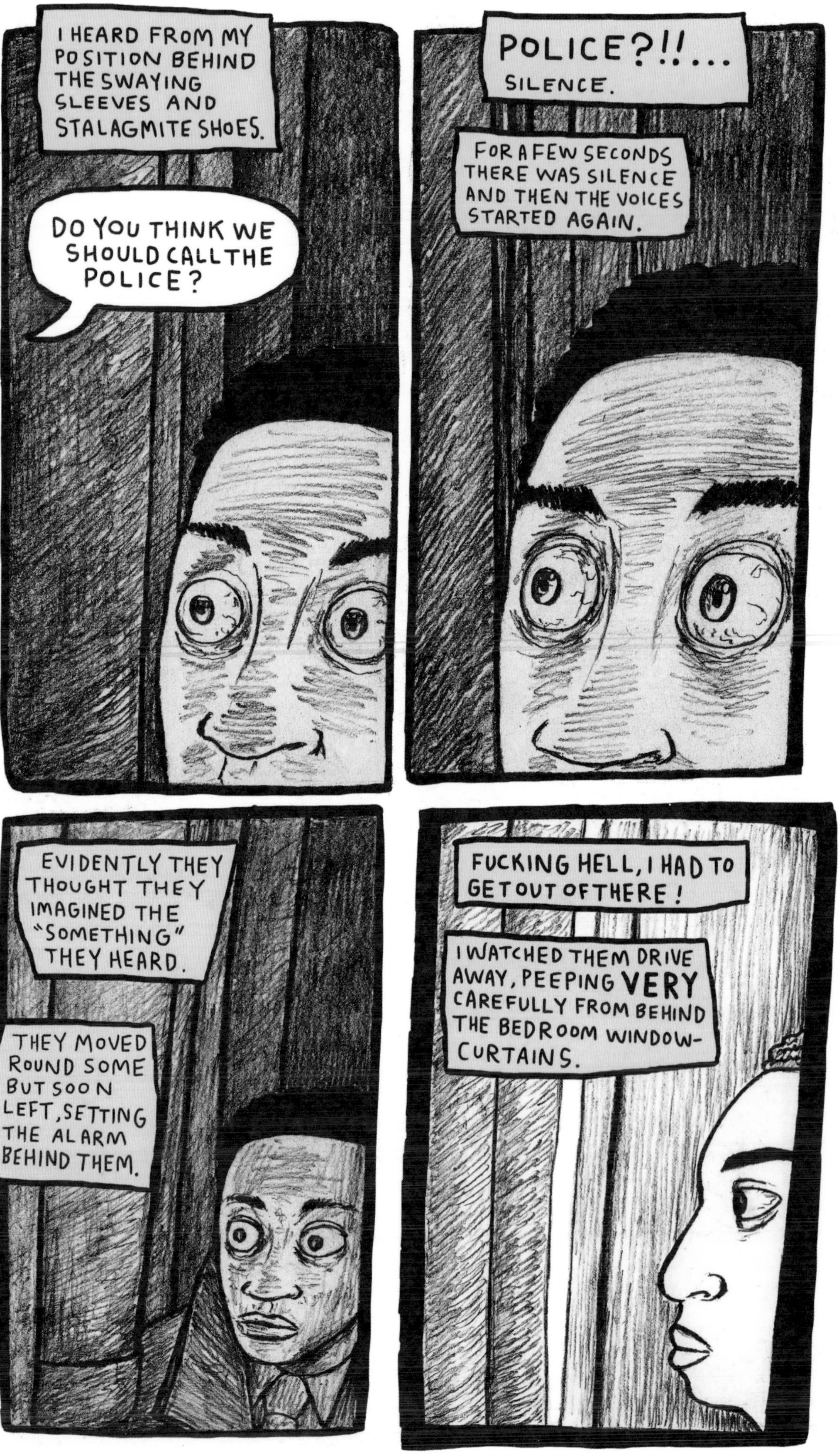
I HEARD FROM MY POSITION BEHIND THE SWAYING SLEEVES AND STALAGMITE SHOES.
DO YOU THINK WE SHOULD CALL THE POLICE?
POLICE?!!... SILENCE.
FOR A FEW SECONDS THERE WAS SILENCE AND THEN THE VOICES STARTED AGAIN.
EVIDENTLY THEY THOUGHT THEY IMAGINED THE "SOMETHING" THEY HEARD.
THEY MOVED ROUND SOME BUT SOON LEFT, SETTING THE ALARM BEHIND THEM.
FUCKING HELL, I HAD TO GET OUT OF THERE!
I WATCHED THEM DRIVE AWAY, PEEPING VERY CAREFULLY FROM BEHIND THE BEDROOM WINDOW-CURTAINS.

I GATHERED MY GEAR, RESET THE ALARM AND HEADED OUT... BUT TO WHERE?

IF THIS WAS A NICE MAKE-BELIEVE STORY I COULD FINISH IT BY SAYING THAT I FOLLOWED MY HEART TO CALIFORNIA AND BECAME A PUNK ROCKER, OR SOME SUCH NONSENSE.

BUT THIS IS A TRUE STORY.

I COULDN'T RIDE THE BUS ALL DAY, COULDN'T GO HOME, COULDN'T STAY AT TOOTSIE'S AND I COULDN'T GO TO SCHOOL. THERE WAS ONLY ONE OTHER PLACE I KNEW ENOUGH ABOUT...

CHICAGO IS BUILT ON PRAIRIE LAND.

I'M SURE THE GHOSTS OF A MILLION DEAD INDIANS HAVE CAUSED THE UNRIVALED VIOLENT INSANITY THAT CONTINUES TO THIS DAY.

IN 1981 THERE WAS A PRAIRIE 3 BLOCKS FROM MY HOUSE.

THAT PRAIRIE WAS BOUNDED BY AN EXPRESSWAY AND RAILROAD TRACKS TO THE WEST, MY NEIGHBORHOOD TO THE EAST, THE FUNTOWN AMUSEMENT PARK ON THE NORTH, AND DISAPPEARED INTO A TRIANGLE AT THE SOUTH I GUESS, SINCE I NEVER WALKED THAT FAR SOUTH.

I SPENT MANY A SUMMER'S DAY HANGING OUT WITH THE NEIGHBOR BOY DAMIEN IN THAT PRAIRIE.

THE GRASS WOULD GROW TWO FEET IN A DAY IN THE SPRING.

INSIDE THE THATCHES AND TREES WERE WILDLIFE. GARTER SNAKES, TOADS, PHEASANTS, BUNNY RABBITS AND MORE.

THE POND TAUGHT ME ABOUT TADPOLES, AND LEECHES AND IT WAS A GLORIOUS COUNTRY LIFE FOR A CITY BOY.

BUT THAT DAY WAS 17 DEGREES. THE GRASS WAS DEAD. THE TREES JUST NAKED BLACK HANDS.

THE POND WAS FROZEN SOLID.

PEOPLE DUMPED STUFF IN THE PRARIE ALL THE TIME.

THANKFULLY THE CITY HAS SINCE HAD THE GOOD SENSE TO BLOCK OFF THAT AREA AS A NATURE PRESERVE, BUT BACK THEN EVERYONE JUST CHUCKED ALL THEIR BULLSHIT INTO NATURE.

THAT INCLUDED CONSTRUCTION COMPANIES BECAUSE AS I WALKED TOWARD THE POND I NOTICED THESE HUGE CONCRETE TUBES, HALF SUBMERGED IN THE FROZEN WATER.

THE WIND WAS CUTTING THROUGH ME, SO I DUCKED DOWN AND WALKED INTO THE CEMENT SEMI-CIRCLE, TO TRY AND HIDE FROM THE HAWK.

I CROUCHED DOWN THERE, BACK AGAINST THE CURVED WALL, WRAPPING MY PEA COAT AROUND MY LEGS AND NOT FEELING MY NUMB TOES AS I STARED AT MY DRESS SHOES.

AND THIS IS WHERE I LEAVE YOU. THE STORY IS DONE. OF COURSE I GOT CAUGHT A COUPLE OF DAYS LATER, PLAYING HOOKY. AND OF COURSE THE BULLYING DIDN'T STOP.

BUT THE NEXT TIME YOU HEAR OF A GIRL CUTTING HERSELF ON PURPOSE, OR YOU SEE SOME KIDS THAT LOOK LIKE THEY MIGHT BE HOMELESS, I WANT YOU TO THINK OF ME, AT 13 YEARS OLD, FREEZING AND AFRAID IN THAT CONCRETE TUBE.

"PROPER" SOCIETY MADE ME WHAT I AM TODAY.

GOODNIGHT.

CASANOVA NOBODY FRANKENSTEIN was a Gen-X latch-key-kid, raised on the incongruous influences of '70s-era Chicago UHF TV-programming and American-hypocrisy. He earned degrees in Fine Art and Metaphysics and produced art, poetry, and comics. (*In The Wilderness*, which he wrote and drew, was published by Fantagraphics in 2019.) He worked a 25-year string of Kafkaesque day jobs while maintaining a strict personal code. Retiring early in 2016 due to health issues, he remains a combination of James Baldwin, Charles Bukowski, and Mad Max—but 20-years ahead of his time.

Born in 1975 **GLENN PEARCE**, INFJ and animal and human rights activist, has been an Australian underground comic artist since 1990.